Wild Bill Hickok
The Man and His Myth

Wild Bill Hickok

The Man and
His Myth

Joseph G. Rosa

 University Press of Kansas

© 1996 by the University Press of Kansas
All rights reserved

Published by the University Press of Kansas (Lawrence, Kansas 66045),
which was organized by the Kansas Board of Regents and is operated
and funded by Emporia State University, Fort Hays State University,
Kansas State University, Pittsburg State University, the University of
Kansas, and Wichita State University

Library of Congress Cataloging-in-Publication Data

Rosa, Joseph G.
Wild Bill Hickok : the man and his myth / by Joseph G. Rosa
p. cm.
Includes bibliographical references.
ISBN 978-0-7006-0773-0 (cloth); ISBN 978-0-7006-1523-0 (pbk.)
1. Hickok, Wild Bill,1837–1876.
2. Peace officers—West (U.S.)—Biography.
3. Frontier and pioneer life—West (U.S.) I. Title
F594.H62R68R68 1996
978'02'092—dc20
[B]   95-54015

British Library Cataloguing-in-Publication Data is available.

Printed in the United States of America

10 9 8 7

The paper used in this publication meets the minimum requirements of the American National
Standard for Permanence of Paper for Printed Library Materials Z39.48-1992.

To the late Charles Leland ("Doc") Sonnichsen
who encouraged me to write this book,
but sadly did not see it reach fruition.
And for Robin May, friend, occasional co-author,
and companion on so many Western ventures.

Contents

Illustrations

A Personal Foreword

I was about seven years old when I first encountered Wild Bill Hickok in the person of Bruce Cabot in the movie *Wild Bill Hickok Rides,* which was released in the early 1940s. At that time Mr. Hickok joined a host of other "heroes" led by my particular favorite Buck Jones, who died in 1942 in the Boston Cocoanut Grove nightclub fire, which took more than five hundred lives. Later, however, Gary Cooper's version of Hickok in *The Plainsman,* in which I saw my hero breathe his last on the floor of Saloon No. 10 at Deadwood, made a great impression on me and inspired an interest in Hickok that has never dimmed.

By my late adolescence, however, I was more interested in the real man rather than the myth. This "magnificent obsession" (as one old friend, a senior judge of the Kansas District Court, once described it with a smile) led me to spend more time than I ever imagined possible in an attempt to confront the myth and find the real man. In many instances I did unearth new materials, confound legends, and clarify events in Hickok's life that had been a mystery. But there are still gaps, many of them unlikely ever to be filled, for no one can hope to learn everything about another person, least of all a highly controversial historical character.

During the past forty years I have covered several thousand miles, spent hours in discussion with Hickok's family, and ranged through historical archives, courthouses, and other likely places seeking factual information about Wild Bill Hickok. Along the way, I have met or corresponded with a large number of people either anxious to help or ready to debate the subject. I unearthed a lot of material, not all of it devoted to what Ethel Hickok might have called "the adventures of my uncle Jim."

In some areas my search will continue—I hope to uncover information on obscure sightings or unexplained disappearances, and I also hope that more photographs may yet turn up—but for now I trust that all those people who have contributed in some way will appreciate the result of my own and their labors.

Preface

His real name was James Butler Hickok. But to friend and foe alike he was better known as "Wild Bill"—a sobriquet that more than a century after his death still commands attention.

No other Western character (except perhaps Wyatt Earp) is as famous or as controversial. Even Buffalo Bill Cody (long the subject of scholarly debate) fails to inspire the same reaction as Hickok, despite the fact that Cody's Wild West Exhibition made him better known worldwide. Yet in an age of changing values and introspective reassessment of Western history and its myriad characters, Hickok, for many people, still epitomizes the deadshot gunfighting peace officer who kept the mob at bay. The manner of his death also contributed toward his legend. He was shot in the back of the head while playing poker in the aptly named town of Deadwood on August 2, 1876. The cards he held are remembered as "the Deadman's Hand." Surely his was one of the most poignant and romantic demises in Western history.

It was inevitable that many legends would center upon Hickok. What for him was a normal existence appears fictional to people of a later generation. Thus his real life adventures inspired what has become an enduring myth. Hickok's character and exploits did outshine those of most of his contemporaries, who are usually famous for specific traits or deeds. Hickok was a complex man, which is why he remains controversial and enigmatic, and why it is difficult to separate the man and his myth.

Legends, by their very nature, are often suspect. Either they are fictions designed to disguise the real image, or they embody a natural progression from admiration to adoration. In Hickok's case, the legend is a blending of both possibilities. The legendary "Wild Bill" was the creation of the fevered imaginations of the press and public; they wove his real exploits into a tangle of fact and fiction that has long confused, confounded and irritated historians, not to mention Hickok himself. It was pure irony that prompted Colonel George Ward Nichols, who interviewed him in 1865, to credit Wild Bill with the remark, "I'm sort of public property." This comment officially thrust Hickok into the public domain, leaving him at the mercy of both eulogizers and debunkers alike.

It is important, therefore, to remember that it was the myth- or mischief-makers who elevated Hickok to a status that later caused him embarrassment and anger. But when we examine his comments, cited as verbatim by Nichols and Henry M. Stanley, we see that Hickok himself sowed some of the seeds that blossomed into a myth of immense proportions, one that survives to this day.

Since magazines and newspapers in Hickok's day lacked the technology to publish photographs, writers had to provide "graphic" pen portraits of their subjects. George Ward Nichols's description of Wild Bill in *Harper's* touched upon his piercing gaze, high cheekbones, sensitive mouth, and when in friendly conversation, eyes as "gentle as a woman's." Henry M. Stanley, writing in the St. Louis *Weekly Missouri Democrat* of April 16, 1867, added more detail: a "face, free from blemish, a light moustache, a thin pointed nose, bluish-grey eyes, with a calm look, a magnificent forehead, hair parted from the centre of the forehead, and hanging down behind the ears in wavy, silken curls, made up the most picturesque figure." The Scholten full-length portrait of Wild Bill, discovered in 1989, confirms Stanley's description. Hickok's personal appearance contributed to his myth, for unlike many of his contemporaries, he looked the part. It might be said "Wild Bill" was the swashbuckling Cavalier to Wyatt Earp's more puritanical Roundhead—Earp's photographs suggest a banker or a mortician rather than a Western gunfighter.

In recent years, Colonel Nichols has been credited with an additional comment on Hickok's appearance and attitude toward killing that has so far defied verification. The late Elmo Scott Watson, a founding member of the Westerners Organization, cited the following attributed to Nichols, but did not give a source: "I thought as I looked at him of eagles, hawks and stallions and John Wilkes Booth, but he had a finer, saner, better balanced, more magnetic face and head than Booth." Similarly, the following comment credited to Hickok: "As ter killing men, I never thought much about it. The most of the men I have killed it was one or t'other of us, and at sich times you don't stop to think; and what's the use after it's all over?" was later edited to read: "As to killing, I never think much about it. I don't believe in ghosts, and I don't keep the lights burning all night to keep them away. That's because I'm not a murderer. It is the other man or me in a fight, and I don't stop to think—is it a sin to do this thing? And after it's over, what's the use of disturbing the mind? The killing of a bad man shouldn't trouble one any more than killing a rat or an ugly cat or a vicious dog."

So far, nothing has been found to connect Nichols with the reference to John Wilkes Booth or Hickok's attitude to man killing; but why anyone should deliberately change Nichols's story can only be a matter of conjecture.[1]

The Western myth is itself complex, which makes the task of the biographer appear daunting. To ignore the myth in favor of the historical record can destroy the balance, for both fact and fiction have contributed toward the conception of character and period. Why did the Old West's characters acquire such mythical status? Curiously, there is no equivalent of a Wild Bill, a Billy the Kid, or a Jesse James in any other nineteenth-century frontier. True, Australia had its Ben Hall, Frank Gardiner, and Ned Kelly, and England boasted a fictionalized Robin Hood, Dick Turpin, and the likes of Jack Shepherd. But that does not explain the universal appeal of the American gunfighter, while the others (except for Robin Hood) achieved only a local fame. One writer has suggested that they were a "typically Anglo-Saxon phenomenon"; the fact that they were immortalized in death was "essential to ensure resurrection of the legend."[2]

The American public's preoccupation in the late 1860s with Wild Bill and other frontier "types" stemmed largely from the escapism that followed four years of civil war. The restrictions imposed by government, the military, and the exigencies of war encouraged people to seek freedom from daily routine, if not physically, then mentally. The written word was one way to escape. Monthly journals and newspapers were crammed with stories of the West and accounts of derring-do among hostile Indians. People anxious to rid themselves of the restrictions of post-war unemployment, recession, and the over crowding in many of the larger eastern cities dreamed of risking the Indians, climate, and other hazards to reach the rich, fertile regions to the West. So when they read about those places and the adventures of the "plainsmen" or "frontiersmen," they formed a vision that was largely fictional yet left them yearning for the "wide open spaces."

Every generation has its heroes and villains, and often one man becomes both. To many of his contemporaries, Abraham Lincoln was as much reviled as he was revered. Similarly, "Wild Bill," as exemplified by *Harper's* appealed to the masses if not to all of his contemporaries. But fame has its pitfalls as well as its rewards, the greater the fame the greater the risk of character assassination. A fickle public can make or break any reputation. It is a quirk of human nature that it seeks to destroy if it discovers that its idol is fallible. It is not surprising, then, that Hickok, vaunted as the greatest of gunfighters, bravest of scouts, and most feared of peace officers should fall from favor.

When we worship heroes, they often become extensions of ourselves—the hero is the sort of person we wish we could be. If this sounds bizarre, then remember the effect heroes have on children. What small boy, or young adolescent, has not imagined the effect it would have if his hero came to his aid when confronted by a bully or a thug? To the many millions of youngsters who roared their approval as their particular hero raced across the silver screen in the days of the Saturday movie matinees, the Hollywood cowboy was real. When we reach maturity, most of us view childhood heroes with nostalgia. But for some incurable romantics, the bond with their hero remains unbroken, and they fantasize into adulthood. Some even visualize situations where the likes of Hickok are employed to uphold the law in a crime-ridden New York or Chicago, blissfully ignoring the impracticability of such a situation. For these reasons it is difficult to analyze a myth, especially one that is as entrenched as Wild Bill's. Great care is needed to separate myth from reality.

When I began researching for my Hickok biography, I had a preconceived idea of the sort of character I was seeking, having been influenced since childhood by the movies and, in particular, Gary Cooper's mid 1930s portrayal of Hickok in *The Plainsman.* I quickly realized that the legend and the man were entirely different. Even so, separating the two was no easy task. I was indeed fortunate that most people or institutions I contacted were happy to assist me; in many instances those research contacts led to lasting friendships. Others, however, were hostile. In my time, I have "crossed pens" with a number of well known writers. Of these the most formidable was undoubtedly the late Mari Sandoz. When I first read her book *The Buffalo Hunters,* in which she was very critical of Hickok, I was amazed at the wealth of detail she seemed to have acquired. Later I realized that her book would be best described as an historical novel, for she had dramatized events that no living person could have known about. Nevertheless, her antipathy toward Hickok and other "long hairs" intrigued me. She did provide me with her main source for her claim that Wild Bill murdered Whistler, Handsmeller, and Fat Badger, three members of the Cut-off band of Sioux then living in the Republican River country of Nebraska. This was an army report that accused a "Wild Bill's Outfit" of the murders. Subsequently, I was to learn from the Nebraska State Historical Society that the main suspect was not Hickok but one Mortimer N. ("Wild Bill of the Blue River") Kress, a local near-desperado, and his partner Jack Ralston. In recent years I have learned that at the time he was supposed to have murdered the three Indians in Nebraska, James Butler Hickok was living in Springfield, Missouri.

The late Senator Arthur Carmody of Trenton, Nebraska, once told me that he and the late Everrett Sutton (who had himself spent many years studying the "Whistler problem") had devoted a great deal of time and energy trying to convince Mari that she had the wrong "Wild Bill." But despite a wealth of evidence to the contrary, she was adamant that her "Wild Bill" was Hickok. Once her mind was made up, Mr. Carmody said, she refused to change it.

Mari Sandoz was by no means alone. Other writers, for whatever reason, chose to fictionalize events in Hickok's life or invent things that conflicted with known facts. Even today, attempts are being made to turn Hickok into some kind of a psychological freak, adding facets to his character and behavior that were not evident during his lifetime.

Miss Sandoz also aroused my curiosity when she inferred that Wild Bill and his brother Lorenzo were both "hot-headed" and that there "were some who said that the John or Curly McCall around town was a brother too, and he did resemble them in a caricatural sort of way." Questioned on this alleged resemblance, she replied:

> About Lorenzo Hickok's photograph: Yes, I've seen a couple purported to be of him but the photographs of the frontier have been so mislabeled so long that I wouldn't offer an opinion. If he looked like the photographs I saw no one could have mistaken him for Wild Bill, although there is a resemblance—but to a sort of coarsened, darkened version of Wild Bill—the kind of thing you see in the photographs of McCall. In fact one of the pictures labeled Lorenzo Hickok is often labeled as Jack McCall's.[3]

In this and as in other instances, Miss Sandoz was unable to lay her hands on any of the photographs she mentioned or suggest where they might be obtained, since her materials were in storage in the West. This is unfortunate, especially because there are *no* authenticated photographs of McCall.

Some time later, in conversation with the late Don Russell, Buffalo Bill's biographer, I learned that he, too, had disagreed with Mari concerning her attitude and allegations about Buffalo Bill and Hickok. He then informed me, with a chuckle, that he believed we had been mentioned, but not by name, in her book *The Cattlemen* in this revealing comment: "What Chicagoans and the British didn't understand was that western gunmen did not shoot important people, whose killing would bring certain action . . . Hickok, the most publicised of gun fighters, would shoot a southerner, a Reb in northern territory in 1861, but never a man of any consequence."[4]

In complete contrast to my relationship with Sandoz was my relationship with the Hickok family. When I first began to correspond with them in the 1950s, they were courteous but not very keen to divulge information to a perfect stranger. Later, though, after they had read the first edition of my book, *They Called Him Wild Bill,* and I had visited them in 1965, we got to know each other very well. James's niece, Ethel, even allowed me access to materials never seen outside family circles. In return, I produced information concerning their English origins. This cooperation, together with additional research on my part, led to the publication of a revised edition of the book in 1974. Hickok's grandniece, Edith Harmon, the family historian, paid me a great compliment when she said that with the possible exception of Lorenzo, I probably knew more about her great uncle James than did most of his own brothers and sisters, whose real memories of their brother were from childhood or adolescence.

This present volume, however, owes its existence to a chance conversation at a Western History Association Conference some years ago. I was asked why Hickok and his myth still commanded so much attention—a good question, but not an easy one to answer. Hickok, as mentioned earlier, is remembered for many reasons besides his "pistoliferous" activities and employment in law enforcement. He was a respected military and government scout, and also (reluctantly) an actor and a dime novel hero. But apart from the manner of his death, it was perhaps his undeserved reputation as a prolific "mankiller" that best explains why he is so well remembered today. Are Hickok's alleged homicidal exploits the reason for the public's continued interest? Or is he seen as an instrument in the eradication of "bad men" in a semicivilized era? It seems clear that his alleged reputation as a "civilizer" did indeed account for much of the attention he received during his lifetime and since. But he himself abhorred his "killer" mantle—it was others who sought to exploit it. Therefore, in the following essays devoted to the origin and significance of Wild Bill Hickok's myth, I hope to resolve some misconceptions and put his legendary reputation into historical perspective.

Acknowledgments

M uch of the material used in writing this book was gathered during the preparation of previous books. My gratitude to the large number of people who helped with those efforts continues. Some of them are given further credit in the present volume. In addition, my special thanks to those whose efforts played a crucial part in the completion of this volume: the late Ethel Hickok, who donated items relative to her "uncle James"; her niece Edith Harmon, for allowing me access to materials that I had not seen before; and to Sandra Sagala, who spent months digging into old newspapers in an attempt to verify all of Hickok's appearances with Buffalo Bill's Combination. Ida Ipe labored long and hard in an effort to to unearth Colonel George Ward Nichols's journals; Brian W. Dippie offered advice and encouragement, as did James McLaird, who produced previously unknown material on Calamity Jane. Similarly, Delbert Bishop, archivist, and Robert Neumann of the Greene County Archives, Springfield, Missouri, unearthed long-lost material on the Hickok-Tutt gunfight and ensured that I was kept informed of their findings. Additional material was provided by John Bradbury of the University of Missouri at Rolla. Robert Knecht of the Kansas State Historical Society also offered many useful suggestions. The following individuals were also very helpful: Harwood P. Hinton; David Dary; the late Col. Paul King; Robin May; Darlis A. Miller; Jessica Nashold; Chuck Parsons; William B. Secrest; and Judge Arthur J. Stanley, Jr. Paul Fees, senior curator of the Buffalo Bill Museum in Cody, Wyoming, and the Wyoming State Archives, Cheyenne, Wyoming, provided invaluable assistance, as did James E. Potter of the Nebraska State Historical Society. Nicholas Rees, a computer wizard, set me on course for using modern techniques in preparation of the manuscript. Paul and Penny Dalton prepared many of the illustrations. And I owe an enormous debt to James Joplin of Springfield, Missouri, for permission to reproduce his unique photographs of Wild Bill and Capt. Richard Bentley Owen. To all these people and to those I may have inadvertently left out, my grateful thanks.

Introduction

"The Man and His Myth"

James Butler Hickok was a legend in his own lifetime, and he has since become immortalized as "Wild Bill" Hickok, one of America's foremost folkheroes. How he achieved such a status has long been the subject of debate.

He was born in Illinois in 1837 and emigrated to Kansas in 1856. During the next twenty years he was regarded by some as the "greatest of all Western scouts" and by others as "one of the most successful Indian fighters that ever crossed the plains." His service as a Civil War scout and spy for the Union and later exploits as a deputy U.S. marshal, acting sheriff, and marshal of Abilene established his reputation as a Western gunfighter or "civilizer." At his death in 1876, he was nationally known and much mourned.

Hickok's physical presence was impressive. He was over six feet tall, broad-shouldered, and narrow-hipped. He wore his auburn hair shoulder length and had a straw-colored moustache. But his dominant feature was his blue-gray eyes, which became coldly implacable when he was aroused. Around his waist he wore a belt from which hung a matched pair of ivory-handled Colt's Model 1851 Navy revolvers. He was rarely without them and was reputed never to miss when he shot at a target or another man.

In 1867, Hickok was the subject of an article in *Harper's New Monthly Magazine* that brought "Wild Bill" before the public and gave birth to the Hickok legend. Therefore, in reproducing the complete text of the original article as an appendix, I hope that the student will appreciate its "flavor" and may be encouraged to use it as a guide when attempting to be objective rather than cynical in seeking the facts behind famous legends.

One

In Search of "Wild Bill"

Although the legend of Wild Bill Hickok was inspired by his real exploits, James Butler Hickok would hardly recognize himself today. He has long been obscured by his legend, a tangle of fact and fiction that hinders objective assessment of his life. The adulation and controversy surrounding Hickok have inspired many attempts to learn more of the real man. Research has revealed that he was no illiterate or unlearned rowdy eking out an existence in a harsh environment. On the contrary, he was educated and had been brought up in an atmosphere of discipline, religion, and morality. He was, in effect, the complete antithesis of many of his frontier contemporaries.

Hickok's personality surprised many of those who met him for the first time, having known him only by reputation. Instead of the raw-boned, bullying desperado described by ill-informed members of the press, Hickok was courteous, soft-spoken, self-effacing, and generally knowledgeable. His eulogizers made much of his courage, integrity, and reluctance to become involved in violence unless "put upon" or in the course of his official duties. His detractors on the other hand, declared that he could be vicious; a man who exacted revenge for imagined insults for which he bore a grudge. It was this combination of appearance and behavior that created so much controversy. Certainly, a boot heel in the face, or a revolver butt across the skull conflicts with the image of Wild Bill so much admired by early writers who rarely discussed the seamier side of brawls and shoot-outs. But in the real world of survival in a semicivilized and hostile environment, such actions were commonplace. Surely, a boot in the face was a lesser evil than the jagged edge of

a broken glass, or the loss of an eye to a gouging thumbnail
grown and "brined" for the purpose, a common feature of the
earlier riverboat and mountain men.

The Hickok family's recollection of James (they remembered
him as a child or young man) understandably differed from that
of others. They recalled him as self-willed and a great leg-puller
with a vivid imagination. His niece Ethel recalled that her aunt
Lydia often told her of his boyhood scrapes, his practical jokes,
and his efforts to "scare us to death" with tall stories. Lydia herself wrote in 1915, "I have to laugh when I read James' stories for
when we were children he was always telling just such yarns to
amuse the rest of us[.] we were always a great family to read
aloud to each other." James, she also noted, swore that one day
he would do things that Kit Carson "never thought of doing."
But he also displayed a marked sense of right and wrong and
fought several of his contemporaries caught bullying others.[1]

Writing as late as 1923, Col. Homer W. Wheeler recalled first
meeting Wild Bill at Fort Wallace in 1869 when Hickok was a
scout for the Tenth Cavalry. Later, he met him again at Abilene
when Hickok was marshal. Hickok had arrested one of his cowboys for discharging a pistol (which belonged to the colonel) and
had released him, after a night in jail, into Wheeler's custody.
"During the time that I knew Hickok," he wrote, "he did not indulge in liquor. He was not a profane man, and was affable to
meet. He had the respect of the citizens, and especially the cowmen."[2]

The colonel's reference to cowmen probably meant ranchers
or drovers rather than the actual cowboys, whom Hickok did not
trust at all. Some might conclude that this distrust was due partly
to the ongoing Rebel versus Yank animosity that followed the
war. Others point to the prolonged psychological stress these
men were under, constantly on their guard against attempts on
their lives by unpredictable, "liquored up" Texans. Others argued
that not all the cowboys were homicidal. Rather, they delighted
in frightening old men and timid women with a show of rowdy-
ism that was their way of letting off steam. Unfortunately, when
loaded firearms were included in the festivities, Wild Bill and
company were probably right to overreact on occasion.

Hickok's liquor intake and his penchant for gambling aroused a mixed reaction among those who claimed an acquaintance. An editor who met him on a train in October 1867 recalled that Wild Bill and his companions were all "more or less affected by frequent potations from their bottles, and Wild Bill himself was tipsy enough to be quite belligerent." He excused their conduct on the grounds that they had just come in from a scouting expedition, and that their lives were in constant danger. Their idea of relaxation was to "blaze away" with their revolvers, and to keep them cocked beside them when they played cards.[3]

If Hickok had one lasting weakness it was for gambling. John Malone, who had known him since the early 1860s and spent time with him on the plains, agreed that he "would rather indulge in poker than eat, and on one occasion . . . played in his last earthly possession[,] a black and tan terrier." This passion was also noted by Charles Gross, who declared that Hickok would "gamble the shirt off his back" if the mood possessed him.

Gambling was to be a lifelong passion for Hickok. When Wild Bill left Abilene late in 1871, he went to Kansas City where he remained until August 1872, boarding at the St. Nicholas Hotel. Each day he passed down the main street just after noon and entered the Marble Hall, where he played poker or faro. His reputation was enough to keep him out of trouble, except where the occasional ordinance was used to fine him and his cronies.[4]

Critics of Hickok's gambling pursuits were also critical of his behavior as a policeman. The fact that many cowtown police gambled, whored, or drank whenever they had a chance was often ignored by the citizens as long as peace was maintained. Even so, when men of reputation indulged, it tended to arouse comment, and the critics were plentiful. Samuel D. Henry (no relation to the brothers Theodore and Stuart) spent some of his youth in Abilene. He was sixteen when Hickok was marshal. Recalling the activities of the pistol-packing Texans, he declared that Hickok was the ideal choice for the job of marshal, for all "the Texas cattle herders at Abilene feared and hated Wild Bill" because of his wartime activities against the Confederacy. Henry stated that Hickok had no real social life:

He was anti-social, cold blooded—had no friends and seemed to want none. So far as is known he never gave a smile or a handshake. His whole bearing was like that of a hunted tiger—restless eyes, which nervously looked about him in all directions closely scrutinizing every stranger. When he played cards, which he did most of the time in the saloons, he sat in the corner of the room to prevent an enemy from stealing up behind him. He drank to some extent but was never known at Abilene to be unsteady on his feet.

Henry, however, did admit that Wild Bill had some redeeming traits. Although a killer of killers, Hickok was never a "bandit or stick up man" like the James brothers, and neither was he a "criminal in a strict sense." His killings seemed "always to have been in self defence, or when in the line of official duty or government service—a sort of Robin Hood. The frontier developed such men—they seemed necessary . . . Wild Bill . . . was a creditable citizen compared with the vicious, soulless gunmen of the present time."[5]

Samuel Henry was in error when he claimed that Hickok was antisocial and friendless. He had many friends spread around the West. Many people discovered that Hickok was self-effacing and anxious to avoid mixing with the masses. But he was not alone in this trait. Frontiersmen as a whole were noted for their dislike of so-called civilization and its crowds.

As for Hickok's mankiller reputation, W. E. Webb, writing in 1875, declared:

> The number of persons I knew him to kill was five, three at Hays and two at Abilene. It seems as if such men as Bill were designed by Providence to act as a sort of carnivore for keeping down the increase of their species. In all of my residence upon the frontier, during which time sixty-two graves were filled by violence, in no case was the murder otherwise than a benefit to society. The dangerous class killed within its own circle, but never courted justice by shedding better blood. Orderly people looked on with something like satisfaction, as at wolves rending each other. The snarl was the click of a revolver, and the bite following the bark. These were the men who gloried in snuffing out a candle or a life at thirty paces.[6]

Writing on the "Death of Wild Bill" in *City Life,* for May 18, 1895, Capt. Jack Crawford made the following observations of the man and his character:

Bill Hickok was regarded as a red-handed murderer by eastern people who did not know him. He never wantonly took human life. It is true that in his exciting career on the borders of civilization he killed several men, but there is no instance on record where he shed blood except in defence of his own life or in the line of duty as a peace officer. . . . While serving as a peace officer in several of the towns along the line of the old Kansas Pacific Railroad he was brought in contact with the very worst element in the country—thieves, thugs and outlaws who would cut a throat for a dollar—and some of them were cut short in their career of crime by his ever ready pistol. It is yet a matter of comment among the first settlers of that now prosperous and peaceful State of Kansas that when Wild Bill started to enforce order and obedience to the laws, he performed that duty in the face of all opposition from the rougher class. All western men know that when a man has made a reputation as a "killer," there are numerous cranks and whiskey-crazed would-be "bad men" who seek to "do him up" just for the notoriety to be gained for having "killed a killer." Bill Hickok's life was ever menaced, and on several occasions his quick eye and dexterity in handling the six shooter alone prevented his mortal light from being snuffed out. In some instances the would-be assassins paid the severest penalty for attempting his murder, while on others he has dropped a pistol and held them until he could read them a pointed lecture on their folly, and has then permitted them to go away unharmed.

Wild Bill had his faults, grievous ones, perhaps, but he never was the human fiend some writers have pictured him. He would get drunk, gamble, and indulge in the general licentiousness characteristic of the border in the early days, yet even when full of the vile libel of the name of whiskey which was dealt over the bars at exorbitant prices, he was gentle as a child, unless aroused to anger by intended insults. Even in his rage he had wonderful control of his temper, and rarely permitted himself to get into unnecessary trouble. He was loyal in his friendship, generous to a fault, and invariably espoused the cause of the weaker against the stronger one in a quarrel. His nature, despite the blood upon his hands, was very sympathetic. He would endure the severest pain with remarkable fortitude, yet tears would fill his eyes when he witnessed the sufferings of another.

One could cite many similar descriptions of Hickok's prowess as a fighting man, his generosity of character, his courage and his

skill with a pistol, his weakness for gambling, his fondness for liquor. From that evidence one could conclude that he was an extraordinary man with human frailties. But for every individual
who eulogized Wild Bill there was one who did not. As early as
1872 an unknown correspondent for the Saline *County Journal*
was cited on January 18 as claiming that Hickok was in Boston,
exhibiting himself to the public for a fee. It was now the turn of
the "credulous New Englanders" to interview "in person the
man who has shot men down in cold blood by the scores and is
as big a criminal as walks the earth. If it is pleasure for those
down-easters to welcome a gambler, a libertine and a rowdy, we
can furnish those of the same ilk, just as deserving, by the hundreds, from our 'wicked plains.'" No evidence has so far come to
light to suggest that Wild Bill visited the Eastern states prior to
August of that year.

On May 11, 1873, a certain Colonel Norton of the *Arkansas
Traveler* was credited by the Topeka *Daily Commonwealth* with
an attempt to discredit Hickok's reputation by exposing the real
man:

> It is disgusting to see the eastern papers crowding in everything
> they can get hold of about "Wild Bill." If they only knew the real
> character of the men they so want to worship, we doubt if their
> names would ever appear again. "Wild Bill," or Bill Hickok, is
> nothing more than a drunken, reckless, murderous coward, who
> is treated with contempt by true border men, and who should
> have been hung years ago for the murder of innocent men. The
> shooting of the "old teamster" in the back, for a small provocation
> while crossing the plains in 1859, is one fact that Harper's corres-
> pondent failed to mention and being booted out of a Leavenworth
> saloon by a boy bar tender is another, and we might name many
> other similar examples of his bravery. In one or two instances he
> did the U.S. government good service, but his shameful and cow-
> ardly conduct more than overbalances the good.

Even a cursory glimpse at the foregoing suggests a certain
amount of malicious hearsay, for if there were any truth in the allegations, names and dates should also have been included. Norton was by no means alone in debunking Hickok, but his was a
contemporary attack. Many of the similar statements were made

years later, and the accusers themselves are often suspected of
mischief-making to boost their own egos.

Still critical, but not so much of the man as the circumstances
that had made him, were comments by those who had known
Hickok personally or by reputation. In assessing the sort of frontier characters he had known, William E. Curtis recalled that
Hickok, when Nichols discovered him and published the article
in *Harper's,* was a "very brave, intelligent and valuable Union
Scout, more dreaded and feared by the rebels than any forty men
of the Union Army. Indeed, most of the early homicides on Bill's
long catalogue were the result of attempts to entrap or betray
him by rebel sympathisers of Missouri." His great failing, however, was gambling and liquor.[7]

C. W. Miller, an early resident of Hays City, recalled in 1931
that Hickok was considered to be "a very likable chap but dangerous if 'crossed.' His law for persons considered dangerous to
the community consisted of a choice of three things: 1. Take the
first eastbound train out of Hays. 2. Take the first westbound
train out of Hays. 3. Or go north in the morning. And North
meant Boot Hill." Miller adds little to what we know of Hickok,
but his reference to "train times" does suggest a hint of Hickok's
known sense of humor.[8]

The real Wild Bill then, was a mixture of strengths and weaknesses like that found in any other mortal. But unlike most
people, who rarely enter the limelight, his strengths and weaknesses were grabbed by others and exposed to public examination.

One other facet of Hickok's relationships concerns the number of women who either shared his blankets or were in some
manner linked to him. In 1874, during the period when Hickok
traveled with Buffalo Bill's Combination, the editor of the
Springfield, Massachusetts, *Republican* remarked on February 21
that Hickok was a secretive individual: "He is a bachelor, and is
supposed never to have been in love, though upon this point, as
on many others, even his most intimate friends do not speak
with assurance, for Wild Bill keeps his secrets closely guarded."
We assume the editor meant "love" and not "married," for in the
case of the former, Wild Bill had his moments of success and failure. The first recorded reference to a youthful romance was with

Mary Owen (the part-Shawnee daughter of John Owen) with whom he was romantically involved at Monticello, Kansas, in 1858. Hickok's involvement with Owen led to a family rift—the family was most concerned that he might marry an Indian. His nephew Howard later recalled that his elder brother Lorenzo was given the task of dissuading him. But the belief that he did marry Owen prevailed in the area as late as 1922, when the editor of the Johnson County *Democrat* stated on August 31 that Hickok "married Owen's daughter but they did not get along and separated, and the wife afterwards married a Dr. Harris." She did in fact marry Dr. Simeon H. Harris, but only when her relationship with Hickok ended. Earlier, on June 6, 1901, Jule Hadley, an early resident of Johnson County, was quoted in the Olathe *Mirror* as stating that

> Hickok was one of the first constables of Monticello township and remained there a year after his term of office had expired in an effort to marry Mary Owen, a farmer's daughter and an eighth-blood Shawnee of great attraction. In 1858 I carried many notes to the lady for him as I made my home with the Owens. The public does not know it but his matrimonial failure and disappointment made him the "Wild Bill" and the most distinguished Son of the Border, the equal of General Funston, in his different and exacting line of duty.

Hickok was later reported to have had a liaison with Sarah Shull at Rock Creek (which she herself denied just before her death) and during the Civil War with a still untraced woman named Susannah Pruitt (or Moore, depending upon the source), who is alleged to have shared some of his Civil War adventures. Even Elizabeth Bacon Custer is said to have fallen for Hickok's charms (but not in a physical sense). She was captivated by him and wrote several glowing descriptions of his manner and bearing. In Ellsworth, an Indian woman generally called "Indian Annie" is reputed to have borne him a son, but this has never been established.

The most publicized relationship, however, was the one Hickok is reported to have had with Martha Jane Cannary, better known as "Calamity Jane." Contemporary reports and the recollections of those who knew both parties very well indicate that they only met weeks before Hickok's death. Wild Bill is reported to have befriended Jane when she joined the Utter wagon train en route for Deadwood. Verification of this rumor came from an unlikely source. In 1878, Thomas McLean Newson published a play in three acts, *Drama of Life in the Black Hills,* that purported to tell a true story of life in the Black Hills. Hickok's death took place in Scene VI, Act III, at which point his relationship with Jane is also explained. She entered the saloon and declared that Wild Bill "is one of my best and dearest friends." Hickok shook her hand and asked, "How are you, my old gal—take a drink." She soon left the saloon. When McCall killed Wild Bill, Jane returned and demanded to know who shot him, and then, watched by an astonished crowd, dropped to her knees and took Hickok's head upon her lap and moaned: "Oh! my God! my best, my greatest friend is gone! Bill! speak to me! Bill! open your eyes! Bill! you can't be dead! When the cold world kicked me, it was you who helped me. When the heart was breaking, it was you who calmed it. Oh! my God! my God!"

Jane then dropped to the floor "in a swoon." That declaration seems to scotch rumors of a romance. But in 1941, a "diary" was produced, allegedly written by Jane herself, which claimed that they were married in 1871 and that the marriage had produced a daughter. Expert opinion, however, quickly exposed the diary as a fake, and when the so-called daughter was interviewed by the Hickok family, she confessed that she had been born in 1880 and not 1873 as originally claimed. Indeed, the latest conclusion, based upon some very intensive research, is that the alleged daughter, Jeane Hickok McCormick, was probably an orphan who decided to create a family and chose Wild Bill and Calamity Jane as her "parents." She is also believed to be the author of the so-called diary, updating it with loose-leaf inserts as new information or potentially "authentic" snippets of information came to light. It was a massive fraud, one that deserves a place in Western legend.[9]

A daughter of a different kind was that of John B. Edwards of Abilene. Some quite extraordinary things happened when she gave the Kansas State Historical Society permission to allow scholars and others access to her father's correspondence, including the letters he received from Charles F. Gross, an early res-

ident of Abilene. Several people cited Gross's comment that
Hickok lived with several women while at Abilene. One of them,
described as "Nan Ross," a former mistress who came to Abilene
to make up with him. Hickok gave her $25 and she moved on
when he told her he was through with her. In the mid 1950s, I received a letter from a gentleman in Texas who claimed that Nan
Ross had been a great friend of his father's, and that she had told
his father many things about Wild Bill that no one else knew. I
was intrigued and asked questions. The answers I received were
sometimes conflicting but always interesting. But when I myself
examined the Gross letters, I learned that "Nan Ross" was a badly
written "no row," meaning the lady did not make a scene, but
took the $25 and departed. This discovery not only removed
Nan from the scene but destroyed much of my faith in *alleged*
reminiscences from some old-timers!

In 1871, Hickok met Agnes Lake Thatcher, widow of a circus
owner. She fell in love with him. They corresponded for several
years before marrying on March 5, 1876, at Cheyenne, Wyoming.
Gross recalled that Hickok said he would not marry her because
she would try to civilize him: "It's me for the West. I would be
lost back in the States."[10]

Like many of the old-time plainsmen, Hickok was not as at
ease with well bred ladies as he was among the hard-working or
hard-living women who populated the West. Mrs. Custer recalled
that Hickok was reluctant to appear before "excursionists." On
one occasion some ladies even gave flowers to bystanders with
the request that they "be given to the renowned scout" in the
hope that he would be tempted to emerge from the back of a saloon. He refused both the flowers and the invitation. "He was
really a very modest man and very free from swagger and bravado," Mrs. Custer wrote. Finally, Custer himself agreed to invade
the saloon and returned with the scout, whose face betrayed the
confusion and embarrassment he felt. "He went through the enforced introduction for General Custer's sake, but it was a relief
when the engine whistle sounded that released him."[11]

A similar incident was recalled in 1876 by "C," who stated that
Hickok was among a crowd of sightseers watching the arrival of a
train at Hays City when a young fashionably dressed "Ohio girl"
turned her lovely gaze upon him and marched up to him:

"Are you Wild Bill the *Harper's Magazine* tells about?" The astonished scout bashfully replied "I believe I am." The mischievous eyes surveyed him complacently from head to foot, while their owner laughingly said, "*are you?* Why, my papa told me to come out here and marry some great man like you." The effect was wonderful, and for once in his life the man who had faced death almost times without number, and who could look into the muzzle of a "Colt's army" in the hands of a murderous assailant without a quiver, was thoroughly frightened, and, too, by the harmless weapons of a pretty woman. Pistols were of no use in such an engagement, and to steal away and "blush unseen" was impossible. So, completely vanquished, he stood like the rural youth at his first "sparking," vainly trying to hide his feet and hands, until, tired of questioning a victim too overcome to answer, she bounded away to tell her capture, and perhaps to find other "sons of the border" to conquer.[12]

In 1927, it was reported in the Junction City *Union* that a woman at Ellsworth had presented the writer Frank J. Wilstach with a mustache cup that she claimed had belonged to Hickok when he was marshal at Abilene. In the center of the cup were his initials J. B. H. Unfortunately, the woman's name was not disclosed, and she was one of a number of elderly women who claimed to have had either a relationship or a friendship with Wild Bill.[13]

Hickok's decision to marry late in life may have been dictated by a number of factors that are no longer known. Only two of his letters to Agnes have come to light, but there were obviously others. She sent several of them to the Hickok family to read and return so that they would know more of James's whereabouts. Nonetheless, the Reverend Warren of Cheyenne, who married the couple, stated in his register that he did not think that they "meant it." But Agnes assured the Hickok family that she loved James and that she mourned him. Less than a year later, however, she and a man named George Carson, described as a "frontiersman widely and favorably known," took out a marriage license on September 27, 1877, which was returned for file the next day. Curiously, the witnesses, S. L. and Minnie Moyer, were the same couple who witnessed her marriage to Hickok. Carson, however, soon disappeared, and in later life, Agnes always referred to herself as Mrs. James B. Hickok. She died in 1907.[14]

Almost as a postscript to Hickok's love life, there appeared in 1985 a photograph of Wild Bill and a poem allegedly written by him to a long lost love. It aroused considerable attention when it came to be auctioned, for the idea that Hickok might have had poetic leanings was something no one had considered.

At first, I thought Hickok might have been the author. But conducting some research and consulting experts I established that the poem was based upon one written by John Saxe, and that it was the young lady who wrote this version, not Wild Bill. The photograph is a tintype, circa early 1870s. It is housed in a brown leather case with reddish and gold embossing, a brass clasp, and is lined with moire cloth. The initials J. B. H. are written inside. Beneath the tintype was found a scrap of paper on which was pencilled:

> Do I love Thee go ask
> The flowers if they
> Love Sweet refreshing
> Showers
>   Sadia
>   James B. Hickok
>   Springfield, Mo.

Saxe's original poem read:

> Do I love thee? Ask the flower
> If she loves the vernal shower,
> Or the kisses of the sun,
> Or the dew, when day is done.
> As she answers, Yes or No,
> Darling! take my answer so.

An extensive examination of available records at Springfield, Missouri, revealed that Wild Bill had been a resident of the St. James Hotel from about late September 1872 until August 1873. Close to his hotel was one that included on its staff a twenty-one-year-old Canadian girl named Salina Stubbs. She had disappeared by 1880. Whether she was the mysterious Sadia, or possibly Sadie, is open to speculation. But whoever she was, she kept her secret well. The photograph and poem came to light at Austin, Texas, about 1965 and remained in a private collection until 1985 when it was sold and later auctioned.[15]

This latter insight into Hickok's love life suggests that at least one of his conquests held him in deep regard, which conflicts with the view of those who consider him and his kind as licentious and contemptuous of women friends. The mid-Victorian view that women were either "good" or "bad"—or "fallen"— the latter existing for the enjoyment of men to be tossed aside when used, was held by many men of Hickok's day. The reality was, of course, more complicated. Women were rare in many parts of the West until the post–Civil War era, and were treated according to their class. Married women were usually left very much alone, and single women in "respectable" occupations were accorded similar courtesies. But those who eked out livings as prostitutes were considered fair game. As a result, the Cyprian sisterhood acquired a reputation for toughness that was rarely applied to the more genteel of their sex.

The Hickoks were able to trace their origin back to Stratford-upon-Avon, Warwickshire, England, where they were contemporaries of William Shakespeare. The New World branch took root when William Hickocks (sometimes spelt Hitchcocks) sailed for Boston in 1635. The Hickocks (later spelled Hickok) soon spread all over New England. During the Revolution they fought on the side of the Americans against the British and again during the War of 1812. James's father, William Alonzo Hickok, was born at North Hero, Vermont, on December 5, 1801, and in his youth considered the church as a vocation before turning to other pursuits. James's mother, Polly Butler, was born on August 4, 1804, at Bennington, Vermont, and came from a well-to-do family who later laid claim to Gen. Benjamin Butler of Civil War fame and more recently to George Bush, forty-first president of the United States.[16]

William Alonzo and Polly married in 1827, and had seven children, five sons (one of whom died in infancy) and two daughters. They were Oliver (1830–1898), Lorenzo (1831), the third child was also named Lorenzo (1832–1913), Horace (1834–1916),

James (1837–1876), Celinda (1839–1916), and Lydia (1842–
1916).

Moving from New York state in 1833, the couple eventually
settled at the village of Homer in La Salle County, Illinois, where
James was born on May 27, 1837. Later, when it was learned that
there was an older and much larger town named Homer in northern Illinois, the name was changed to Troy Grove. Illinois at that
time was just recovering from the Black Hawk Indian War, and
the removal of the tribes west of the Mississippi River meant that
the state was open to settlement. By the 1850s it was recognized
as farming country.

James Hickok and his brothers and sisters were brought up to
believe in God and themselves, and their parents ensured that
they received as good an education as possible. Family tradition
also asserts that James displayed a liking for the outdoors and
preferred shooting game for the family pot rather than pushing a
plow or other chores. His father ran a store until the financial
panic of 1837, when he was forced to give up storekeeping and
hire himself out to neighboring farmers to eke out a living. Between schooling and home chores, the four boys worked for
neighbors to boost the family income. By the early 1850s the
family had a small farm, and his father also became involved in
the Abolitionist movement, helping fleeing slaves to escape to
the north. The family claims that James probably heard his first
"shot fired in anger" when, while helping his father and friends
move some fleeing slaves, they were chased and fired upon by
bounty hunters.

The first written reference to James dates from 1851, when his
father paid a visit to relatives back East. Oliver had left home that
year and gone to California in the wake of the gold rush. James
was anxious to follow him, but his parents thought him too
young. His time would come. "James," his father wrote, "I shall
hope to have a good acount of you when I get home. Horace, I
depend much upon you in my absence [and I] hope you and
James will be friendly & steady & stay at home as much as possible & do all you can for your Mother & be kind to the Girls."[17]

In view of later statements by members of the family, James at
fourteen years of age, was already showing the independent side

of his nature. When his father died less than a year later, on May 5, 1852, James's ambition seems to have been set on leaving home at the first opportunity. He may have been driven away by the possessiveness of his mother, Polly, following her husband's death. In later years his sisters would recall Polly's actions with sadness. Horace and his wife Martha found that with age Polly grew increasingly difficult to live with, and they were left to care for her with little financial assistance from the rest of the family. Lorenzo returned home from the West in 1871 and joined Horace in running the home and sharing expenses (Lorenzo had in fact been sending money home during his service as a wagonmaster in the Civil War and later on the plains). James, during his short life, probably earned more than his brothers did for most of theirs. But he did not send money home. Instead, on his one authenticated visit home in 1869, he brought his mother and sisters expensive gifts of clothing. His grandniece, Edith Harmon, recalls that her grandmother Martha told her of his visit when she was a child. But she said that was the only criticism of him made by any members of the family. Rather, they went to extraordinary lengths to defend him in public or in print. Nevertheless, we do detect a conflict of personalities between James and his mother. Both appear to have been strong-minded individualists. It is true that in later years she expressed pride and at the same time felt considerable anxiety for her youngest son; but she did not hide her thoughts on some of his actions.[18]

James and Lorenzo left home in June 1856, bound for Kansas Territory. There they hoped to lay claim to some of the available farming land. There was talk of the rest of the family following if they were successful. But Lorenzo returned home when letters intimated that their mother was ill. It is not clear whether she was genuinely ill or simply wanted them to return home. James decided to stay on. Polly later chided him for not writing more often, hinting that he, too, should return to the fold. In response, James wrote: "You say write us often[,] how can I when it has been more than three months since I left home and only received t[w]o letters from home . . . the excitement is purty much over. I have seen since I have been here sites [sights] that would make the wickedest hearts sick[,] believe me mother[,] for what I

say is true[.] I can't come home till fall[,] it would not look
well.''[19]

By 1859, when James had left Monticello, Kansas, and moved
to nearby Olathe to be with his cousin Guy Butler, Polly was not
averse to Horace visiting his brother. But when Horace wrote
home to inform her that James had borrowed his best shirts and
gone off to Pike's Peak with a freighting outfit for thirty dollars a
month, she was concerned:

> I was sorry to hear that James had gone to Pike's Peak[.] I do not
> know what he means by doing [so] as he has in writing to us[,] we
> have had but one letter from him since you went away[.] If you
> hear from him I want you to let me know for I am verry [sic] un-
> easy about him[.] did he appear glad to see you or was he cold and
> distant[?] has he got anything or made anything or is he in de[b]t
> for his board[?] do tell me all about it[.] I was pleased when I heard
> that you had gone to Kansas in stead of the Peak[,] for I thought it
> would be better for you and James both if you were together[.] But
> it seems that you did not stay together long[.][20]

Polly's apparent insight into James's character is interesting.
Was he in fact inclined to be standoffish, aloof, or simply unso-
ciable if the mood possessed him? In later years it would be recalled that he did not make friends easily, but when he did he
would lay his life on the line for them. In a letter addressed to
Horace dated November 24, 1856, he displayed a dramatic
change of mood. Horace had asked ''What is going on in Kansas?'' James remarked that he had read Horace's letter on his way
home. ''I looked ahead of me to where the roads crossed and
saw about 500 soldiers agoing on and I looked down the river
and saw some nice steamers, and they wear [were] all agoing on
and that is the way with all the people in Cansas[,] they are all a
going on.'' But in a postscript dated November 27, he seemed
depressed. Noting that he was suffering from a cold but was otherwise well and weighed 180 pounds, he declared that he was a
hermit, ignoring girls, beer, and people. But he still had his fiddle, a dog, and a gun that ''I almost worship.'' He added, ''I hold
no intercourse with the world around[,] everything looks dark
about me and a round but there is a bright spark ahead. . . . it I

persue til my fiddle strings brake and my dog dyes and my gun bursts this is so."[21]

James's reluctance to return home further suggests that his relationship with his mother was fostered by absence. Had he remained at Troy Grove, they may well have fallen out entirely. As it was, the occasional letter seems to have bridged the gap. But this minimal communication was not enough for the whole family. They felt that he should have made more of an effort to keep in touch. So far only one of the letters he wrote during the Civil War has come to light, and once James became a noted character, his family hardly heard from him at all. Some indication of James's attitude toward his family can be gleaned from remarks made by Lorenzo. On December 2, 1867, writing from Fort Lyon, Colorado Territory, Lorenzo declared that James's life was so full of excitement that he hardly had time to write: "If you can get letters from him you will do better than I can or anyone else[.] this is not because he does not think of you or me but it is a great bother to him to write[.] if he could sit down and write a letter in one minute he would do it but he has led a life of activity and excitement and the common acts of an everyday life are a bother and a bore to him[.] he sends me some word every chance he has but no letters and is anxious to know how I am getting along."[22]

Despite his exciting life and his selfish pursuits, James was still concerned over his brother's welfare and anxious not to cut himself off entirely from his family. He displayed the independence of so many people who leave home to live their own lives, yet keep in touch, however remotely, with their kin.

Polly's intimation that James might have been a cold character is not borne out by reminiscences of those who knew him in later years. But if she implied that he tended to make no secret of his likes and dislikes, then perhaps she was right. James never suffered fools gladly.

In demeanor, James Butler Hickok bore himself with a pride that might have been interpreted as arrogance. He was egotistical, but not in the manner of Buffalo Bill (who craved attention). Rather, he imparted the impression that he was a man who was well aware of his reputation yet self-confident enough to admit his faults and foibles. Above all was his sense of humor, evident all through his life. From the tricks he played upon his brothers

and sisters to the tall tales he spun for gullible scriveners or innumerable barflies who hung on every word, he enjoyed himself
immensely. And even his audience appreciated the humor when,
having told a particularly outrageous story, there was always one
innocent who remarked, "But Bill, how did you escape?" "I
didn't," he would reply, poker faced. "I was killed!"

It is doubtful that Buffalo Bill fully appreciated this side of
Hickok's character when Hickok was a member of the Combination. Had he done so, perhaps he might have reacted a little less
harshly to Hickok's penchant for shooting close to the legs of the
"supers." What to Wild Bill was a farce was, for Cody, a serious
matter. Hickok retired from the stage in disgust, whereas Cody,
following some minor disappointments, eventually became an
accomplished character actor, playing himself and other characters on stage. Hickok, however, must have realized very early on
that he was no actor. He did not take himself or the role he was
playing as seriously as his companions would wish. So rather
than continue to "make a fool of himself," he quit.

From the wealth of material devoted to Hickok, there is still
one facet that defies total clarification—how and why did he
earn the name of Wild Bill? W. E. Webb, writing in 1875, noted
how prevalent was the name Bill when it came to reputations:

> The most astonishing crop the plains ever produced was the
> one of "Bill" heroes. If an ambitious frontiersman named William
> chanced to see an Indian or kill a few bison, he at once took unto
> his name an addition, and became a character. But let it not be
> supposed he was a hero among his companions. To them he ever
> remained plain Bill, or, at the best, with a Jones or Brown added,
> as the case might be. . . .
>
> Buffalo Bill and Wild Bill, whom I met often on the plains,
> much more fairly deserved their names. The former I knew first as
> teamster, then bar-tender, and finally scout. He certainly knew
> more about the plains than any one I ever met. Wild Bill, during
> the years that I was cognizant of his actions, filled at intervals the
> positions of scout, saloon-keeper, refugee, and sheriff.[23]

During his later years, Hickok was generally known as Wild
Bill, and only on occasion did scriveners thoughtfully add James
B. Hickok or other variants of his name (as did Col. George Ward

Nichols, who described him in *Harper's* as "William Hitch-cock"). Reference to Hickok in army records after 1866 also tend to refer to him as Wild Bill in correspondence and as J. B. Hickok in the quartermasters' returns.

The name "Wild Bill" suggests a violent or at least an unruly character. Some of those similarly dubbed have been just that, while others have been tame by comparison. Several individuals in more recent times have been called "Wild Bill" either in jest or for some spectacular action. These include the noted jazz musician William Edward Davison. But the best known is the celebrated William J. Donovan, who served with distinction against Pancho Villa in 1916 (earning the name "Galloping Bill"), in World War I, and in the Office of Strategic Services during World War II. He was later called "Wild Bill" because of his wartime exploits as the most highly decorated soldier in American history—all of which goes to show that the name had a certain class as well as notoriety.[24]

The late Waldo E. Koop found reference to more than thirty individuals with Western connections called "Wild Bill," and since 1971, when he compiled that list, I have been able to add several more. Koop's earliest candidate was a youth who was born in 1800 and died in 1818. He came from Pinckneyville, Mississippi, and was also known as the "Mississippi Orson." On October 20, 1859, the Westport, Missouri, *Border Star* published a letter from one "Wild Bill" offering to fight two of the most famous pugilists of the day, John Morrissey and John Camel Heenan, for $1,000 a side. According to the editor, this "Wild Bill" was white by birth but a Cheyenne by choice.

A rebel guerrilla known as "Wild Bill" Price from Westport is reported to have been killed at Fort Scott, but he may have been confused with one William H. Gardner, "sometimes known as 'Wild Bill,'" who was shot at Fort Scott on July 28, 1863, by Capt. William S. Tough. Gardner, a private in Company F, Third Wisconsin Cavalry, was said to be frequently "crazy drunk" and dangerous. On the day of the shooting he picked on a small man named Pat Hamlin and tried to make him fight. Tough interceded and Gardner mounted his horse and rode off, only to gallop back moments later with a pistol in his hand. He fired at Tough, but the cap snapped. Meanwhile Tough grabbed a pistol from a by-stander and shot this "Wild Bill" out of the saddle.[25]

A candidate put forward as the "original Wild Bill" by James R. Cunningham, a former guerrilla with Quantrill, was "Wild Bill" Thomason, alleged to be an uncle of Jesse James who had served as an army officer during the Mexican War of 1846–1848.[26] Closer to Hickok's time, and of far greater significance, was William J. Heffington, who deserted from the First Arkansas Infantry and formed a guerrilla band that fought for the Union in the mountains of Arkansas. He, too, was known as "Wild Bill," and the area where he operated was known as "Wild Bill's Mountain." He was killed in action in August 1863.[27]

In March 1868, there were reports that "Wild Bill" had thrown a tantrum at Lawrence, Kansas, chopping down the cabin door of a lady named Mary Ann Winfrey and then throwing the ax at her. Some concluded that this was Hickok, but a search of the local press revealed that the culprit was a Negro thief named William or Bill Smith known locally as "the black Wild Bill." By April, when Hickok was known to be in Leavenworth, another "Wild Bill" was reported to have been arrested for some misdemeanor at Omaha.[28]

William P. Longley, the noted Texas "bad man" who was hanged in 1878 for murder has, in recent years, been dubbed "Wild Bill" Longley. His descendants, however, have vigorously protested. In 1972, his eighty-nine-year-old niece, Mary Longley Hooker, declared, "I never heard my father call uncle Bill 'Wild Bill Longley.' None of the family ever called him 'Wild Bill.' " She claimed that a modern writer coined the term.[29]

By far the most important of the other "Wild Bills" who populated the West during Hickok's time was Mortimer N. Kress, a native of Williamsport, Pennsylvania. Kress had served in the Civil War and later emigrated to Nebraska, where he settled on the Blue River in 1870. He was known locally as "Wild Bill of the Blue," to distinguish him from his more famous namesake. His was the "Wild Bill's Outfit" that the army held responsible for the murder of the Sioux chief Whistler and two other Indians, Fat Badger and Handsmeller, in the fall of 1872, for which James Butler Hickok was later blamed. Local recollections of Kress were not good. In September 1871, he was involved in a train robbery but escaped prosecution when no evidence could be produced. He was generally called a "grandstander" by his neighbors.[30]

According to Hickok family sources, James Hickok was sometimes known as "Billy Barnes," but no definite source has been found. However, in the *Harper's* article he is reported to have told Nichols that he adopted the name Barnes when it suited him, passing himself off as the brother of a Texan he had known from Austin who had been killed sometime before. But no trace of such an individual could be found in local records. There is ample evidence, however, to prove that James Hickok was addressed as William or Bill soon after his arrival in Kansas in 1856.[31]

A search of early Kansas newspapers covering the Leavenworth area where Hickok first settled revealed that by 1858 he was known locally as William Hickok. The Englishman Robert H. Williams, one of the founders of Monticello, recalled being accompanied on his site-hunting trip by one William Hitchcock, though in later years he never realized that this man was the Wild Bill he had read about. According to the *Kansas Weekly Herald* of January 30, 1858, the citizens of Monticello were organizing a grand dress ball to take place on the evening of February 15. A member of the Committee of Invitation was William Hickok. In March 1858, Hickok was one of four constables elected to serve the four local magistrates. Surviving court records indicate that he was referred to both as J. B. Hickok and as William Hickok. On one occasion when he managed to evade jury service (he kept the court busy for three years trying to find him), he was described as "J. Hickox."[32]

For generations, the Hickok family has believed that during his early days in Kansas, James was known also as "Shanghai Bill." This information reached them via J. W. Buel, who claimed in his book *Heroes of the Plains* that James had joined Gen. James Lane's anti-slavery force known as the Red Legs. When he displayed his superior marksmanship, "the regiment gave James the title of 'Shanghai Bill.' " Buel was mistaken on all counts. The Red Legs was not formed until 1861, and Lane had no connection with them at all. "Shanghai Bill" was an alias for one William Hanschen, whose name appears regularly in early court records, mostly on charges of

grand larceny. By the time James Hickok reached Rock Creek, Nebraska Territory, in late April or May 1861, he was known locally as
Dutch Bill for a still indeterminate reason. Because the name was
misspelled as "Duch" on a couple of the court records relative to
the so-called McCanles Massacre, some writers have interpreted it
to mean "Duck Bill," an appellation allegedly fastened upon him
because of the shape of his nose.[33]

According to legend, James Butler Hickok won the name Wild
Bill in 1862, when he stopped the lynching of a bartender at Independence, Missouri. The source of this story was George W.
Hance, a fellow wagonmaster and family friend. He served during
the war in this capacity, sometimes with Lorenzo Hickok, and
first met both brothers at Rolla, Missouri. Tradition asserts that a
woman in the crowd yelled, "My God, ain't he wild!" and Wild
Bill was born. Hance's talks with the family and his recollections
(published in 1901 and 1912) reveal some discrepancies. There is
no mention of this incident. But Howard L. Hickok, James's
nephew (the son of his brother Horace), evidently gave this story
to Connelley, and an examination of some papers presented to
this writer by Howard's son, the late James Butler Hickok, suggests that there was confusion on somebody's part. Howard asserts that it was Lorenzo who actually put a stop to the lynching
but disclaimed any part in the affair. He is unsure of the source of
the name: "In some manner the name was given to uncle Jim in
Springfield and kept by him throughout his life." But in 1901,
Hance stated that when he first met the Hickok brothers at Rolla,
"in order to distinguish them they were called Wild Bill and
Tame Bill and as such they were known and called by everyone
from the summer of 1862 until the close of the war."[34]

Howard's remark that James became Wild Bill at Springfield
may be closer to the truth than he could have imagined. Following the trial of Jack McCall in 1876, attempts were made to discredit Hickok's reputation in an effort to get McCall pardoned.
William Pound, the prosecutor, wrote a spirited reaction to the
suggestion that Hickok was a "notorious character" whose real
name was only disclosed by the evidence:

> A reference to the indictment will show that both his real name
> and alias of "Wild Bill" were used in it. But the name "Wild Bill"

had been given to him and fastened upon him so that he was really better known by that than by any other, and without discredit to himself. It is a part of the history of the war, that this man, by reason of his fearless and efficient service as a Union Scout among the guerrillas of Missouri, Arkansas and Eastern Kansas, and by his contests with these same guerrillas even after the war closed, when they so persistently pursued him, won this name of "Wild Bill," and he certainly had no reason, during his life to be ashamed of it.[35]

No matter how one approaches the origin of the name Wild Bill in relation to James Butler Hickok, one is constantly reminded of his Civil War activities. Indeed, William Pound's earnest defense of Hickok suggests that perhaps he was aware of information that is sadly lacking today. In effect, he was able to talk to people who had known Hickok for years, some who no doubt had ridden with him during the war or as a scout with the army afterward. Therefore, allegations that he was a self-styled "Wild Bill" or so named by the likes of Ned Buntline are without foundation.

The first known published reference to Hickok as Wild Bill appeared in the Springfield, Missouri, *Weekly Patriot* of July 27, 1865. When reporting Hickok's shooting of Dave Tutt in a duel on Public Square, the paper also noted that Hickok was "better known in Southwest Missouri as 'Wild Bill.' " From that time on, Hickok lost his regional notoriety and became known nationally (and later internationally) as Wild Bill Hickok.

Two

A *Hero of* Harper's

Late in January 1867, copies of the February issue of *Harper's New Monthly Magazine* began circulating in the West. The inhabitants of places as far apart as Junction City, Kansas, and Springfield, Missouri, were startled to find that the lead article "Wild Bill," written by Col. George Ward Nichols, was a highly colored story about an individual familiar to many of them—James Butler Hickok.

Hickok had spent much of the period between 1861 and 1866 in parts of Missouri and Arkansas. He was well known in Rolla and Springfield as a wagonmaster and government scout. Some folks remembered him because of a recent gunfight, while others, particularly those who had worked with him during the war, remembered his exploits behind enemy lines. And there were some who were appalled that his deeds should receive national attention.

Initial reaction from the press was very mixed. On February 1, the Atchison *Champion* recalled that "Bill was formerly a driver on the Overland Stage Line, and is well known to many old residents of this city. Few, however, would recognize him in the romantic picture Nichols draws. He was simply a desperado, and dozens like him can be found among the employees of the O.S. Line." On February 5 the editor again discussed "Wild Bill" and hastened to correct an error on the part of Colonel Nichols, who had described his subject as "William Hitchcock":

> The real name of "Wild Bill" . . . is William Haycock, and not Hitchcock [he later amended this to "William Hickok"], and [he] . . . is, as stated in the Magazine, a splendid specimen of physical

manhood, and is a dead shot with a pistol. He is a very quiet man, rarely talking to anyone, and not of a quarrelsome disposition, although reckless and desperate when once involved in a fight. There are a number of citizens of this city who know him well.

This opinion was shared by the Leavenworth *Conservative,* which, on February 1, had also repudiated the language and grammar that Nichols credited to his hero.

On February 26, the Atchison *Champion* again referred to Hickok and noted that he had paid a visit to the city. This time attention was given to his personal appearance. The *Harper's* woodcuts were "remarkably accurate," the editor remarked, and Hickok himself was a "fine specimen of physical manhood, and although courage and determination are imprinted on every feature of his countenance he is quiet and unassuming in his manners, and evidently not disposed to be quarrelsome."

Both editors made the point that the Hickok they knew bore little resemblance to the character portrayed in the magazine story, emphasizing instead his self-effacing, quiet manner—an impression gained by many of those who met him in later years. And even in Springfield Hickok escaped criticism. But not Nichols. His description of Springfield infuriated its citizens:

> On a warm summer day I sat watching from the shadow of a broad awning the coming and going of the strange, half-civilized people who, from all the country round, make this a place for barter and trade. Men and women dressed in queer costumes; men with coats and trowsers made of skin, but so thickly covered with dirt and grease as to have defied the identity of the animal when walking in the flesh. Others wore homespun gear, which often times appeared to have seen lengthy service. . . . The most marked characteristic of the inhabitants seemed to be an indisposition to move, and their highest ambition to let their hair and beards grow. . . . When people moved in this lazy city they did so slowly and without method. No one seemed in haste.[1]

These and other disparaging remarks prompted the editor of the Springfield *Missouri Weekly Patriot* in his January 31 issue to make the only known direct criticism of Nichols and the article and some of the feats attributed to its hero. Yet in condemning

Nichols, the editor thought it fitting to defend Wild Bill and to point out that in Springfield at least, they knew his real name:

> James B. Hickok . . . *is* a remarkable man. . . . the portrait of him on the first page of *Harper* for February, is a most faithful and striking likeness—features, shape, posture and dress—in all it is a faithful reproduction of one of Charley Scholten's photographs of "Wild Bill," as he is generally called.[2] No finer physique, no greater strength, no more personal courage, no steadier nerves, no superior skill with the pistol, no better horsemanship than his, could any man of the million Federal soldiers of the war, boast of; and few did better or more loyal service as [a] soldier throughout the war. But Nichols "cuts it very fat" when he describes Bill's feats in arms. We think his hero only claims to have sent a few dozen rebs to the farther side of Jordan; and we never, before reading the "Colonel's" article, suspected he had dispatched "*several hundreds* with his own hands." But it must be so, for the "Colonel" asserts it with a parenthesis of genuine flavourous Bostonian piety to assure us of his incapacity to utter an untruth.

The *Patriot*'s stirring defense of Wild Bill prompted the Leavenworth *Bulletin* of March 1 to declare that the paper's "review" was not only more readable than the article but also more truthful, "emanating, as it does, from the residents of the town in the vicinity of which 'Wild Bill's' exploits are laid." Moreover, it was written by some one who knew Hickok personally, and not by an individual with only a few days' acquaintance.

This reaction was shared by Henry M. Stanley, the young Welsh-born reporter for the St. Louis *Weekly Missouri Democrat* covering the Hancock Indian War. He interviewed Hickok at Fort Zarah on April 4. In his account published on the sixteenth, Stanley concluded that the *Harper's* story was a "slight exaggeration" in parts, but otherwise correct, adding that Hickok "is neither as coarse and illiterate as *Harper's* portrays him."[3]

Where the *Patriot* and other Western newspapers were skeptical of some of the feats attributed to Hickok, newspapers as far away as New York were less critical. On January 24, the *Daily Tribune* declared that Hickok "realized the legends of Samson and Hercules combined. . . . the deeds of Wild Bill are equalled only by the accomplishments of his miraculous horse, and the

Discovered in 1989 in an album of photographs once the property of Richard Bentley Owen, this carte de visite *of Wild Bill is thought to be the work of Charles W. Scholten, who photographed him several times. It exemplifies the "legendary Wild Bill" more than any of his other photographs. (Courtesy James Joplin)*

whole narrative affords a rich illustration of the romance of border life." And by July, DeWitt's Ten Cent Romances were enthral-
ling their readers with *Wild Bill, the Indian Slayer,* to be followed in the December by *Wild Bill's First Trail.*[4]

Already the real Hickok was being woven into the web of
myth, which makes us wonder about his own reaction to his
overnight fame. Curiously, no one has so far discovered a published interview with verbatim quotes from Hickok. Some may
well believe that it suited him to ignore the criticisms and bask in
the glory, for there is no doubt that his *Harper's* appearance influenced those who employed him as a scout and later as a peace
officer. However, as early as April 27, 1867, a correspondent for
the influential *Army and Navy Journal* claimed to have spoken
to Wild Bill on the subject and he was alleged to have denied
"two of those Munchausen tales related of him, viz.: the horse
story and killing twelve men. He once killed three ranchmen
who attacked his house, but he had the door between him and
them." We must assume that the "ranchmen" was a reference to
the McCanles incident, which will be discussed elsewhere.

Even those closer to Hickok—his family at Troy Grove—cannot say just what effect the *Harper's* story had on him. In the
1960s James's nephew Horace told me that he had never seen
any letters from his uncle concerning the incident, but his father
(James's brother Horace) used to "tell us as children how Uncle
Jim would get mad when anyone mentioned the Nichols story."
Unfortunately, Horace was unable to confirm whether James
made his feelings known orally or by mail. His sister Ethel also recalled the stories, and it was her memory that brought to light a
hint of criticism from an unexpected quarter. It was Oliver, the
eldest brother who had left home for California in 1851, who
first questioned his younger brother's exploits. Whether he initi-
ated the correspondence or his brother Horace brought the magazine to his attention is not clear. But after a gap of four years the
family again established contact, and on April 11, 1867, Oliver
wrote:

> In that description of James there is some things that I do not
> understand[.] I did not know that he ran away from home or that
> he had been fifteen years amongst the trappers and then there[']s

some things in that piece that does not correspond with my way of thinking about James. I suppose he is a very stout and active man[,] but I think that I am almost as stout and active as his [he] is[.] I have weighed two hundred and ten Pounds but I do not weigh that now[.] then I was the stoutest man in this county and there was a good many of them in it[.] I would like to try him a shot or two with a rifle.[5]

Oliver's skepticism was evidently shared by the family, for they well remembered James's sense of humor and leg-pulling. But James was never known to tell deliberate lies to his family. It was unfortunate, therefore, that his own thoughts were not recorded. Nevertheless, it was made very clear that the family made no attempt to elevate James above the rest of the family members—a point reiterated many times by Ethel. She recalled that her father (Horace) had spent a lot of time and money in postage writing to various editors and others refuting some of the more bizarre stories of his late brother's exploits, but with little effect. The legend was already too well established.

Back in the 1860s when *Harper's* first publicized the exploits of Wild Bill, there must have been considerable confusion among his friends and former scouting companions, together with those who had employed him. The *Missouri Weekly Patriot* noted that his activities as a scout and spy had been efficiently conducted and he had rendered "signal service to the Union cause, as numerous acknowledgements from the different commanding officers with whom he has served will testify." But they would soon become even more bewildered by the wealth of stories woven into the growing web of fantasy.[6]

Hickok entered Union service in August 1861 and is said to have taken part in the Battle of Wilson's Creek near Springfield, Missouri, on August 10. The Union general Nathaniel Lyon, in command of 5,500 federal troops, was killed, and the one-day conflict ended in victory for the Confederates under the command of Gen. Benjamin McCulloch. The Union force fell back to Rolla, leaving the Confederates in control of the area. On February 13, 1862, Gen. Samuel R. Curtis recaptured Springfield, which remained in Union hands for the remainder of the war. But no record has been found that confirms Hickok's alleged participation in the battle. Informed opinion suggests that he may have been one of the civilian teamsters, men hired to transport provisions and kept well out of the battle area. According to Nichols, Wild Bill admitted to being "so frightened" the first time he was under artillery fire (when a Confederate battery opened up in front of him and shells screamed within six inches of his head) that for some moments he was rooted to the spot. When he returned to his companions, they thought he had seen a ghost.[7]

Official records, however, disclose that at Sedalia, Missouri, on October 30, 1861, J. B. Hickok was hired by quartermaster agent N. P. Cook as a wagonmaster at $100 per month. On November 28, he was transferred to Capt. J. A. Swain, assistant quartermaster at Warsaw and Sedalia. By January 1862, however, Hickok's wage was reduced to $60 per month, and on February 10 he was transferred to Capt. S. L. Brown, assistant quartermaster at Sedalia. On March 26, Hickok was made chief wagonmaster and his pay was increased to $100. On June 30, he was again transferred, this time to Lt. S. C. Peck, acting assistant quartermaster at Rolla. Here he remained until September 20 when he was dropped from the rolls, no discharge or transfer being noted.[8]

The only known letter written by James to his family during the war is dated Springfield, July 8, 1862, and was addressed to his sister Lydia. At that time he was still employed as a wagonmaster. In acknowledging two letters from her, both received when he was unloading the last sections of his ox trains, he said he was glad to hear that all was well.

I expect to have Ruff [rough] times for some time On account of General Curtis['s] Supplys Being cut off. I may be ordered to Platesvill[e] NBR [.] as soon as I reach Rolla and I start for Rolla in the morning. . . .

When next you write direct [it] to Rolla[.] Thare Was a farmer Just after me for Pay for 12.00 Rales my men Burnt of[f] his fence yesterday and to day I told Him I Would make him some Rales next fall when it got Cool And feed His Corn for him to Boot[.] He walked off saying He was as good a Younion man as I was[.] I told him he could afford to loose the Rales[,] then He went to cusin [cussing] then and some of my men Put in the Variations[.] By Laughfing I guess he likes me Purty Well . . . . When I get to Rolla I

will write Again so Good By for the Presant From your Affection-
ate Brother

Capt. J. B. Hickok[9]

Hickok's name appeared several times in the Rolla *Express* during 1862 and 1863 in connection with unclaimed letters at the
post office. His brother Lorenzo, himself a wagonmaster in government service, confirmed that the pair occasionally met either
at Rolla or Springfield. Writing from a camp eight miles from St.
Louis on July 16, 1863, Lorenzo informed the family that "I left
J B at Rolla." On March 4, 1864, he wrote that "J B is in *Batesville*
no Fayetteville at work for Capt Squires who is Chief of the Detective Police [, and he] gets about $100 per month." At that time
Lorenzo, following a row with his quartermaster, had his pay cut
from $60 to $30 per month. Lorenzo's remarks make it clear that
the "W. Hickok" listed as a Special Policeman under the direction of Lt. N. A. Burns, acting provost marshal, District of South-
West Missouri, at Springfield, in March 1864, was indeed Wild
Bill. However, according to abstract accounts dated July 20, audi-
tor William Patrick, on the orders of a Colonel Sanderson, disal-
lowed payment of $60 owed to Hickok "for the reason that no
authority was issued by the Prov. Mar. Genl. Dept. of the Mo., for
his employment."[10]

Brig. Gen. John B. Sanborn, who had authorized Hickok's
payment as a policeman, then decided to employ him in another
capacity. On April 3, he issued Special Order No. 89 requesting
that "J. B. Hickok will be taken up on the Rolls of Capt Owen,
A.Q.M., as Scout, at these Head Quarters, from this date and will
be furnished a horse, and equipments while on duty as Scout.
His compensation will be five dollars per day."[11]

Twenty years later, Sanborn was to state publicly and in print
that

> my principal scout was William Hickok, 'Wild Bill,' the real hero
> of many exploits, and, according to the dime novels, the imagi-
> nary hero of many more. Bill was a fine scout and detective. He
> entered the rebel camps, was arrested as a spy, and even taken be-
> fore Gen. Price; but his inordinate nerve and great self-possession
> not only saved him, but made him an orderly on Price's staff. He

eventually escaped and returned to me with valuable information during the battle of Newtonia."[12]

In 1867, the Leavenworth *Daily Conservative* of February 1 added the following comment on Hickok's involvement with the Battle of Newtonia:

> There has been a determined research in memory by those who participated in the closing scenes of the war in Northern Arkansas. Since the subject of the sketch in Harper has been prominently given to the country we have furbished our recollections, and the result is that we knew Bill Hitchcock in 1864 and recognize his portrait in the magazine. . . . "Wild Bill," as he is called, rode in company with the writer, and with the Adjutant Mackle and Lt. Col. Hoyt from Newtonia, subsequent to the battle in October, to the Arkansas river, we think, but perhaps he remained at Fayetteville . . . He came into Gen. Blunt's camp on the morning after the battle of Newtonia, having previously been with Price, and having spent several months in the camps in Arkansas, as stated in the article in question. . . . "Wild Bill" has made his mark in the war for the Union, and we accord him full credit for his risks and reward for results attained.

In January 1864, the Seventeenth Illinois Volunteer Cavalry was formed, and at one time was under the command of General Sanborn, as were the Eighth Missouri State Militia. Both regiments are reported to have employed Hickok as a scout at some point, although official records have not confirmed this. Nonetheless, F. A. Carpenter, formerly of Company K and author of the Seventeenth's history, went to great pains to describe the similarity in manner and character of Hickok and Lt. Philip McRae, who commanded Company C when it was engaged against General Price in the fall of 1864. He concluded that they were "thrusting, daring, fearless men, both did good work for their country and took pride in so doing." According to this account, Wild Bill saved a number of the regiment from capture by Price. He later described Hickok riding with the regiment's commander, Col. John L. Beveridge, in pursuit of enemy troops: "Wild Bill is with us, his horse running with a long easy stride, the front of his broad brimmed hat standing out of his line of vision."[13]

In the early 1930s a young man living in Oswego, Kansas, was befriended by Alfred Brock, who was then in his 90s. Brock told him he recalled seeing Hickok when he scouted for his regiment. Brock served in Company L, Seventeenth Illinois Volunteer Cavalry. His recollection of Wild Bill was revealing. He only saw Hickok once. He

> rode past on a mule. The man was dirty & unshaven, his clothing was dirty & needed repairs, so a young recruit made some disparaging remarks to the man about his appearance. The man made no answer but looked the young fellow over as tho he wanted to remember him. After the man was out of hearing, one of the cavalrymen said: "Young fellow, you're lucky to be alive. That man you smarted off is Wild Bill Hickok, one of our scouts & he doesn't take that kind of talk from anybody."

Brock recalled that the kid was scared for weeks that Hickok would come back and look him up, "but he never did." Hickok's presence with the Seventeenth Illinois has not been verified. It is a matter of record, however, that scouts could, and were, seconded without official documentation, the record simply noting the "period of his employment and the compensation received."[14] Wild Bill, officially headquartered at Springfield, continued to spend some of his time in and around Rolla. It was there on September 10, 1864, that Lorenzo recorded James's remark that "if the War Ever stops he will go Home and stay for a month or two[,] but as long as his services are needed here he will remain.[15]

Official references to Wild Bill, J. B., or William Hickok are few, but they are informative. On February 10, 1865, he addressed a note to General Sanborn (how he actually despatched it is a matter of conjecture) informing him that he was at Cassville, Missouri, and had visited Camp Walker and Spavine and learned that there "are not more than ten or twelve rebels in any squad in the southwest that I can hear of. If you want me to go to Neosho and West of there, notify me here. It was cold; I returned back." Sanborn replied on the 11th, "You may go to Yellville or the White River in the vicinity of Yellville and learn what Dobbin intends to do with his command now on Crowley's Ridge, and from there come to this place."[16]

Wild Bill from a family tintype made ca. 1863 when he was a contract scout for the Union Army. Believed made at Springfield or Rolla, Missouri. (Courtesy the late Ethel Hickok)

On April 20, one of Sanborn's scouts reported that Archibald S. Dobbin, a Confederate officer, was still in command of an estimated fifteen hundred men, many of them on furlough, and accompanied by four pieces of artillery. Sanborn doubted this, as he did the suggestion that, despite the end of the war on April 9, the Confederates were preparing for an offensive. The general remained convinced that they would follow the terms of surrender and present themselves at Batesville on May 1. "There is general quiet in the District at present," he wrote.[17]

By now, the machinery of war was slowing down and the planning for peacetime began to take precedence. Consequently, among the first combatants to be demobilized were scores of civilian employees, among them Hickok and Thomas Martin (the *Patriot* noted that he had been Wild Bill's "mate" during the latter part of the war). Both men were dropped from "the roll of scouts" on June 9; it was now up to the legend builders.[18]

A cursory review of the foregoing account of Hickok's known service to the Union reveals its romantic potential. Sanborn's remarks add further luster to the publicity, the oral tradition, and the fiction published during and after Hickok's lifetime. It is not difficult to imagine how the legend snowballed in a comparatively short time. But we must not lose sight of the important part played by Colonel Nichols in promoting "Wild Bill," transforming him from a local character into a national celebrity. His rich and imaginative descriptions of both Hickok and his adventures captured the public's imagination and inspired many imitators. But when Nichols's narrative is examined, it becomes clear that he glibly interwove fact and hearsay so that the whole reads like a fireside yarn. Many have suggested that Hickok, ably assisted by others, had no difficulty in convincing Nichols that he was some kind of Superman. But to suggest that Hickok maliciously deceived Nichols is nonsense. Nichols was no fool. He had seen action in the war, witnessed death in all its forms, and was a close observer of men under wartime stress and their reactions later. Yet he clung to the belief that the individual could surmount the most daunting odds. And when he was confronted with Hickok, he probably thought that he had found his "Beau Ideal." This is apparent when he described Hickok's appearance and declared that when he looked into his eyes he found it difficult to believe that they had "pointed the way to death to hundreds of men. Yes, Wild Bill with his own hands has killed hundreds of men. Of that I have not a doubt. 'He shoots to kill,' as they say on the border."

For a man of Nichols's experience and worldliness to be faced by such a character as Wild Bill and have his leg pulled without being aware of it would be difficult to accept. But in hindsight we know some of the stories to be fiction. Therefore, it is unfortunate that so far (and despite some intensive research) his original notes or journal have not been found. If they are discovered, they may answer many questions. Nevertheless, Nichols did make the point that not all the stories came from Hickok:

> Whenever I had met an officer or soldier who had served in the Southwest I heard of Wild Bill and his exploits, until the stories became so frequent and of such an extraordinary character as quite to outstrip personal knowledge of adventure by camp and field; and the hero of these strange tales took shape in my mind as did Jack the Giant Killer or Sinbad the Sailor in childhood's days. As then, I now had the most implicit faith in the existence of the individual; but how one man could accomplish such prodigies of strength and feats of daring was a continued wonder.[19]

The real wonder, of course, is a mind-boggling list of heroics that is rarely matched, even in fiction. But it would be naive to suggest that Nichols invented his interview with Hickok. Much of it was based upon first-hand comment—some of it direct from Hickok, and the remainder from "Captain Honesty" and others. Nichols sought to distinguish between his characters by inserting a crude dialect for some and passable English for others. For instance, when he quoted a "lieutenant of cavalry" who declared that Hickok was "the most remarkable character I have met in four years' active service," his informant's grammar was perfect. The lieutenant then mentions a feat that was "beyond description" yet proceeds to describe it anyway. Hickok and a companion had been pursued by rebels and were faced by a wide ditch:

> And when they turned I thought they were going to give themselves up. But no; in the face of that awful fire they deliberately turned back to get space for a good run at the ditch. This gave time for two of their pursuers to get within a few yards of them, when they stopped, evidently in doubt as to the meaning of this retrograde movement. But they did not remain long in doubt, for the two men turned again, and, with a shout, rushed for the ditch, and then we were near enough to see that they were Wild Bill and his mate. Bill's companion never reached the ditch. He and his horse must have been shot at the same time, for they went down together and did not rise again.

Bill did not get a scratch. He spoke to Black Nell, the mare we saw just now, who knew as well as her master that there was life and death in that twenty feet of ditch, and that she must jump it; and at it she went with a big rush. I never saw a more magnificent sight. Bill gave the mare her head, and turning in his saddle fired twice, killing both of his pursuers, who were within a few lengths of him. They were out of their saddles like stones, just as Black Nell flew into the air and landed safely on our side of the ditch. In a moment both the daring scout and the brave mare were in our midst, while our men cheered and yelled like mad.

Asked why he had not waited and stolen through the enemy lines in the dark, Hickok replied, "Mate and I wanted to show them cussed rebs what a Union soldier could do."[20]

Thomas Martin, who was generally regarded as Hickok's "mate" during the latter part of the war, declared in 1867 that Nichols's "pathetic description of his murder in 1863 was not true."[21]

The story of Black Nell is not true either, and only the appearance of Nichols's notes or some other clue will establish who invented Hickok's miraculous horse. Hickok denied the story, so we must conclude that Nichols introduced the animal to add color and establish a bond between man and beast in the best tradition of literature. Remember, Dick Turpin was allowed his Black Bess, and other popular heroes down to present-day movie heroes had a special horse that shared their adventures.

According to Nichols, he first saw Hickok mounted upon her as he dashed "furiously across the square and down the street. The rider sat perfectly erect, yet following with a grace of motion, seen only in the horsemen of the plains, the rise and fall of the galloping steed. There was only a moment to observe this, for they halted suddenly, while the rider springing to the ground approached the party which the noise had gathered near me." Later, he describes how Hickok arrived outside his hotel and "swung his right arm around with a circular motion. Black Nell instantly stopped and dropped to the ground as if a cannon-ball had knocked life out of her." Remarking that the mare would do anything for him, Hickok turned to the animal, which "winked affirmatively the only eye we could see." Explaining how much he owed his life to his horse, Hickok then bet that she would get up onto a billiard table and lie down. This she did, and allowed others to sit on her back before Hickok ordered them down. When she got down from the table, Hickok sprang upon her back, and "dashed through the high wide doorway, and at a single bound cleared the flight of steps and landed in the middle of the street."[22]

This remarkable performance may have delighted outsiders and the New York press, but it was not shared by the locals who were both amused and irritated. The editor of the *Patriot* on January 31, 1867, declared that Black Nell was not a mare, but a

> black stallion, blind in the right eye, and a "goer," that would not "fall as if struck by a cannon ball" worth a cent, or wink on request. As for standing on billiard tables or allowing herself to be mounted in Ike Hoff's saloon so that "William" might "with one bound, lit in the middle of the street," he would have got a severe fall in the doorway of the bar-room, sure, to make no mention of clearing at "one bound" a porch twelve feet wide, and five feet high, a pavement twelve feet, and half the width of the roadway (twenty-five feet by actual measurement) making a total of forty-nine feet, without computing any margin inside the room from which she (or he) "bounded."

Unfortunately, the *Patriot* did not enjoy the same sort of wide readership as did *Harper's,* so its criticisms were ignored until many years later, and by that time Black Nell was an established part of Hickok's legend. It did not help when others later claimed that Hickok had become the owner of the animal in 1863 when he killed her rebel rider and paid the government the sum of $225, her value as a prize of war. She is reported to have died at Kansas City in 1869.[23]

If Black Nell was fiction, then so must have been "Captain Honesty," who contributed so much to Nichols's knowledge of Hickok. Certainly, the name "Honesty" immediately suggests just the opposite. But it was the editor of the *Patriot* who provided a clue to his real identity when he declared in his review of the Nichols story that "Captain Honesty" had forgotten more than Nichols ever knew, and that he spoke very intelligibly and with good English. His capability as an assistant quartermaster led to his retention by the War Department after his regiment was

Capt. Richard Bentley Owen, the quartermaster who employed Hickok during the Civil War and later on the plains, from a carte de visite *made by R. F. Adams, St. Louis, ca. 1864–1866. He was the celebrated "Captain Honesty" of* Harper's *fame. (Courtesy James Joplin)*

mustered out, to serve in one "of the most important posts in the country." This was the clue that led me to identify "Honesty" as Capt. Richard Bentley Owen. The 1865 issues of the paper carried advertisements signed by Owen offering government property for sale. The paper later announced his departure for Fort Riley, Kansas, and with him went the good wishes of his many friends in Springfield. Obviously the editor had no wish to embarrass Owen (who had retired from the army late in 1866 and returned to live in Springfield, where he died in 1872) by divulging his real name. Owen held Hickok in high regard and had known and employed him at various times since the early part of the war. He was also one of those who stood bail for him after Tutt's killing. And when Owen was posted to Fort Riley, he appointed Hickok as post guide and scout, and later as a government detective.[24]

Nichols's occasional lapses into a crude dialect when quoting Hickok and "Captain Honesty" is curious. We can only assume that in Hickok's case it added color; but since Honesty was supposed to be a commissioned officer, he at least should have spoken correctly. As we have noted, Henry M. Stanley was critical of this ploy, and others doubtless expressed similar opinions. In-

deed, in the following yarn from the February 1867 *Harper's*,
Hickok emerges not only unscathed, but his diction is much improved. His comment in the second sentence is significant.

> I hardly know where to begin. Pretty near all these stories are
> true. I was at it all the war. That affair of my swimming the river
> took place on that long scout of mine when I was with the rebels
> five months, when I was sent by General Curtis to Price's army [as
> a Union spy in the Confederate Army]. Things had come pretty
> close at that time, and it wasn't safe to go straight inter their lines.
> Everybody was suspected who came from these parts. So I started
> off and went way up to Kansas City. I bought a horse there and
> struck out onto the plains, and then went down through Southern
> Kansas into Arkansas. I knew a rebel named Barnes who was killed
> at Pea Ridge. He was from near Austin in Texas. So I called myself
> his brother and enlisted in a regiment of mounted rangers.

Nichols went on to quote Hickok's verbatim account of how
he outwitted a particularly tough and obnoxious sergeant by per-
suading him to join Hickock in a daring raid to get close to the
Union lines. But first Hickok had alerted men of the "Missouri
cavalry" who joined him and other "Rebels" in an exchange of
coffee and tobacco during a lull in the fighting. Watched by "ten
thousand men," Hickok and the sergeant got close to Union
lines, and suddenly a "Yankee" shouted out: "Bully for Wild
Bill!" At that moment the sergeant "suspicioned" him, but
Hickok outdrew him and shot him out of the saddle. He then
rode into the river, taking the sergeant's horse with him. After
dodging bullets, with the help of covering fire from his own side,
Hickok emerged without a scratch.

> "It is a fact," said the scout, while he caressed his long hair, "I
> felt sort of proud when the boys took me into camp, and General
> Curtis thanked me before a heap of generals.
> "But I never tried that thing over again; nor I didn't go scouting
> openly in Price's army after that. They all knew me too well, and
> you see 'twouldn't a been healthy to have been caught."[25]

That yarn typifies Nichols's mixture of fact and fiction—although it would be some time before anyone questioned its ac-

curacy. An examination of Gen. Samuel R. Curtis's available papers has failed to reveal any mention of Hickok, which is not surprising. It would have made more sense had Hickok (or Nichols) mentioned General Sanborn rather than Curtis. Sanborn would have linked Hickok's escape from Price's army with information that influenced the Battle of Newtonia. And Hickok's alleged statement that he never tried such a trick again makes one wonder how someone as well known in Union circles as Wild Bill could possibly hope for anonymity.

Legends, however, pay little attention to detail. To gain any understanding of Hickok's reported Civil War heroics, and their influence upon his status as a latter-day folk hero, we must first have a clear picture of the danger that characterized parts of Missouri, Kansas, and Arkansas during the war. Some remote areas escaped much of the murder and mayhem of those four years; but for southwest Missouri, much of Arkansas, and areas along the Missouri-Kansas border, the savagery and misery suffered could only be fully appreciated by those who endured it. Indeed, the surviving residents of all three states would have had much in common with those who lived through the French Revolution or occupation by Nazi Germany in World War II. The murderous activities of the guerrillas, both Union and Confederate, led to a Reign of Terror. No one knew for sure who his or her friends were, and even an act of humanity toward an injured person could be construed as treason. On both sides, death was the punishment for those convicted of being guerrillas. Drumhead court martials occasionally led to imprisonment when it was felt that the miscreants had been misled. But, as one historian has remarked:

> Several prominent Union leaders made very pointed remarks regarding the punishment of guerrillas. Secretary of War Stanton advised, "Let them swing;" General J. A. Dix, "Shoot them on the spot;" General J. M. Schofield, "Execute them immediately;" General J. G. Blunt, "Give them no quarter;" and General H. W. Halleck, "Let them be tried immediately by a drumhead court, and punished with death." He also noted that the Confederates also treated Union guerrillas as common criminals, "which in many cases they were." A similar fate awaited so-called Kansas Jayhawk-

ers who had been active during the pre–Civil War battles in Kansas Territory.[26]

The federal army often described rebel guerrillas as "bushwhackers," a term that originally meant the lowest and meanest of persons and, in the Wild West era, came to mean ambusher or assassin. The original bushwhacker was a nondescript character in drab clothing and slouch hat, mounted upon a fast horse and armed with a double-barreled shotgun and a pair or more of Colt's revolvers. This image also fit the earlier Missouri "Border Ruffians," men with long, greasy hair who were reported to be "undersized rather than oversized," humorless—never known to laugh but only to "chuckle"—and who lived off a diet of tobacco and corn whiskey. The Kansas Jayhawkers were similarly described.[27]

Some historians and folklorists have ignored the horrors of the era and concentrated on the alleged heroics of individuals or organizations devoted to the cause of the Union or Confederacy. The idea that a band of armed men displaying a Union or Confederate flag should descend upon a homestead and destroy it, murdering its inhabitants in the name of such a cause, is abhorrent. But it happened, and all manner of excuses were put forward by combatants on both sides to explain why it was necessary. But for every individual who sacrificed himself in order that good would triumph over evil, there were those whose inclinations were opportunist or downright murderous simply because they hated Yanks or Rebs.

The Kansas-Missouri border wars of the 1850s that presaged the Civil War have been portrayed as a simple fight between good and evil—Kansas being on the side of the angels. In reality, both sides were guilty of acts of brutality and murder. Slavery was an issue, but power politics also played a part. For too long Missourians have been dismissed simply as marauding Border Ruffians when in fact many of them were not slaveowners; neither, for that matter, were all Kansans Jayhawker "nigger-stealers." But the seeds of violence that bore the fruit of guerrilla warfare are better understood when one examines the earlier Kansas-Missouri conflict.

The intense feeling between freestate and proslavery factions along the eastern and southern borders of Kansas and Missouri "left a fertile foundation for the development of a partisan conflict. Parts of Kansas became a battleground during the Civil War as Confederate guerrillas engaged upon a campaign against both the Union army and the civilian population." And Kansas as a "frontier state" in the 1860s influenced the development of the guerrilla conflict. The editor of the Kansas City, Missouri, *Western Journal of Commerce* claimed on December 1, 1859, that the place was beset by a "set of the most desperate characters that ever infested any country, we believe is admitted by all." "Jayhawkers," according to the editor of the September 5, 1861, White Cloud *Kansas Chief,* was a "term peculiar to Kansas" and was interpreted to mean parties of guerrillas who "generally make sure that they strike in the right place, then come with a swoop quick and sudden, wreaking such vengeance upon wrong-doers as is not likely soon to be forgotten."

The Fort Scott *Weekly Monitor* of May 13, 1868, however, suggested that the term "Jayhawker" was first used by proslavery Missourians to mean "thief" and was eventually applied to all freestaters within the territory. Another source credits its origin to a wagon train that left Illinois in 1849 to join the gold rush; members of the train boasted that they would "jayhawk" their way across the plains. Regardless of origin, however, the term is now a part of Kansas mythology.[28]

It has even been suggested that had the Confederacy discarded its Old World chivalry, as practiced by the landed gentry who controlled the fortunes of the South, she might well have won the war simply by relying upon guerrilla tactics. But Christian values prevailed. While the likes of Quantrill and "Bloody Bill" Anderson were tolerated as a necessary evil, the exploits of John Singleton Mosby's Rangers, a disciplined force, were applauded. Similarly, the Kansas Red Legs originally formed to hunt down Quantrill, degenerated into a band of cutthroats and brigands and were outlawed. They were eventually replaced by a band of "buckskin scouts" under the command of William S. Tough and attached to the Fifteenth Kansas Regiment. However, it was the murder and mayhem created by the likes of Anderson and Quantrill that aroused the most hatred.

Official attitudes toward guerrillas ranged from tolerance, be-

cause of their usefulness, to disgust. The views of the Union
Army, however, were clear. In a general order issued from its
headquarters at St. Louis, Missouri, in May 1863, guerrillas were
defined as troops not of a regular army, mostly volunteers, raised
on the authority of their acknowledged government. They received no regular army pay, in fact none at all. This left them to
live off the country. They engaged in raids against the enemy; did
not take prisoners, gave no quarter and were considered dangerous. They were easily able to fade into the background; swiftly
forsaking the musket for a hoe. In short, they soon degenerated
into "simple robbers or brigands."[29]

Gen. John B. Sanborn was one of the few Union Generals to
implement the notorious General Order No. 11 issued on August
25, 1863, by Brig. Gen. Thomas E. Ewing following Quantrill's
raid on Lawrence on August 21. This order called for the depop-
ulation within fifteen days of areas known to be guerrilla strong-
holds. Sanborn believed that General Price was more concerned
with "Bloody Bill" Anderson's worth to him than his ethics.
Early in October 1864, wrote Sanborn, "Price sent Bill Anderson, the most cruel and merciless of the guerrilla leaders, back
across the river, with a written order to operate against the North
Missouri Railroad, directing him to 'go as far east as practicable.'
Two weeks later Anderson was killed and this order was found
on his body." Anderson was among several killed in a skirmish
with troops of the Missouri State Militia led by Major Samuel P.
Cox.[30]

One can imagine the confusion created when it was alleged
that guerrillas sometimes dressed in the uniforms of Union and
Confederate troops operating in Missouri and Arkansas. The mid-
night knock; the appearance of troops dressed in "friendly" uniforms and the shock of betrayal that led frequently to male members of a household being led away in the dark to be shot or left
hanging in the woods. Small wonder that with the passing of the
years, the horrors of guerrilla warfare and all its miseries were replaced by glowing stories of personal heroics and fights for the
"noble cause." Until the early years of this century, veterans of
both sides met to remember old times. In defeat the rebels were
ennobled; in legend the likes of Jesse James, who appeared
briefly as a guerrilla late in the war, continued the fight, only this

time it was not the Union he was fighting but the robber barons of the railroads and banks.[31]

Nichols's article was obviously well intentioned, for he was an honorable man, but he could not possibly have realized what its twofold effect would be: sudden fame for Hickok and as a result, early death. It also inspired many writers to fictionalize some already romanticized exploits. The most noted of these early "biographers" was J. W. Buel, who probably met Hickok in Kansas City in the early 1870s but certainly knew him when Hickok was a temporary resident of St. Louis and Buel was an editor of a local paper. Buel also claimed to have met Hickok's widow, who gave him her husband's diary or journal (a document unknown to Hickok's family but hinted at in the contemporary press). Buel introduced selected quotations from the diary into his own narrative. One entry alleged that Wild Bill had been captured and while waiting to be shot as a spy, planned his escape: "I am in a bad pickle; it may be that they will shoot me to-morrow, but somehow I feel that some means of escape will offer." To his credit, Buel did state: "How this entry was made in his journal, while he was under close guard, is not explained, but it is probable that he wrote it after his escape to indicate his feelings while under conviction, when the chances of escape were least favorable." Naturally, Wild Bill found an old clasp knife with which he cut his bonds, overpowered and killed his guard, and escaped to warn General Curtis of the enemy's plans.[32]

Buel's whole approach to Hickok's Civil War exploits is so fictionalized that any attempt to verify it is an impossible task. Yet those who would condemn him as a liar and a rascal should also bear in mind that he was writing for a readership that demanded blood and thunder rather than hard facts. And perhaps it never occurred to him that the day would come when historians would investigate both Hickok the man and his myth. So far, and despite some intensive research, no trace has been found of Buel's papers.[33]

Hickok's presence at Springfield when Nichols arrived proved opportune. The colonel reached the place in September 1865, in company with Gen. Thomas Church Haskell Smith, the inspector general of the District of South-West Missouri; but in what capacity is uncertain. Having experienced and written about the

Kansas-Missouri border wars as well as the horrors of the Civil
War, Nichols would have known that Hickok would be good
copy for a future article.

Nichols himself was quite a character. Born at Tremont, Mount
Desert, Maine, on June 21, 1837, he was only a month younger
than his subject. Nichols, however, spent his formative years in
the more civilized East—in Boston, to be exact. At the age of
twenty-two he went to Paris, and on his return he joined the New
York *Evening Post*. Following his Kansas experiences, he became
the *Post's* art editor and contributed material to other publications. On April 26, 1862, he was commissioned a captain in the
Union Army and became an aide to Maj. Gen. John C. Fremont.
Subsequently, he worked in the provost general recruiting de-
partments before joining the staff of Maj. Gen. William Tecumseh
Sherman, in 1864, with whom he formed a friendship. Nichols
participated in the campaigns in Georgia and the Carolinas (and
wrote several best-selling accounts of them). He was breveted a
major on January 12, 1865, and a lieutenant colonel on March 13
of that year for meritorious service.[34]

Prior to his interview with Hickok, the colonel mentioned the
prevailing "climate" in and around Springfield:

> In Southwest Missouri there were old scores to be settled up.
> During the three days occupied by General Smith—who com-
> manded the Department and was on a tour of inspection—in
> crossing the country between Rolla and Springfield, a distance of
> 120 miles, five men were killed or wounded on the public road.
> Two were murdered a short distance from Rolla—by whom we
> could not ascertain. Another was instantly killed and two were
> wounded at a meeting of a band of "Regulators," who were in the
> service of the State, but were paid by the United States Govern-
> ment. It should be said here that their method of "regulation" was
> slightly informal, their war-cry was, "A swift bullet and a short
> rope for returned rebels!"

Nichols added that General Smith himself had told him that in
the "six months preceding not less than 4,000 returned Confederates had been summarily disposed of by shooting or hanging.
This statement seems incredible; but there is the record, and I
have no doubt of its truth." Unfortunately, despite intensive re-

search, this claim has not been verified. Nichols further declared that Hickok was not one of the Regulators, but had "buried the hatchet," and would not fight unless "I'm put upon."

Hickok may not have been a Regulator, but according to Pvt. William James Smith of Company M, Second Ohio Volunteer Cavalry, he was employed in hunting down ex-rebels. Smith's regiment garrisoned at Springfield in the summer of 1865, and its commanding officer, Maj. Albert Barnitz (who had witnessed the fight between Hickok and Tutt on July 21 and ordered Hickok's arrest) was advised by Hickok that several members of Quantrill's gang were headquartered a few miles from Springfield. Thirty troopers were sent in pursuit with "Wild Bill as guide, to look after their welfare." After scouting around for some time and lying low in some woods until dark, Hickok took Smith and another man and set out to reconnoiter. Smith described what happened next:

> We found them in a BIG log house, in a small clearing, back in the woods, some distance from any road. Then leaving us two soldiers to watch, Bill went back and brought up the Company, dismounted and placed them in front of the doors. Then BILL went up and rapped on the door. They asked who was there, and he said Wild Bill. One of them swore that WILD BILL had better GIT out of there. But Bill laughed, and told them that the house was surrounded by soldiers, that they had better come out without any trouble, as we had come after them, and would GIT them, trouble or no trouble.
>
> They seemed a little BASHFUL at first, but when one of them came, GUN IN HAND, and took a look out at the door, and saw a line of soldiers, with GUNS UP ready to pull the trigger, they decided to come out, like little MEN. So we got the whole GANG without a gun being fired. There was one of them got away and escaped after we started with them, but WILD BILL brought him in a few days later. We took them to Springfield, I think they were turned over to the civil authorities but I never learned what was done with them.[35]

Nichols departed from Springfield with his notes, an excellent photograph of Hickok, and an assurance that his subject did not mind being written up. It is doubtful, however, that Nichols paid much attention to the public reaction to the published article. Since his notes have not been found, we are left to conjecture whether Nichols added the "color" himself or *Harper's* did. But the answer is now academic, for what really counts is the effect of the article.

With the end of the Civil War, and the recriminations, heartbreak, and hardships that were to follow, people tended to seek escape from their problems. In the same manner that cinema audiences are today inundated with war movies that claim to be based upon real events, so, too, did the periodicals and magazines, books and dime novels of the time devote space to Civil War heroics. *Harper's* merely followed a trend, and "Wild Bill's" adventures up against cunning and desperate "Rebs" were eagerly read by the victorious northerners. And with time, assisted by dime novels and frequent retelling, Hickok's deed as a Union scout and spy were grossly magnified. That he did perform some of the feats credited to him is not in dispute; but the deliberate falsification of his role in the conflict rankles historians and fuels the fire of envy among his detractors. For there were many who performed their duties as well or better than Hickok but declined to discuss their role or, as the cynics might claim, failed to find the right press agent.

Hickok, therefore, emerges from the Civil War as a kind of demigod with superhuman strength and powers that place him in the forefront of frontier heroes. That he was no such thing was irrelevant to the masses because what he represented was so important: a larger-than-life character with the courage and determination to fight for what he believed in. And that is the image that remains even after a century of controversy. According to Nichols, Hickok wanted his mother to be assured that "I'm not a cut-throat and a vagabond, and I'd like the old woman to know what'll make her proud. I'd like her to hear that her runaway boy has fought through the war for the Union like a true man." To which the editor of the *Patriot* for January 31, 1867, added that he imagined Hickok's reaction to that remark would be: "'O! hell! what a d——n fool that Nichols is.' We agree with 'Wild Bill' on that point."

Three

Tall Tales and Tangled Truths

Henry M. Stanley credited Wild Bill Hickok with the admission that he had slain "considerably over a hundred" white men. He also included in the St. Louis *Weekly Missouri Democrat* of April 16, 1867, an allegedly verbatim account by Wild Bill of how he came to kill the first one:

"I was twenty-eight years old when I killed the first white man, and if ever a man deserved killing he did. He was a gambler and counterfeiter, and I was in a hotel in Leavenworth City then, and seeing some loose characters around, I ordered a room, and as I had some money about me, I thought I would go to it. I had lain some thirty minutes on the bed, when I heard some men at my door. I pulled my revolver and bowie-knife and held them ready, but half concealed, still pretending to be asleep. The door was opened, and five men entered the room. They whispered together 'let us kill the son of a b——h; I'll bet he has got money.'" "Gentlemen," said he further, "that was a time—an awful time. I kept perfectly still until just as the knife touched my breast; I sprang aside and buried mine in his heart, and then used my revolver on the others right and left. Only one was wounded, beside the one killed; and then gentlemen, I dashed through the room and rushed to the fort, procured a lot of soldiers, came to the hotel and captured the whole gang of them, fifteen in all. We searched the cellar and found eleven bodies buried there—men who were murdered by those villains." Turning to us, he asked: "Would you have not done the same? That was the first man I killed, and I never was sorry for that yet."[1]

Hickok's heroics on that occasion, aided by his reputation as a fighting man, prompted Stanley to suggest that anyone foolish enough to tangle with Wild Bill, unless they possessed "almost superhuman strength," would come off worse. This yarn (which has so far defied a search in the local press), presaged the notorious Bender family, accused of similar practices several years later, and highlights the frontier tradition of tall stories. Therefore, it is not difficult to understand how Hickok's reputation as a fighting man should later became a "murderous mantle" once the press enlarged upon his exploits.

In available press reports and so-called biographical treatments a pattern emerges in the physical conflicts of Western heroes: their fights with men are also interspersed with fearsome battles against wild animals, notably various species of bear. In his book, journalist J. W. Buel examines the early lives of several noted plainsmen besides Wild Bill, among them California Joe, Kit Carson, and Buffalo Bill. Cody is excluded from wild animal antics, but the other two men performed spectacular feats. Wild Bill is reported to have encountered a large, ferocious cinnamon bear with two cubs while driving a freight wagon in the Soccoro range. The bear stood her ground, forcing the team to a halt. Hickok jumped down and approached the bear assuming she would move off. Instead, she attacked him. In the fight that followed, Hickok fired a number of shots into the animal, and then set to work with his knife, cutting its throat and literally disemboweling the creature, so that she "became so tangled in her intestines that she thus assisted in her own quick destruction." Hickok had "his shoulder . . . torn dreadfully, his left arm crushed from the elbow, his breast furrowed by the long, poniard-like claws, and his left cheek was split open." At the end of this gory encounter, "it was difficult to decide which presented the more horrifying spectacle, Bill or his dead antagonist; they were both saturated with blood, and their flesh was in shreds in several places." Not surprisingly, it was several months before Hickok was able to resume work of any kind![2]

California Joe (Moses E. Milner) came off lightly by comparison. His battle with a "Mexican couger, or spotted panther" was as courageous but less bloody. The starving animal leapt upon Joe and began tracing its stiletto-like claws in patterns all over his back and biting chunks out of his neck. The force of the animal's attack had knocked Joe's rifle from his hands so he, too, had to rely upon a knife to survive. He disemboweled the cat then examined his own terrible injuries. If it hadn't been "for his great knowledge of the medicinal virtues contained in several plants in convenient proximity, he would surely had died of his wounds." Joe prepared a "balsamic poultice" for his neck wounds, taking advantage of the "properties of the plants" to stem the flow of blood and absorb any poison. Joe was left with a "very large and prominent scar" on his head, a mark he carried until his death.[3]

Kit Carson shared Wild Bill's experiences with a bear, only his antagonist was a full-grown grizzly. Unlike Wild Bill, however, he emerged unscathed—the animal chased him up into a tree and kept him there until companions arrived and scared it off.[4]

The only importance to be attached to such tales is their emphasis upon the hero's cunning, courage, and boundless strength when dealing with all manner of perils. By matching their own strength in a fearless encounter with a foe that was rarely beaten in hand-to-hand combat, the frontiersmen emerged as a race apart. The fact that their own contemporaries knew the truth of such stories, and probably enjoyed the joke, was tacitly ignored. Samson's exploits with the jawbone of an ass seemed tame in comparison with the deeds of the bear-battling plainsmen.

Hickok's encounter with the bear took place in 1859, according to Buel, and others have suggested that it happened in 1860. But the date doesn't matter, since it is now accepted that the story is fiction. At that time Hickok was employed as a teamster by Jones & Cartwright between Leavenworth and Denver City, Colorado Territory. Nevertheless, Hickok's arrival at Rock Creek, Nebraska Territory, early in 1861 was locally believed to be a direct result of the alleged bear fight. Even the usually skeptical Charles Dawson, in *Pioneer Tales of the Oregon Trail,* noted that Hickok had been sent to the stage station to "recuperate from wounds which he had received the year previously in an encounter with a bear." But he was healthy enough when, according to Nichols's account in *Harper's,* McCanles and his gang reportedly rushed the cabin where Hickok was holed up. McCanles was shot dead as he jumped through the door. Hickok then prepared to fight and die as he picked up his revolver: "Only six shots and nine men to kill. Save your powder, Bill, for the death-hug's a-comin!" When the gang rushed him, he shot four of them dead.

Then despite being blasted by "birdguns" that stung him all over, Hickok launched into a fierce hand-to-hand encounter that left the remainder of the gang dead and Wild Bill bleeding profusely. When Nichols suggested that he must have been "hurt almost to death," Hickok is reported to have declared, "There were eleven buck-shot in me. I carry some of them now. I was cut in thirteen places, All of them enough to have let the life out of a man. But that blessed old Dr. Mills pulled me safe through it, after a bed siege of many a long week."[5]

Hickok's alleged fight for survival against impossible odds was not unique. Fights with wild animals and hostile Indians were an established part of the frontiersman's mythology. But occasionally one encounters a true story that bolsters the myth. In December 1854, the *Daily Alta California* began a series of reports concerning a Capt. Johnathan R. Davis of South Carolina, who was involved in a shoot-out with twelve men who had attacked his party of four. He and one member of his party survived, leaving the twelve villains dead or dying. Despite witnesses' testimony to his feat, there were doubters. Davis, however, dismissed his critics and stated that "I did only what hundreds of others might have done under similar circumstances, and attach no particular credit to myself for it."[6]

Wild Bill emerged from the so-called McCanles Massacre unscathed despite what he or someone else told Nichols. But in later years, close friends and acquaintances made a point of describing the scarred state of his body. George Hance, who had known him since the early years of the Civil War, recalled in 1901 and again in 1912 how Hickok received "seven full grown buckshot" into his "right side and breast, two of which entered his lungs causing him to spit frothy blood." Later, he claimed that he carried seven shotgun pellets to the grave. Hance intimated that during the time he worked alongside Hickok and they bunked and bathed together, he observed the scars on Hickok's body. A similar statement was made by Edwin P. Mitchell, a newspaperman who had met Wild Bill when he appeared with Buffalo Bill's Combination at Lewiston, Maine, in February 1874: "There was nothing of the faker about Bill. He stripped to the waist for my benefit and allowed me to count the dozen or score of unmistakable bullet scars upon his person. There could be no doubt of the genuineness of his record. Two years after this the already well-riddled Pistol Prince was shot and killed at Deadwood."

A bizarre footnote to Mitchell's comments was published in the Longview (Tex.) *Democrat* of September 28, 1881:

> Although he carried a dozen bullets, more or less, deeply imbedded in his flesh, Wild Bill never sustained an internal wound. He was killed, while playing cards, by a scoundrel who, for $500 blood-money paid him by gamblers, sneaked up behind Bill and blew his brains out. . . . The post mortem examination of his remains explained his immunity from penetrative bullet-wounds. It was discovered that his ribs were welded together, the intercostal cartilages and muscles having ossified. His lungs and heart, therefore, were naturally protected by a cuirass of bone.[7]

No such post mortem was conducted. Such a claim would attract attention, but it would have been impossible for Hickok to have escaped without some body scars. Nevertheless, Hickok did emerge unscathed from all of his authenticated gunfights.

It comes as no surprise that Wild Bill's alleged exploits not only caused confusion but aroused passion among his contemporaries. For example, Abilene businessman Edward C. Little published an article in *Everybody's Magazine* titled "A Son of the Border" that sketched Hickok's life. But his story emphasized Wild Bill's Abilene exploits. Here he met criticism as well as praise. Sen. Fred Dumont Smith took it upon himself to attack Little, basing his own remarks upon the original Nichols story in *Harper's*. In effect, he made a fool of himself by asserting that Hickok's real name was "William Hitchcock" and not "James Butler Hickok" as stated by Little. Little's response was to point out that a cursory glance at the Abilene city records would confirm Hickok's name. Little also attacked the senator's comments by listing some relevant facts (and a couple of near misses), ending with the remark, "What is the matter with you anyway? I have the honor to remain. Your most obedient servant." Next came a blast from Percival G. Lowe, who admitted that he had not read Little's article, but insisted that Hickok's name was "William Hickok" (not Hitchcock), and went on to dismiss Nichols's version of the McCanles ("MKandlas") fight as "bare faced nonsense." Unfortunately, Lowe injected himself into the story by

claiming to have arrived at the stage station in company with Ben
Ficklin, the line superintendent. Little deserves an "E" for effort,
despite some unfortunate errors; but Little, Lowe, and Smith all
display yet again a tendency for some old-timers to get into the
act, sometimes with embarrassing results.[8]

Wild Bill's alleged gambling difficulties are legion. He seems to
have attracted card sharps as a honey pot attracts bees. Some of
the stories are amusing, and others hint at confrontation. But
apart from Wild Bill's fight with Davis Tutt, none of the stories
record actual gunplay. Hickok's acknowledged passion encouraged such stories. Those who knew him back in his early Monticello days recalled that he liked to gamble, and similar reports
came from Rock Creek. And following the war, he was reported
to have run a gambling "hell" at Junction City for a short period.
During 1872, following his departure from Abilene, Hickok lived
at the St Nicholas Hotel in Kansas City and spent most afternoons
at the Marble Hall. There he played poker, faro, or whatever game
took his fancy. When local ordinances against illicit gambling
were passed (seriously affecting the legitimate establishments as
well), Wild Bill's gambling career in Kansas City came to an end.
He moved on to Springfield, Missouri, where he remained for
some months. Following a brief sojourn with Buffalo Bill's Combination in late 1873 and early 1874, Hickok returned briefly to
Kansas City before making tracks for Cheyenne, Wyoming Territory, where he was a familiar figure for the next two years. And it
was Cheyenne that was to be the scene of one of Hickok's best-
known gambling stories.

On March 12, 1904, *The Saturday Evening Post* published
one of Alfred Henry Lewis's amusing yarns that was about half
fact, half fiction. This was "How Mr. Hickok Came to Cheyenne,"
or "The Epic of an Unsung Ulysses." Unfortunately for Lewis, his
humor was not appreciated in some quarters. In Kansas City the
editor of the *Journal* declared in his March 12 issue that the language Lewis had attributed to Hickok was "slang" and turned a
"quiet-spoken, fairly well educated fellow who never boasted,"
into an inarticulate frontier illiterate. Nevertheless, the article,
which followed in the tradition of Buel and others, was widely
read.

Lewis described how Hickok, "ruminating the loss of his final dollar, which had fled across a faro layout in the Marble Hall Saloon," was rescued from poverty by someone who owed him his life and wished his help again, and to prove his good faith sent him $200. Having spent $43 in thanking his benefactor and telegraphing editors along the railroad route to Cheyenne that he wore his hair long as usual, Hickok proceeded to Cheyenne, arriving late at night. He disguised his appearance, swept his hair under his hat and donned dark "goggles." Armed with a sawed-off rosewood billiard cue (for "rheumatic reasons"), he "crept about" on his cue to examine the place. He entered the Gold Room where his gaze fell upon a well-stocked bar and games of faro "raging in the rear."

Having been addressed as "sport" and being charged double for rot-gut whiskey, Hickok sat in on a game and soon found that he was being cheated like some greenhorn. He decided to take action. He laid out the dealer and the lookout and calmly leaned across and picked up the pot. He then backed up against a wall, tore off his hat and goggles and advised everyone present to "fill his hand." Then "some one sophisticated" yelled, "It's Wild Bill!" Lewis went on:

> There was no dispute over Mr. Hickok's identity. The public at once conceded it, and began going through the doors and windows in blocks of five. Mr. Hickok, thus deserted, limped slowly toward the front door. As he passed the bar its once supercilious custodian raised his head above the sloppy levels and asked in meekness: "Mr. Hickok, will you have a drink? It's on the house."

The following day the proprietor of the place, one Bowlby and the city marshal approached Hickok over the question of the take. It was agreed on an even split and the three passed arm in arm to the local oasis.

It is a good yarn and Lewis made the most of it; but his version came along much later than most. Buel's account lacks Lewis's melodrama and the saloon owner is named "Boulder," not "Bowlby." Later, on October 15, 1911, the Chicago *Inter-Ocean* published an article by Walter Noble Burns citing Buffalo Bill Cody's recollections of the "Greatest Gunfighter of the Frontier" and adding details to the story. According to Cody, Hickok "could stand flat footed and jump sixteen feet," which athletic prowess presumably had something to do with his survival rate, or the oft-stated comment that Hickok's movements were quick and "catlike." He also noted that Hickok's eyes were bothered by the calcium light used during their stage performances, which is why he donned the dark goggles. "But I think he merely planned to play a little joke on his Cheyenne friends. Judging from the number of men he killed after he left the stage, there wasn't anything serious[ly] the matter with his eyes."

Describing the events that led to the saloon incident, Cody said that the place was known as "Boulder's saloon and gambling house, one of the biggest places of its kind in Cheyenne," which suggests that he (or Walter Noble Burns) was using the accounts by Buel and Lewis as his source. Cody also claimed that Hickok's "take" was $800, but that this time he refused to return any of it. Later, a brother of Phil Coe's turned up with a companion and tried to kill Wild Bill, but using a "six shooter I had given him when he quit the theatrical business," Wild Bill killed them both.

The truth (or as close as we are probably going to get) is this: According to an article in the Topeka *Daily Commonwealth* of July 21, 1874, Hickok was on a train that stopped at North Topeka on the 18th. He was en route to Cheyenne to join Cody and Texas Jack in a hunting trip for the benefit of some English tourists. It was reported that he was suffering from an "affection of the eyes caused by the colored fire used during his theatrical tour," but it was not stated whether he wore glasses. Later that same day, Hickok arrived in Kansas City. The *Times* of July 19 said he was promptly hired by a party of "twelve English Lords and noblemen" who were headed 200 miles west on a "general hunting excursion."

According to the Cheyenne *Daily Leader* of July 22, he went instead to Cheyenne, where it was reported he rented a room above Dave Miller's Jewellery Store. He then became a familiar figure at the Gold Room. There were actually two such establishments. James Allen's "Variety Show" included the Gold Room as a separate attraction for gamblers and it ran from 1867 until about 1878, when he sold out because of the decline in Black Hills gold rushes. The place later became a meat market and was demolished in 1932. Another Gold Room was opened in the 1880s by G. H. Pierce and

Robert D. Murray. This place was the best remembered of the two, and it lasted into the present century.[9]

According to J. W. "Doc" Howard, a former sergeant in Company B of the Fifth Cavalry who had served with Hickok in the Carr-Penrose expedition of 1868–1869, Hickok was only peripherally involved in the Gold Room fracas. Howard was serving on the city police force at the time. When he heard raised voices in Allen's Variety Show, he shifted his pistol from its holster into his right hand pocket and he entered the hall:

> I noticed Wild Bill leaning up against the door jamb. I passed by him to see what the quarreling was about. I saw Charley Rich grab the table to turn it over. The men around the table held it down, so that he could not. He had been loser and wanted to put an end to the game. There was quite a lot of money on the table when I entered. I said, "What's the matter? Stop that!" With that Charley whirled around, grabbed me by my slipknot necktie and tried to choke me. Then Wild Bill jumped in and grabbed me around the arms, so that I could not use my gun. Charley Boulder, a noted gambler, stuck his gun right into my stomach. I grabbed his gun and stuck it in my left coat pocket. I said, "Bill, let loose of me," and he said, "Doc, if Boulder had got you, I'd have got him." I took Boulder out and turned him over to Fallon, another cop, who was peeping in the window, afraid to come in.

Returning for Rich, Howard was persuaded not to press charges against him or Boulder. Rich was to achieve fame as one of the men seated opposite Hickok when he was killed, while Boulder, according to Howard, later killed two men and served ten years in the penitentiary for his crime. Another version suggests that his name was Collingwood Boulter, and that he fell out with one "Kansas Jack," a refugee from Dodge City. But before either gent could unlimber his artillery, "City Marshal" Howard and his able assistant Dan Fallon disarmed him and ordered him out of town. The only valid element of this story is the link with legend provided by the names Bowlby, Boulder, and Boulter.[10]

Cody and others have left accounts of Hickok's gambling activities. Some recalled that his reputation as a gambler was "bad," and others assert that he was easy meat for cardsharps. The *Ellis County Free Press* of January 5, 1887, copied an item from the Chicago *News* claiming that one McDonald tried to pull a fast one on Hickok. Finally, when Wild Bill was all but cleaned out, McDonald decided to call.

> "I've got three jacks," said McDonald, throwing down his hand.
> "I have an ace full on sixes," said Bill.
> McDonald, coolly turning over his opponent's cards, "but I see only two aces and a six."
> "Here is the other six!" suddenly roared Bill, whipping out a Navy revolver, "and here"—drawing a bowie knife—"is the one spot."
> "That hand is good," said McDonald, blandly arising. "Take the pot."

The artist N. C. Wyeth once illustrated a card game in which Hickok was depicted, pistol in hand, remonstrating with a crooked dealer. Others, however, have suggested that Hickok took pleasure from exposing cheats or those who took advantage of someone they presumed to be a greenhorn. When Hickok appeared with Cody's Combination at Portland, Maine, Cody recalled that Hickok was unable to sleep because of the noise from a poker game in the room next door. When his requests to quiet down were ignored, Hickok joined them in their game, under the pretext that he was unfamiliar with it. By morning he was $700 in profit and departed with the remark that one should "never wake a man up and invite him to play poker."[11]

In 1929, Judge C. B. Arnold of St. Mary's, Kansas, recalled that back in 1870, when he was a young man working in a repair shop in Hays City, he got to know Wild Bill very well. He reported that Wild Bill would occasionally turn up with packs of cards, borrow Arnold's trimming shears, and "trim the cards of low numbers so the deck could be more easily 'thumbed.' Then with the face cards untrimmed the dealer could detect the cards he wanted to deal himself more easily. . . . Nowadays such procedure would be regarded as cheating, but it was the way the game was played in those times."[12]

These stories add color to the character of Wild Bill, and again stress his human frailties rather than suggesting legendary prowess at the gaming tables. And despite criticisms leveled at him and his ilk for gambling, that activity was not generally viewed unfavorably. For many people, gambling was an antidote to boredom. Its popularity encouraged those more adept with the cards to become professional gamblers. And it was also regarded as a means of raising revenue to support local taxes. While some historians concentrate upon the game's social significance, others dismiss gamblers as akin to desperadoes or opportunists who preyed upon human weaknesses. In a social context, where prostitution satisfied a physical need, gambling sated a mental obsession. Unfortunately, the unsavory characters attracted to gambling tainted the others, many of them honorable men who prided themselves on being honest players. To city residents and members of city councils, fines for gambling and exorbitantly priced licenses and taxes compensated in part for the "immorality" practiced within their midst. As for the gamblers themselves, the lure of the game and the suspense about the outcome counted far more than the opinions of those who neither played themselves or bothered to understand the motives of those who did—a situation that still exists.

Hickok's myth is made up of many elements, but without doubt it centers on two basic points: his reputation as a mankiller and as a pistol shot. His mankiller status is discussed elsewhere; here we examine his alleged revolver skills, because they feature very high on his list of accomplishments.

Controversy marred Hickok's reputation as a pistol shot, as it did other elements of his reputation. In the early years of this century, it was reported that he had been known as "The Prince of Pistoleers" during his own lifetime. The title is still used to describe his reputedly miraculous skill with a revolver. More recent research, however, suggests that this description was first used by the writer Frank J. Wilstach in the title of his biography of Hickok published in 1926. We suspect that Wilstach's experience as a press agent influenced its use and that it was in fact inspired by Prentiss Ingraham's *Wild Bill, the Pistol Prince*, first published as a dime novel in 1891, which purported to tell Hickok's life story from birth to death. The original yarn may be forgotten by all but a few devotees of the genre, but the description of

Hickok as the "Prince of Pistoleers" is now a firmly established part of his myth. Nevertheless, it is true that Hickok's "pistoliferous" accomplishments are not confined to latter-day reminiscences. They were already legion during his own lifetime. Some of the short-range feats credited to Hickok have been duplicated by modern marksmen, whereas the more bizarre stories involving long-range accuracy have been dismissed as tall tales.

In 1931 the motion picture *Cimarron,* starring Richard Dix (a Wild Bill look-alike), was making the rounds. J. E. ("Jay") House, a journalist of reputation, was cited in the Hays *Daily News* when he sought to debunk the legendary feats of such as Wild Bill and criticized the "hip shooting" displayed by Dix and others in the movie. Someone, identified only as "I. B.," wrote to inform House that he knew nothing about gunplay, and that he "had an uncle once who could put six bullets within half an inch of each other at seventy-five yards. He's dead now, but you may remember him. His name was William Cody. And old Wild Bill Hickok could do the same any old time, and just as lief in a redskin's carcass as in a wooden rail."

House's response was predictable. He recalled that William Cody was otherwise known as Buffalo Bill and that he was not remembered as a revolver shot but was good with a rifle. "We don't think I. B. knows much about his 'uncle.' Otherwise he would not hold him up to the ridicule of all six-gun men by claiming he could put 'six bullets within half an inch of each other at a distance of seventy-five yards.' A man ought not to go around talking about his 'uncle' in that way."

As for Hickok, House's comments are worth repeating in full because they put the subject into perspective:

> It may be Wild Bill Hickok would as lief have plugged a redskin as a wooden rail. But there is no evidence in support of the contention. In the first place, there were no wooden rails in Wild Bill's section [*sic*]. In the second, Wild Bill did not traffic in Indians. White men were his dish. In Wild Bill's heyday in Abilene, Hays, Wichita and Deadwood, Indians were not considered worth shooting. And who actually knows just how accurate he was with a six-gun? The answer is, nobody. Wild Bill was killed in the Black Hills . . . more than fifty years ago. How many are alive today who

really know anything about his prowess as a marksman, and who are they?

Very likely—and there is no evidence to contravene the point—all of Wild Bill's shooting affrays were at close range. He is supposed to have killed anywhere from seventeen to thirty-five men, but there is no certainty about that. Buffalo Bill was not a gunfighter at all. He was a scout, a courier, a buffalo hunter and, in his later years, a showman. The supposedly deadly accuracy of the six-gun man is all a matter of tradition. And the accepted traditions of one generation usually are the lies current in a previous generation. No man need take our word for the fact that the accurate shooting ascribed to the gunmen of the old days is pish posh. Let him engage in a little revolver practice on his own account. Let him try to hold his weapon steady and overcome its tendency to "jump."

Mr. House's last comment infers that he knew little about ballistics. Pulling or "jerking" the trigger instead of "squeezing" it accounted for the "jump" and contributed to poor results. Mr. House said that Emmett Dalton agreed with him in his criticism of the pistol prowess displayed in *Cimarron* and declared that he never knew any man who shot from the hip. But Mr. House's remarks are questionable when we consider some of the alleged eyewitness accounts of Wild Bill's pistol skill.[13]

On the subject of hip shooting, there is possibly some confusion between hip shooting and pointing. Hip shooting is usually understood to mean that the pistol is held against the body and fired with no real attempt to aim, whereas "point" shooting was entirely different. The weapon was "pointed" toward the target, the shooter lining up the barrel in the same manner a person would point to draw attention to an object or an individual. Sam Colt had this in mind when he designed his pistol to be an extension of the hand. In 1860, the English explorer Richard Burton also confused hip and point shooting, but did emphasize the fact that pistols were worn butts forward:

> The pistol should never be absent from a man's right side—remember it is handier there than on the other—nor the bowie knife from his left. Contingencies with Indians and others may happen, when the difference of a second saves life: the revolver should therefore be carried with its butt to the fore, and when

drawn it should not be levelled as in target practice, but directed towards the object, by means of the right fore-finger laid flat along the cylinder whilst the medius draws the trigger. The instinctive consent between eye and hand, combined with a little practise, will soon enable the beginner to shoot correctly from the hip; all he has to do, is to think that he is pointing at the mark, and pull. As a precaution, especially when mounted upon a kicking horse, it is wise to place the cock upon a capless nipple, rather than trust to the intermediate pins [set between chambers and fitting into a corresponding slot in the hammer face].[14]

Burton's suggestion that the index finger should be laid alongside the cylinder and the center finger used to pull the trigger does not work well in practice. The secret of the "plains" or "reverse" draw was both its safety and its speed. When the hand grasped the butt, the thumb slipped over the hammer spur and the index finger went into the triggerguard. As the pistol was pulled upward and spun forward, the barrel lined up on its target; the hammer was cocked and could be released in one movement. But to pull the pistol in the manner described by Burton is impractical. It would slow down the whole operation.

By the time Colonel Nichols publicized Hickok's alleged skill in *Harper's*, point shooting was commonplace. Yet he claimed that Hickok, "in an off-hand way, and without sighting the pistol with his eye," fired at a letter "O" on a sign board more than fifty yards away, remarking that he would put the "six balls into the inside of the circle, which isn't much bigger than a man's heart." Nichols confirmed that all six bullets were within the circle. Writing in 1910, Bat Masterson credited Hickok with a similar feat at Kansas City, only this time he upped the distance to one hundred yards. And others copied him with variations. Neither individual, of course, produced eye-witnesses or explained how Hickok could discharge firearms within city limits without incurring official censure. People who knew Hickok intimately declared him to be a "dead shot." Major Barnitz, who witnessed the fight between Hickok and Tutt and recorded his recollections only hours later, declared that the pair opened fire simultaneously at about one hundred paces; Tutt missed, but Hickok shot him through the chest.[15]

Jay House was not alone in doubting Hickok's skill as a pistol shot. Luther North declared that his own brother Frank, who once commanded the famous Pawnee Battalion, was one of the finest pistol shots on the plains. Luther was noted for his prejudices in his late brother's favor, but he did made some pertinent remarks concerning Hickok's marksmanship. He recalled that in 1873 (he probably meant 1874 or 1875), his brother Frank and Hickok would get together about twice a week and "shoot at targets at John Talbot's roadhouse between Cheyenne and Fort Russell and Talbot would shoot with them. Frank would nearly always win with Talbot second and Wild Bill third." Luther also recalled that "I never saw Wild Bill shoot with his left hand either, although he was always called a two-gun man, and as to shooting from the hip, I never did see a man shoot from the hip, although I have seen such gunmen as Wild Bill, Jack Hays, Doc Middleton, Joe Hall and others." Irish-born Major John Talbot was regarded locally as a crack shot and even in old age wore his hair long, frontier fashion. Curiously, in later years when interviewed by the press, no mention was ever made of any shooting matches with Wild Bill. Talbot died in 1910 at age seventy-seven. Luther also claimed that his brother Frank said he never saw Hickok "try to shoot with his left hand and the day I saw him shoot he was very deliberate and took careful aim closing his left eye. If he could shoot from the hip he never did it there."[16]

Further doubts concerning Hickok's marksmanship were cast by the late Charles B. Roth, who wrote that at one time he possessed specimens of Hickok's targets. These were 4" x 4" envelopes: "The stamp was affixed on the back, in the exact center, and was around an inch square. The stamp was the 'Bullseye.' They [marksmen] customarily shot at ten yards, 30 feet. With the distance and target of this kind, a modern pistoleer would shoot the stamp completely away, but [none of] the Hickok targets I had . . . showed more than one shot in the stamp, with the others scattered clear around the sixteen square inches of white space." None of these targets have been produced for examination, so they must themselves be relegated to hearsay.[17]

Nevertheless, skeptical reaction is healthier than a total acceptance of alleged miraculous feats. Charles F. Gross was both a critic and an admirer of Wild Bill. He was employed as Joseph G. McCoy's bookkeeper at Abilene. For a short period he bunked with

Hickok and got to know him well. He once accompanied Hickok outside city limits and was privy to an impressive impromptu shooting exhibition. Wild Bill fixed a piece of paper about 6 inches by 4 inches in size to a tree and made a spot in the center. He then stood facing it and ordered Gross to carry on talking and then to say "*Draw* (kinder qu[i]ck)." Gross said that he "shot six times so quick it startled me, for his 6 was in his Holster when I said 'Draw[.]' I was looking directly at him and only saw a Motion & he was firing. No use to ask how he drew [.] I don['t] Know[.] I only know his arm was not straight & stiff[.] there was a perceptible Curve to his arm, but very slight." Every shot was in the paper, two of them clipped the spot. Hickok next tried with his left hand, and although every one was in the paper, none of them hit the spot. He admitted to Gross that he had never "shot" (he did not say "killed") any men firing a pistol with his left hand. But from what Gross reported, he was ambidextrous. What Gross meant by a "perceptible curve" to Hickok's arm is not clear. Did he mean that there was a curve when Hickok drew the pistol (such as one would expect with a reverse or plains twist draw), or when he took aim at the target? I suspect the latter.[18]

Another early resident of Abilene who said that he witnessed Hickok's marksmanship is himself the subject of controversy. D. R. Gorden was the Abilene telegraph agent in 1871, but by 1901 was described as a jeweller and a "great friend of Wild Bill's in the good old days."

According to the Topeka *Mail and Breeze* of June 28, 1901, Gorden

> was shooting at a mark down at Mud creek and Bill came up and joked him on his shooting. He offered to bet a dollar he could out-shoot Bill. The marshal said all right and pulled out a magnificent gun and firing rapidly and without aim put six shots in the end of a log across the creek in a small space. Gordon [*sic*] says "I lost, have no dollar but here's my gun." "No," said Bill, "I wouldn't have your darned old gun. Keep it to practice with and when you can shoot that log head full of holes I'll give you a new one." Gordon has never claimed the new gun.

Twenty-eight years later, however, this "great friend" of Wild Bill's intimated that he was a cowardly cold-blooded killer who

relied upon his reputation to "put fear in the hearts of offend-
ers."[19]

Another skeptic was Gen. Eugene Carr, who recalled that
when he asked Hickok to shoot for him he refused; but this may
have been because of a personality clash. Evidently, Wild Bill
turned down opportunities to exhibit his skill if he felt so inclined, while on other occasions he willingly obliged. It is a part
of family mythology that when Wild Bill visited his mother's
home in 1869, he put on an amazing display of marksmanship.
His nephew Howard knew one of the young lads who had
watched the performance and told him all about it. But he did
not go into detail. However his niece, Edith, remembers her
grandfather's recollection of the incident. Her grandfather, William Andrews, was born in 1861 and lived close to the Hickok
family as a boy. He told her that Wild Bill took the young children walking along a line fence between properties and set up
some small coins on the posts. He then made them all stand well
back and proceeded to shoot each one from the fence with no
apparent effort. That feat would not be spectacular to most
marksmen, but to a small child, already awed by the man and his
reputation, it was an unforgettable experience.

An essential part of Hickok's "pistoleer" status was his ability
to get a pistol into action at speed. Several contemporary reports
refer to Hickok's "quick" reaction (the word "fast" was never
used) to any situation. They tell how he drew two pistols at once
and opened fire with both of them. Perhaps he sometimes did (as
happened when he fought Phil Coe). But like most of his contemporaries, Hickok carried two pistols because of the unpre-
dictability of the ammunition—black powder and percussion
caps. Because even prepared paper or metal foil cartridges suffered from dampness and misfired, a second pistol was a necessity. Gross also recalled that he watched with some puzzlement
when Hickok stepped out of his shack one morning and fired six
shots, walked inside, reloaded, and then fired off the other pistol
and reloaded that. Asked if the pistols had gotten damp, Hickok,
who had painstakingly measured the powder, poked a pin
through the nipple vent, and carefully inspected the caps before
loading them, replied that he was not ready to "go yet," and
when he drew a pistol he had to be sure it would work.

As for Hickok's "quick draw" reputation, many confused reaction time with speed, because both required positive and instant action. In a gunfight, however, intelligent reaction to a situation counted far more than speed—a thinking head was much better than a nervous trigger when a gunfighter was faced with a potential life or death situation. Nichols was the first person to hint at Hickok's speed, but other journalists quickly jumped on the bandwagon. Writing in 1865, Thomas J. Dimsdale noted the six-shooter prowess of the characters who infested Montana Territory, in particular the villainous Henry Plummer. His description of Plummer's expertise could easily have applied to Wild Bill: "Plummer was the quickest hand with his revolver of any man in the mountains. He could draw the pistol and discharge the five loads in three seconds." That sort of speed would not impress contemporary "fast draw" addicts, but it doubtless had an affect upon his companions.[20]

Following Nichols's comments, others noted Hickok's reaction to a situation. The most publicized response was part of Capt. Jack Crawford's poems devoted to the burial of Wild Bill. In the third verse of "Wild Bill's Grave" Crawford declared, "Quick as chain-lightning with rifle or pistol— / Custer said, 'Bill never backed!'"

In 1879, the Cheyenne *Daily Leader,* one of Wild Bill's foremost critics, itself succumbed to his already snowballing myth. On July 1 it published the following spurious story following an allegation that the original grave had been robbed and his pistols stolen:

> His ivory handled revolvers . . . were made expressly for him and were finished in a manner unequalled by any ever before manufactured in this or any other country. It is said that a bullet from them never missed its mark. Remarkable stories are told of the dead shootist's skill with these guns. He could keep two fruit cans rolling, one in front and one behind him, with bullets fired from these firearms. This is only a sample story of the hundred which are related of his incredible dexterity with these revolvers.

Others, however, while accepting that Hickok was a remarkable shot, scoffed at such claims. Writing in 1872, W. E. Webb, who had met Hickok at Hays City three years before, declared: "I do not believe, for example, that he could hit a nickel across the street with a pistol-ball, any more than an Indian could do so with an arrow. These feats belong to romance. Bill is wonderfully handy with his pistols, however. . . . His power lies in the wonderful quickness with which he draws a pistol and takes his aim."[21]

Less discerning writers and others who had never witnessed his skill happily accepted some of the tall tales spread about Wild Bill and assumed that he and other renowned gunfighters spent half their time practicing with their pistols. In fact, few of them did. Rather, it was the tyros and those anxious to prove a point or boost their own reputations who practiced drawing and firing at speed. When it came down to it, of course, speed and accuracy took second place to the most important ingredient of all: the mankilling instinct—to shoot to kill while being shot at. Without that ability, skill with a pistol meant nothing.

It is evident, however, that Wild Bill was well aware of his reputation as a "shootist" (a term used to described both a mankiller and a target shot), and when it suited him, he relied upon his skill—as he did when he was first introduced to an audience by Buffalo Bill. On that occasion he put on a dazzling display that greatly impressed all those present. However, it is not clear if Hickok shot at targets (using underloaded ammunition) or fired blank ammunition and created a lot of noise and smoke. Either way, the uninitiated would be impressed, adding further grist to the mill of mythology.[22]

Buel and others have fostered the belief that Wild Bill's pistol skill was little short of miraculous, even suggesting that he could hit targets at any distance with a revolver or a derringer. Anyone who has fired a derringer pistol will know that its effect is deadly but its range is short. To suggest that it could be accurate at seventy-five feet is nonsense. Nevertheless, Buel claimed to have a first-hand account of such a display from Dr. Joshua Thorne. Buel said the good doctor told him that he had removed "eleven bullets from the body of Wild Bill, nearly all of them were shot into him at the Rock Creek fight, but that during all of the painful operations Bill gave expression to none other than sympathetic words for the ferocious enemies he had slain in that memorable encounter." Buel continues:

On one occasion, during his residence in Kansas City, he gave
Dr. Thorne examples of his wonderful shooting. It was a sultry
Sabbath afternoon, when the two were sitting out in the side yard
connected with the Doctor's residence engaged in desultory conversation. A flock of chickens were strolling about the place,
among their number being a large rooster whose propensity was
for chasing every other gallinaceous male off the place. Dr.
Thorne having informed Bill of the troublesome qualities of the
fowl, expressed a wish that, as it was too old to eat, some one
would kill it out of compassion for the other male chanticleers.
Thereupon Wild Bill remarked:

"I'll bet you five dollars, Doctor, that I can cut the rooster's
throat with my derringer, at thirty paces, without breaking his
neck or touching the head or body."

"You can't do it," responded the Doctor, "and I'll take the bet."
The chicken was chased to the required distance, and while it was
still walking Bill raised his pistol and fired, without even bringing
the weapon to his eye. The rooster ran a short distance and then
dropped and fluttered about until it died. Upon examination it
was found that the chicken's throat and windpipe had been cut
with the same cleverness as if a knife had been used, while its
neck was evidently not touched.

The doctor thought it was an accident, so Hickok "fired several
times from the two cartridge derringers he carried, first at small
objects and then at sparrows in the trees; each shot went directly
to the mark, not a single miss being made. The Doctor was satisfied."[23]

Such shooting with a derringer pistol is immediately questionable. But note that this time Buel shortens the range to within a
few feet of the objects; others preferred the long-range stories.
There is no evidence to support Hickok's use of derringers in
fights, but it was generally understood that he carried a pair of
.41-caliber Williamson derringers either in his coat pockets or inside his waistcoat or vest. Yet, when Hickok pulled a pistol with
serious intent or to shoot at a target, he used revolvers.

There is something almost hypnotic about Hickok's marksmanship. His eulogizers have created the impression that he
never missed and, what's more, was so quick that his motion defied description. His detractors, on the other hand, insist that he

was really a poor shot and that his skill lay entirely in his ability to react quicker than his opponents in a kill-or-be-killed situation. The truth, of course, must lie between extremes.

No amount of personal description and old-timers' reminiscences can overcome the mechanical limitations of the firearms themselves. Although it is now possible for a good marksman armed with a Colt's .36-caliber Navy pistol to place six shots into a two-foot circle at 50 yards (firing from a rest or with very carefully aimed shots), and perhaps at 100, these achievements can be bettered when using modern weapons with improved sights and ammunition. Similarly, modern pistoleers can and have performed some of the less bizarre stunts credited to Wild Bill. Yet one has to be practical. My personal experience when shooting a Colt's Navy revolver revealed it to be an extremely accurate weapon. In the hands of an expert, some quite remarkable shooting can be achieved. But so-called hip shooting can be dismissed. Such antics might work in a barroom shoot-out when the combatants are about six feet apart; but serious shooting at distances of twenty-five yards and up to a hundred yards or more requires a steady hand, proper aim, and practice before good results can be achieved. Consequently, stories that suggest Hickok could hit dimes at fifty feet, drive corks through the necks of whiskey bottles at that distance, or perform other miraculous feats at similar ranges should be discounted. The effect of such shooting at ten or fifteen feet is more important. Regardless of the shootist's target skills, his reputation generally hinged upon his close encounters of the revolver kind, when the squeeze of a trigger made or broke a reputation and determined the outcome of the very serious game of life and death.[24]

The preoccupation with speed and accuracy is not the invention of present day film buffs and avid readers of Western novels. It stems from a similar reaction among nineteenth-century dime novel readers and a public anxious for the spectacular rather than the practical. Writing in 1910, the Birmingham gunmaker and firearms expert William W. Greener described at some length the relative merits of single- and double-action pistols, acknowledging the superiority of the former but admitting to the faster firing and loading capabilities of the latter. As to accuracy, he pointed out that the dueling pistol, such as that made by Gastinne Renette

of Paris, was "capable of wonderfully accurate shooting." He
noted that at sixteen paces "there are no less than eleven persons
who have put ten consecutive shots into a centre 3 centimetres
in diameter, *without cutting the line.*" One of the few people to
accomplish this was Ira Paine, one of America's finest nineteenth
century pistol shots. A gold medalist among the dueling pistol
shots, Paine made perhaps the best score with such a weapon
ever recorded. He

> put ten consecutive shots with a mean deviation of only 0.39
> inch, the pistol used taking a 9–millimetre spherical bullet and
> about 12 gr[ain]s of powder. With his .230 pistol he has achieved
> greater wonders, cutting for the author a pencil line drawn on a
> playing card and fixed at 20 feet distance. He could also make sure
> of piercing the ace of hearts at 30 feet twice out of three times,
> and repeatedly split the edge of a card held edgeways at 20 feet
> distant. Such marvelous shooting may be a special gift or the
> result of continuous practice, or both.

With a revolver, however, Greener declared such accuracy to
be impossible because of recoil experienced with some makes of
weapons and the need to change the grip when cocking the hammer. But with regular practice, some marksmen achieved excellent results. Among the best of these was the legendary Walter
Winans. In 1896, while advancing on a target at a marching pace,
from fifty to fifteen yards, put six shots into a four-inch bull's eye.
Winans was one of the few truly great pistol shots. He urged use
of the pistol in combat and even offered his services to the British War office, claiming that he could train officers to shoot with
effect (kill) in less than three seconds. According to Winans, being a good shot was not enough:

> In my opinion, revolver shooting at stationary targets, espe-
> cially at long ranges, is all wrong. To begin with, the revolver is
> not accurate enough for such work. While with the rifle a highest
> possible score at twenty yards at a two-inch bull would be child's
> play, as also at a four-inch bull at fifty yards, in revolver shooting it
> is a very different matter.
> When a revolver is used practically, either in war or self de-
> fence, the shooting is done generally at a few yards' distance and
> at a rapidly-moving object. Further, it often happens that a succes-

sion of shots has to be fired in a few seconds. The man who can make a possible at twenty, or even fifty yards but takes from one to ten minutes for each shot, would be killed long before he had time to get off his first shot, presuming, of course, his assailant is a practicable revolver shot who can shoot without taking a long time over the individual shots. For instance, a man who can hit a target, say, eight inches square at five yards' range, in snap shooting is a good practical shot. It therefore seems to me that deliberate shooting at the revolver clubs and at Bisley is worse than useless, because it teaches a man to shoot in the wrong way.

Winans went on to dismiss most of the existing competitive shooting and suggested instead moving targets and an emphasis upon instant decisions rather than protracted concentration when shooting. In another time and another place, he might have achieved a deadly reputation as a gunfighter, for what he suggested made sense. He would have been entirely at home with the average frontier pistoleer.[25]

In the United States, the Winans and Paine tradition was carried on by a number of people, among them Ad and Elizabeth Topperwein, a husband and wife team. Ad duplicated all the known feats of the likes of Doc Carver and Annie Oakley. Elizabeth was considered the greatest female shot of all time, an accolade allegedly bestowed upon her by Annie Oakley herself. But the one man to whom most Western enthusiasts turned for reassurance when it came to the reputations of Western gunfighters was Edward McGivern, a small, chubby, almost penguin-shaped individual who was one of the greatest fast-and-fancy pistol shots of this century.

The obsession with speed in some quarters has produced some interesting reactions among those who considered the whole business of gunfighting in the Old West to be grossly exaggerated. They claimed that the pistols themselves were useless, clumsy things that could at best only damage an opponent if fired belly-to-belly. Ironically, about 1910, Bat Masterson, who had personally ordered eight Colt Single-Action Army pistols from the company, was persuaded to write a story on the worth of the new Savage Arms automatic pistols in comparison with the old-time Colt's and other makes of revolvers. He wrote:

With the clumsy monstrosities which they were able to obtain, from the heavy "monkey-wrench" cap-and-ball revolver to the more modern but just as cumbersome six-shooter, men all learned to "throw lead" quick and straight without taking sight. To do this, even if he had the natural gift of the born dead shot, required a man to practice hard and long; for although he might have the necessary sense of direction well developed, the hand and the wrist had to be trained to the pistol, since the pistol did not fit the hand.[26]

This is nonsense, of course, for the old cap-and-ball Colt, Remington, and other makes of pistol had been designed to fit the hand. Colt's Navy pistol (its grip was retained for later models, including the Peacemaker) allowed the hand to grip the stock and thumb-cock the hammer without changing position. As for accuracy, reports of the weapon's failings so disgusted sharpshooter McGivern that in the early 1930s he conducted a series of tests that not only amazed his friends but stifled many of the critics. He was of the opinion that the single-action Colt Army or "Peacemaker" would "perform almost any necessary regulation shooting service about as well as any other hand gun available." In his book he described how he put his own theories to the test.

From his boyhood, McGivern had been fascinated by stories of the likes of Wild Bill, and once he was old enough to own a gun he set out to duplicate some of their alleged feats. With a great deal of patience and practice, together with a natural ability, he did just that, adding a few tricks that the old-timers never thought of. He would have won Walter Winans's approval, for he specialized in aerial targets, some "tossed one at a time, with a gun in either hand," or after much practice, "two tossed in the air at a time," using two pistols. Such antics when credited to Wild Bill have been dismissed as nonsense. McGivern proved that they could be done, but he attained the best results using modern double-action pistols.

That much publicized and criticized myth of Western gunfighting, "fanning the hammer," also came in for some examination. To fan the hammer, the shooter gripped the pistol in one hand, with the trigger finger pressing the trigger back against the triggerguard, and, with the palm of the other hand, rapidly fanned the hammer spur to cock it and to discharge all six shots at speed. McGivern noted that this form of shooting was useless against aerial targets. But in the hands of an expert such as himself, fanning at a normal target produced some impressive results. Firing at a target ten feet away, McGivern fanned a series of shots, with accuracy, at speeds of 1–1.2 seconds. But the fact that a modern-day expert can do it does not mean that old-timers could—or that they even cared to spend time and energy in the attempt. More up-to-date revolvers work better for such feats. However, aimed accuracy with an old Colt was good, and that was what mattered.

When assessing Hickok's reputation as a pistol shot, McGivern noted that Wild Bill performed most of his feats and fought his gunfights with cap-and-ball pistols. There seemed to be little information on how he carried or used them. "However," McGivern wrote, "there can be little doubt about his proficiency with his pistols. He certainly could not have survived all of the gun battles chalked up to his credit if he had not been a more than average expert in the handling of his guns."[27]

The U.S. government conducted trials of the Peacemaker in 1872 and 1876, which disclosed that the weapon had a mean absolute deviation at 50 yards of 3.11 inches. By comparison, the Smith & Wesson "American" model was 4.39 inches, and the Remington Model 1875 was on a par with the Smith & Wesson. Penetration tests at 25 yards resulted in 4.1 inches for the Colt and 3.33 inches for the "American" model. Much later, in 1898, the Ordnance extended its trials of the Peacemaker and officially declared that the mean absolute deviation at 50 yards was 5.3 inches, at 100 yards it was 8.3 inches, at 150 yards 12.3 inches, at 200 yards 15.9 inches, at 250 yards 24.9 inches, and at 300 yards, 28.7 inches. A blade formed the front sight and a "V" groove milled into the top strap served as the rear sight. The pistols were "sighted in" at 25 yards in the early 1870s, but by the 1890s the distance had been increased to 50 yards. To simplify matters still further, the army reckoned that a trooper aiming at a point 150 yards away with a pistol should compensate for trajectory and "drift" by aiming four feet above the target. At 200 yards, this distance was increased to eight feet. Little of this "applied science" meant much to the average gunfighter, however, for long-range shoot-outs were not normally his forte. Wild Bill and his contemporaries were much more concerned with events taking place within twenty feet.[28]

Despite all attempts either to verify, qualify, or even debunk stories about Wild Bill's alleged exploits, most people prefer the mythical version. For them, it is a comforting reminder of childhood and their dreams and fantasies. Academics may well frown upon such attachments, and cynics may wring their hands in dismay, but Wild Bill, both as a man and a myth, belongs to history and no amount of revision can change that.

Four

"The Scout of the Plains"

Wild Bill Hickok's reputation as a plainsman and Indian scout places him high among those legendary frontiersmen who have enthralled generations worldwide. The lure of these characters knows no boundaries. Colorful figures clad in buckskin, they are depicted as independent of the restrictions of civilization, wandering as they pleased among the forests, mountains, and plains of a vast wilderness. Their self-reliance and courage in the face of adversity, whether they faced the elements, wild animals, or hostile Indians, captivated the imaginations of millions. Men such as Lewis Wetzell, Daniel Boone, Kit Carson, Jim Bridger, and a host of others, some entirely fictional, were heroes to the masses who lived east of the Mississippi River. It is no surprise, then, to learn that Hickok's initial press publicity refers to him as a plainsman or scout rather than a mankiller. Most posthumous accounts of Hickok's life and adventures, on the other hand, devote little attention to his plains skills but concentrate almost entirely upon his peace-keeping or gunfighting roles.

It took a motion picture to balance the image. Aptly named *The Plainsman,* the film is loosely based upon published accounts of Hickok's life. It conveys the impression that Hickok's scouting reputation was second to none and his mankilling notoriety the result of too much fame and too many tyros anxious to prove themselves his equal. Yet despite changing attitudes toward both Hickok and his reputation, his plains exploits still take second place to his feats with a pistol against both human and inanimate targets.

In his own lifetime Wild Bill's reputation as a scout and Indian

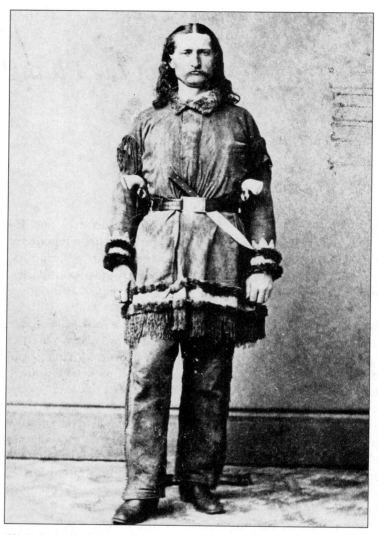

Hickok dressed in a plains-style buckskin suit and wearing his Colt's Navy pistols in the butts forward or "reverse draw" position, credited to Blakeslee of Mendota. The photograph is now believed to have been made in 1869 when Hickok was reported in Mendota in March of that year enroute to his mother's home at nearby Troy Grove. (Courtesy Kansas State Historical Society)

fighter was acknowledged and featured prominently in the publicity devoted to his appearance with Buffalo Bill's theatrical combination. And many of his contemporaries, notably Custer, publicized it. Yet a cursory examination of early biographies and articles built around Hickok's adventures reveals that they paid scant attention to his plains experiences. Instead, one finds glowing accounts of his own and Buffalo Bill's alleged involvement in the Washita fight, where Hickok was credited with the death of Black Kettle. Buel is thought to be the first person to publicize this yarn, and to his discredit, Cody himself was quite happy to include it in the souvenir programs sold at each performance of his Wild West.[1]

Although Hickok's plains experience was respected by his peers, evidence of the same sort of adulation is not contained in the official records, which report only dates, rates of pay, and when and where he was employed. Opinions were left to individuals. But by combining the official and personal views of Hickok, one can begin to understand why he achieved so much notoriety as a scout, guide, and Indian fighter, epitomized as a "Beau Ideal of the Plains."

James Butler Hickok's introduction to the frontier began in his childhood in Illinois. In 1837, the year of his birth, the state was still part wilderness. Only five years had elapsed since the Black Hawk Indian War of 1832, the last major conflict between Indians and the whites within the state. Black Hawk, leader of a faction of the Sauk and Fox tribe, had refused to recognize the treaty of 1804 (and later treaties) that ceded to the United States (for a pittance) the whole of their territory east of the Mississippi River, an area comprising present day northwest Illinois, southern Wisconsin, and a part of eastern Missouri. White settlement alarmed the Indians. Led by Black Hawk, they tried to form a confederation to curb the influx of settlers and preserve their tribal lands. Despite one major victory against the whites, Black Hawk's bid failed. Most of his followers were annihilated at the mouth of the Bad Axe River in Wisconsin as they attempted to cross the Mississippi River. Five hundred Indians reportedly died by the end of the fifteen week war, while the whites claimed only seventy lives lost. The Indians sued for peace and ceded yet more land in return for government help.[2]

Family recollections of James Hickok's childhood exploits as a
hunter are naturally tainted with hearsay, but he did display a
marked ability as a hunter and achieved a local reputation as a
marksman and provider of meat for the family. Some credence is
given to this by a comment James himself made in a letter written
from Kansas on November 24, 1856 to his brother Horace:

> you talk as if you thought if you were here that I would hunt with
> you[.] I have something else to do[,] I can kill all the game we want
> before sunrise and by moonlight so what would be the use for me
> to hunt animore[.] and that you could not do for you don't get up
> early enough[,] and you never scouted any[,] so you could not
> hunt well at night.[3]

The Kansas Territory in which James Hickok found himself in
1856 was in turmoil. On May 30, 1854, President Franklin Pierce
had signed the Kansas-Nebraska Act, opening up the territory to
settlement. In doing so, he set a match to a powder keg of intoler-
ance, hypocrisy, and downright wickedness.

Kansas Territory was to be the scene of much of the violence
between military and guerrilla bands that presaged the Civil War
conflict in the border states of Missouri, Arkansas and parts of
eastern Kansas. The act set out the boundaries of Kansas on the
west of the Missouri state line to the continental divide and included part of the Rocky Mountains and present-day eastern Colorado. It was a vast expanse of land, 700 miles by 200 miles, encompassing prairie, streams, and mountains that were home to
roaming herds of buffalo and other animals as well as nomadic
tribes of Indians.

According to the original act, the people of the newly created
territory would have popular sovereignty and decide their own
destiny. High on the list of difficult decisions they faced was the
question of slavery. In 1820, the Missouri Compromise ensured
that newly created states entered the Union as "free" or "slave"
states in equal numbers. In essence, the Missouri Compromise
provided that Missouri could practice slavery but could not ex-
clude free Negroes and mulattoes. California was admitted to the
Union in 1850 as a free state, so Missourians assumed that the
new Kansas Territory would become a slave state. Many of the

newly arrived immigrants disagreed. But slave-owning Missourians feared that a free Kansas would become a haven for runaway slaves.

Soon, proslavery Missourians began arriving in the territory and quickly earned themselves the hated name "Border Ruffians." In return, Missourians dubbed the Kansans "Jayhawkers" after a mythical bird that was noted for its thievery. The conflict heated up, but the possibility of violence did not deter would-be settlers. They poured into the territory seeking land and a new life. With them came opportunity-seekers whose object was to speculate rather than participate. Both sides soon resorted to violence to achieve their aims, and there were pitched battles between factions. Men like "General" James Lane, leader of the so-called Free State Army and John Brown became household names. Lane believed that his military activities benefited the state, while Brown, hiding behind religious fervor, declared himself dedicated to freeing the slaves, and did help many of them to escape as far as Canada. But when he murdered a number of unarmed Missourians, both sides hated him. Finally, his attack on Harpers Ferry led to his arrest and subsequent trial and hanging in 1859.

The so-called Free Staters were as much to blame for the violence as were the Missourians. They included a number of religious leaders, among them the Reverend Henry Ward Beecher, whose contribution was boxes of "Bibles" that turned out to be Sharps' rifles and carbines. They are still remembered as "Beecher's Bibles."

By the time he emigrated to Kansas in 1856, James was evidently at home in a wilderness. He soon familiarized himself with the area around Leavenworth, where he first settled. His original intention was to take up farming—or at least to look for potential farmland. But that plan was sidetracked for some time by the problems caused by the pro- and antislavery factions, which were already preparing to assert their convictions by force of arms. On September 13 Federal troops fought a brief engagement at Hickory Point with a band of Free Staters. The two-day battle left one man killed, nine wounded, and a number taken prisoner. James Hickok may well have been present, for in his letter of November 24 he also stated that "thare is 29 of our com-

pany in custody at Lacompton [Lecompton] yet. I have been out
to see them once." It is also possible that he was at the Battle of
Bull Creek where, for the first time, outnumbered Free Staters
were able to defeat a superior force of Missouri Border Ruffians
by using the Sharps' rifle.[4]

Late in 1856, James made the acquaintance of Robert H. Williams, an Englishman who had come to Kansas seeking land. He
persuaded Hickok (whom he recalled as "William Hitchcock") to
join his expedition into what would become Johnson County,
and in July 1857, the village of Monticello was established.[5]
(James Hickok, as previously stated, was known by most of his
Kansas contemporaries as William or Bill. This name also appears
in the local press and court documents, although most of the latter refer to him as J. B. Hickok.)[6]

Local elections were held early in 1858, and on March 22,
Hickok was one of four constables elected to serve the local magistrates. It was during this period that he also formed a relationship with Mary Jane Owen, the half-Shawnee daughter of John
Owen, and laid claim to 160 acres of farmland. By 1859 he had
problems. Family interference put an end to his romance, and
Mary Jane married another. But most galling was the loss of his
land. While in Leavenworth he had tried unsuccessfully to obtain
some acres in the Delaware lands. Having squatted on Shawnee
land since 1857, he filed a preemption claim in February 1858
for a quarter-section. Unfortunately for James, the land was also
claimed by Samuel McCulloch, a Wyandot Indian, under the pro-
vision of an 1842 treaty with the Wyandot. The treaty allowed
certain influential members of the tribe to claim sections (640
acres) of land which was then held for Indian tribes west of the
Mississippi River. These "floaters" as they were called (due to the
fact that they were not tied to any large tracts set aside for the
Wyandot) could be singularly (one parcel of land per person)
claimed for any Indian Land. Hickok's was one of six claims pre-
empted, and since McCulloch filed his claim on April 1, 1857,
Hickok found himself homeless. He then moved to Olathe,
where his cousin Guy Butler had a homestead.[7]

At this point, Hickok's movements become blurred. According
to most accounts, he joined Russell, Majors & Waddell and
worked for several years as a teamster on their Santa Fe route. As

early as July 27, 1865, the Springfield *Missouri Weekly Patriot* reported that he had been "engaged since his sixteenth year, with the exception of about two years, with Russell, Majors & Waddill [*sic*]." But family sources have disclosed that this was not correct. Writing on May 26, 1861, from Black Jack, Kansas, Guy Butler advised Horace Hickok of some startling news:

> I take this opportunity of writing to you not knowing when I may get another chance as I am about to enlist. I heard last week that James was dead[.] I do not know but that you have heard of it before[.] I got it from Mcintire [George W. McIntire] of Monticellow[.] he said he died with a disease called the newmonia a disease that has proven very fatal here in Kansas. I had not heard of his sickness before[,] if I had I should have gone up and taken care of him[.] He died at Salt Creek Valley four miles west of Levenworth[.] the sircumstances attending his death I know nothing about[.] he was in the e[m]ploy of Jones and Cartwright in whose employ he had been nearly two years[.] I suppose they must have been owing him considerable[.] when I left him last summer they were owing him about a hundred dollars[.] I will inquire into the matter more particular and let you know as soon as possible.

The family was appalled. Horace immediately wrote to Jones & Cartwright at Leavenworth, and in their reply of June 6, 1861, they stated:

> Mr J. B. Hickock has not been in our employ since 20th April, at which time we settled with him and paid him what was due him. The Wagon Master under whom he worked, Geo. H. Ross, can probably tell his whereabouts, but he has now gone to Denver City and will not be back for two months. We will send your letter out to him when he can probably give you the information desired.

George H. Ross (sometimes spelled Rose) was well known to the Cody family, with whom he lodged for a period in the late 1850s. He would have been familiar with Hickok, who also stayed with the Cody family occasionally. Ross probably hired Hickok some time late in 1858 or early 1859.[8]

Whether James Hickok did seek employment with Russell,

Majors & Waddell following his break with Jones & Cartwright is open to debate. But his employment with the latter outfit until April refutes the claim that he first appeared at the Rock Creek, Nebraska Territory, stage station in March 1861. It is likely that he arrived at the place late in April or early May and remained until the so-called McCanles Massacre.

Following the incident at Rock Creek, Hickok went to Leavenworth where he joined the Union Army in a civilian capacity and served as a wagonmaster, scout, and spy before returning to the plains in 1866. His quartermaster, Richard Bentley Owen, who had been posted as assistant quartermaster to Fort Riley, Kansas, requested his presence at the post. Here he was employed as a government detective from late January until early the following year.

In May 1866, Hickok was detached from the post to guide Gen. William T. Sherman and Gen. John S. Pope to Fort Kearny, Nebraska Territory. There the command split, and Pope went on to Santa Fe, New Mexico. Hickok accompanied his party as a scout and guide. Enroute to the fort, the command camped for the night on Little Sandy, not far from Rock Creek. Frank Helvey, who had known Hickok at Rock Creek back in 1861, recognized him immediately when he rode over accompanied by General Sherman. They requested that Helvey not let any of the troops have any whisky, a promise Helvey kept despite entreaties from the soldiers. The following morning, as the command moved off, Sherman and Hickok stopped by and thanked Helvey for the favor. In later years, Helvey was to recall that in his opinion Hickok was much maligned over the Rock Creek affair. He also stated that he had witnessed a shooting contest between Bob Spotswood, division agent for Russell, Majors & Waddell, and Wild Bill. Spotswood was Hickok's equal, he said, but in his opinion, "the honors were even."

When General Pope returned to the post in September, Hickok resumed his normal duties. Many years later, General Sherman confused Buffalo Bill with Wild Bill when, on June 29, 1887, he wrote to Cody recalling the time when "you guided me honestly and faithfully in 1865–'6 [sic] from Fort Riley to Kearney in Kansas and Nebraska."[9]

The publication of Nichols's "Wild Bill" story in *Harper's* had a decided effect not only on the public, but also on Hickok's reputation. Early in 1867, Gen. Winfield Scott Hancock organized an expedition to convince the tribes in Kansas that the government wanted peace and was prepared to use force to preserve it. When the news spread that Hickok would accompany him, a number of comments appeared in the press. Henry M. Stanley, who interviewed Hickok at Fort Zarah on April 4, described him as "one of the finest examples of that peculiar class now extant, known as Frontiersmen, ranger, hunter and Indian scout." Later he was to report that Wild Bill had been pursued by Indians and had killed two of them, which was verified by another noted scout, Thomas H. Kincaid. One editor even commented: "Wild Bill is out after the Indians. If his history as published in 'Harper' is correct, we suppose he will eat three or four of the red prairie birds every day before breakfast! Ugh!"[10]

General Hancock and his second in command, Gen. George A. Custer, spent fruitless weeks in pursuit of the Indians. But despite the efforts of their agent, E. W. Wynkoop, to convince them of the peaceful nature of the expedition, the tribes remained wary. Their concern was understandable, for Hancock's command consisted of about 1,500 men made up of six companies of the Seventh Cavalry, a battery of the Fourth Artillery Battalion, and seven companies of the Thirty-seventh Infantry, together with supply wagons and a number of Delaware Indians and white scouts and couriers. Hancock's efforts to arrange meetings with the Indians were frustrated when the Indians failed to show up. Reports of Indian depredations against settlers did not help. Neither did his decision to burn one of their deserted villages in reprisal. Custer was later court-martialed for deserting his command without leave in order to visit his wife at Fort Harker during a cholera outbreak. He was suspended from duty without rank or pay for one year. Finally, in October 1867, a meeting was arranged with the tribes at Fort Dodge, and a semblance of peace was restored.

General Custer, despite what has been written concerning his military capabilities, did appreciate the need for experienced plainsmen. He recalled that every detachment of troops that proceeded against hostile Indians was accompanied by experienced scouts or guides; men who were employed by the government because of their knowledge of the country or their ability to speak the languages of the various tribes. Payment for them was far in excess of the common soldier's pay: A private's pay was $13 per month while a good scout or guide could command between $75 and $100 per month—some were paid as much as $125. Before they were hired, the men were asked, "Do you know the country thoroughly, and can you speak any of the Indian languages?" Depending on their reply, they were employed either as interpreters, scouts, or couriers.

Custer also noted that most of these men were of superior judgement or common sense, generally better educated than the average frontiersman. They did not need maps, and their intimate knowledge of the country and the Indians, for whom most of them bore a "deep hatred," along with their skills with firearms and horses, set them apart. They needed all their skill and bravery when pitting their wits against an intelligent and skillful foe.[11]

Custer's claim that most of the scouts hated their Indian foes was reiterated by Henry M. Stanley, who declared that Hickok had an "inveterate hatred" of Indians. Plains Indians were regarded as "hostiles," and stories of their alleged depredations against the whites were common. It is a sad fact that in the parlance of the time, Indians perpetrated "massacres," while similar acts of aggression by whites are claimed as "victories."

Most of the scouts either worked alone or with a particular "pard" or "pal." Many of these partners were themselves noted individuals. "California Joe" (Moses E. Milner), himself one of the truly great scouts, guides, and trackers of the West, had as his partner John ("Jack") Corbin, who was mentioned several times by Custer. Where Joe, who sported one revolver and his favorite long-barreled "Springfield breech-loading rifle," preferred to ride a mule, his "pardner" carried two revolvers and a Sharps' carbine, and in place of the army mule he rode a "fine gray charger."[12]

Hickok sometimes partnered with one "Wentworth" (a scout for the Tenth Cavalry), who may have been a Conrad Wentworth. (An individual known as "Little Buckshot Wentworth" appeared in Nebraska in the early years of this century, but it is not certain that it was the same man.) Hickok's best-known partner, however, was John ("Jack") Harvey, a native of New York State who had fought in the Civil War as one of General Blunt's scouts and may have first met Wild Bill in that capacity. By 1867 Harvey and Hickok were regarded as partners and were both employed by the quartermaster at Fort Riley. It was there in January of that year, that they were responsible for the capture of two mule thieves and the return of stock.

Harvey, according to Stanley, was more "reckless" than Hickok. Although his service record has not so far been found, contemporary newspapers refer to Jack as one of Hancock's riders or scouts. That he did serve in such a capacity is not in doubt; but his adventures with Hickok as recounted by Connelley are not corroborated. Taken ill with "consumption" (tuberculosis), Harvey died at Ellsworth on March 13, 1868. Hickok at that time was employed as a deputy U.S. marshal and was reported to be at Atchison when his friend died.[13]

Custer's reference to California Joe's preference for a mule instead of a horse is important. The legendary image of Wild Bill, dressed immaculately in a fringed buckskin suit and careering across the plains mounted on Black Nell, is not only erroneous but misrepresents both his status and the conditions under which he and his fellow scouts lived. A faded tintype made in the summer of 1867 depicts William Comstock, Thomas Kincaid, Thomas Atkins, and California Joe. It shows them all, with the exception of Comstock, mounted on mules. And each man is dressed in ill-fitting and ragged clothing, ideally suited to the circumstances. Glimpses of Hickok from various sources suggest that he dressed in a similar fashion rather than in the "dandified" manner remembered by Theodore Davis. On the subject of mules, Custer noted:

> Scouts usually prefer a good mule to a horse, and wisely too, for the reason that in making their perilous journeys, either singly or by twos or threes, celerity is one principal condition to success. The object with the scout is not to outrun or overwhelm the Indians, but to avoid both by secrecy and caution in his movements. On the plains at most seasons of the year the horse is incapable of performing long or rapid journeys without being supplied with forage on the route. This must be transported, and in the case of

scouts would necessarily be transported on the back of the horse, thereby adding materially to the weight which must be carried. The mule will perform a rapid and continuous march without forage, being able to subsist on the grazing to be obtained in nearly all the valleys on the plains during the greater part of the year.[14]

Hickok's reputation was enhanced by his involvement in the Hancock Indian War, and "Wild Bill" was featured in a number of accounts. One in particular is firmly entrenched in his legend. In September 1868, a number of men at Gomerville, Colorado Territory, were under siege by Cheyenne and Arapaho Indians. Wild Bill, who happened to be on hand, volunteered to ride for help. Mounted on a fast horse, he evaded the Indians and managed to bring help, saving thirty-five lives. This yarn was repeated (and still is) as late as 1909 by Alva Gomer, son of the founder of Gomerville. Only one contemporary account has so far come to light that identifies the rider as "Wild Bill." Others disclose that it was one "Texas Bill" or William Carrolton who deserved the credit.[15]

Early in the Hancock Indian war, a stagecoach got stuck in a snowdrift. When the driver took his horses and rode off in the hope of reaching the next station, the passengers, accompanied by the messenger (guard or conductor) agreed to wait with the coach, as did a special artist for *Harper's New Monthly Magazine,* to await his return. They made themselves as comfortable as possible in a small cave while they awaited rescue. They were amazed when their game of "draw poker" was interrupted by Custer (whom they did not recognize) asking if they had seen any Indians. Receiving no information of any value, the general withdrew. One of the players looked up and remarked: "Fellers, did you ever see 'Wild Bill?' That was the chap; purty boy, wasn't he? Looked as ef he wanted a hand in, didnt't he?"[16]

No one else seems to have confused Hickok and Custer, but it is an understandable error, for both men were in the habit of wearing their hair long and dressing in buckskins. There the resemblance ended. But in 1872, General Custer himself added to Hickok's growing reputation as an Indian fighter and plains scout by mentioning him in a series of articles written for *Galaxy* that were published in book form in 1874 as *My Life on the Plains.*

And John Wallace Crawford, the self-styled "Poet Scout" in one of several poems dedicated to Hickok, overromanticized their relationship by including the following lines in his "Wild Bill's Grave": "Custer—brave Custer—was lonely without him, / Even with God."

Elizabeth Bacon Custer, the general's wife, in later years also spoke well of Hickok, especially his looks and bearing. On one occasion she declared:

> I remember watching Wild Bill, as he reported at the Commanding Officer's tent to get despatches for my husband, and wishing with all my heart that I could go with him. I know this must seem strange to people in the States, whose ideas of scouts are made up from stories of shooting affrays, gambling, lynching and outlawry. I should have felt myself safe to go any distance with those men whom my husband employed as bearers of despatches. I have never known women treated with such reverence as those whom they honored.[17]

Mrs. Custer's remarks might explain why some have suggested that Hickok was the general's favorite scout. If that were true, it might account for his reputation as a scout and Indian fighter. But Custer himself did not suggest anything of the kind. His comments are nonetheless revealing: "Among the white scouts were numbered some of the most noted of their class. The most prominent among them was 'Wild Bill.' . . . He was a Plainsman in every sense of the word, yet unlike any other of his class . . . then and now the most famous scout on the Plains."[18]

Custer's assessment of Hickok as the "most prominent" and "most famous" of the white scouts is tantalizing in its lack of detail, for he seems to be more concerned with Hickok's growing reputation as a mankiller, and his strength of character than his plains skills. For it was Wild Bill's dominance of his companions that intrigued him. On several occasions when things might have gotten out of hand, Wild Bill (the general never called him by his given name) simply reminded his companions that "this has gone far enough." Anyone who disregarded that comment, he said, "must settle it with me."[19]

It is evident that a number of Custer's fellow officers shared his opinion that Hickok could be relied upon. On April 19, 1867, when Custer's command reached Fort Hays, Kansas, it was discovered that there was no spare forage for his horses and mules, and supplies for his men were also limited. Custer immediately wrote a dispatch for the post commander at Fort Harker requesting supplies. He ordered Hickok to take it and he was given a "fresh mule" and urged to make all haste. Capt. Albert Barnitz, who had known Wild Bill at Springfield (where he had ordered his arrest following the shooting of Dave Tutt), promptly loaned him a carbine and reported to his wife that Hickok was "sanguine that he could make the trip (60 miles) by daylight this morning, unless driven out of his course by the Indians," vowing that he was good for a dozen Indians "at all events." Wild Bill reached the post at "1 1/2 p.m." and after a brief rest returned to Custer with a despatch advising him that five wagons loaded with forage (all that could be spared) were on their way.[20]

According to Francis Cragin (probably an early Colorado settler who kept notebooks on his travels and events), in the summer of 1867, Monument Station, Kansas, was the scene of much activity during the Hancock Indian War. An Oliver Wiggins and his family were sent to the station, and it was guarded at one point by a full company of Seventh Cavalry troopers. There was no telegraph line open between Fort Hays and Fort Wallace, so for a period Wild Bill was employed in carrying weekly dispatches between posts, with a night stopover at Monument Station. Here he bunked with William Comstock, the post guide at Fort Wallace. When the cavalry was removed, ten civilians arrived, described as former Denver jailbirds who had volunteered to guard the station. Their leader, a man named Dolan, made the mistake of insulting Mrs. Wiggins while her husband was away. In a fistfight, he was soundly beaten by Hickok, who added insult to his injury by "jumping on his face with both feet" and reminding the fellow's companions that if they were still there when Wiggins returned, he would kill them all for insulting his wife. This is the first intimation this writer has found to suggest that Hickok and Comstock were known to each other personally and not by reputation alone.[21]

Capt. George Armes of the Tenth Cavalry, who employed Wild Bill in 1867 and again in 1868, was impressed by his knowledge of the country. On August 21, 1868, at a camp on Big Timber, he noted that his bitter enemy, Maj. M. H. Kidd (who was later relieved of his command and discharged from the army at his own request), had "failed to pay attention to the advice of Wild Bill our scout and guide, in regard to the course we should take when we left camp yesterday, he appearing to know more about the country than those who have lived here for years." As a result, the command was ten miles off course with no sign of Indians.[22]

In a letter written from a camp on the Arkansas River dated August 5 and published in the Leavenworth *Daily Times* of August 13, 1867, a correspondent commented upon the way the campaign was going. He noted that Lo (the Indians) had managed to relieve the army of "a few scalps and surplus ponies, and at the end of four months [we] return to our respective homes, covered all over with glory, each the hero of some hair-breadth escape—a second Lew Wetzel, Adam Poe or Wild Bill, forsooth."

But Hickok also had his critics. The most serious of these was Gen. Eugene A Carr. Although Carr would publicize Buffalo Bill Cody's expertise as a scout, guide, and tracker, he did not share either Custer's or Barnitz's positive view of Hickok. In fact, when Carr first met him in Gen. W. H. Penrose's camp on the Palo Duro in December 1868, he took an instant dislike to him. Hickok was one of several scouts accompanying Penrose's command. But he was not "Chief of Scouts" as Carr claimed; that honor went to Charles Autobees, who also had two of his sons along. Carr claimed that Hickok refused when requested to take dispatches to Camp Supply because he thought that it was "too dangerous." Finally, Hickok agreed to go, for if he had flunked that test "he could never have held up his head again as a frontiersman." Wild Bill set off and reached Camp Supply safely. The dispatches were then carried to Fort Dodge in care of Lt. C. Martin, Third Infantry, accompanied by several scouts and soldiers who reached the post late in the evening of January 10, 1869. Lieutenant Martin informed the post commander that the previous Wednesday " 'Wild Bill' came into Camp Supply with Dispatches from Bvt Brig. Gen. Penrose & Command for Major Genl. Sheridan." Other couriers reported contact with Comanche Indians and that the army had captured a village. Hickok's return journey to Carr's camp was made through deep snow and wintry conditions. En route his overcoat, which was lashed to his saddle and held about thirty letters, dispatches and a map, got loosened and the correspondence was lost. Carr was furious. In his official report, he mentioned this loss, but in his manuscript, written years afterwards, he also alleged that Hickok had not delivered his dispatches to General Sheridan because he had gotten drunk and lost his letters. He seems to have confused the outward and return journeys.[23]

Carr does not explain his dislike of Hickok. But it may be that Wild Bill's reputation did not appeal to the general, and it is clear from his manuscript that he included hearsay evidence in his assessment. He implied that Wild Bill was a great liar. One story in particular annoyed him. Hickok told him that during the late war he had been with General Price during a battle and within days was back behind Union lines with information. Obviously, Carr was unaware that Hickok had in fact been close to Price before the Battle of Newtonia and had slipped away to report to General Sanborn who, as related elsewhere, made good use of the information.

Hickok's gambling also annoyed Carr. He alleged that a number of his officers were in debt to Hickok, but he did not say whether his annoyance was due to the gambling itself or the fact that men of rank should gamble with mere civilians. It was a fight with the Mexican scouts (Carr claimed that Hickok had been bullying and dismissing them as "mongrels") that really brought matters to a head. Convinced that Hickok was the aggressor, he ordered him to return with the wagon train the next day. Wild Bill then told him that on the personal order of General Sheridan he was to keep an eye on the "colored" troops with the command, and if there was any problem to go direct to him. Evidently, this posed problems for Carr. Hickok's service with the Tenth Cavalry, where he apparently got on well with the black troops, had probably come to Sheridan's notice. No written orders have been found to confirm Wild Bill's claim, but Sheridan was known to make oral requests. So Carr must have been in a quandary, for his own antipathy toward Negro troops was well known. Reluctantly, he allowed Hickok to stay. At this point, Charles Autobees and his son Mariano presented themselves before Carr with the request that Hickok should not be dismissed.

Buffalo Bill Cody's version of this incident differs from Carr's.

He claimed that the fifteen Mexicans with the command had "often threatened to clean us out; but they postponed the undertaking from time to time, until one day, while we were all at the sutler's store, the long-expected fight took place, and resulted in the Mexicans getting severely beaten." Later, when Carr heard his own and Hickok's version of events, it was admitted that there had been a lot of "tanglefoot" on board that evening, so he took no further action.[24]

A rather bizarre version of the same event was recorded by Hiram Robbins, who had at one time managed Cody's Combination and wrote several of the plays. He alleged that Hickok killed three of the Mexican scouts because Cody had got himself into a fight with them and Hickok was forced to save his life. "Billy Cody would get hurt if he didn't stop fooling around," grumbled Hickok. Carr, understandably, was incensed. He ordered Hickok out of camp. Wild Bill marched into Carr's tent and leveled a pistol at him, remarking that if he went, Carr would go too unless he rescinded the order. The general looked from the pistol to Hickok and declared, "The order is rescinded." "That's right, General," replied Wild Bill. "I knew that there were good spots about you."[25]

The only newspaper reference to the difficulty between the American scouts and the Mexicans appeared in the Pueblo, Colorado Territory, *Chieftain* of January 28, 1869. In reporting the return of the expedition to Fort Lyon, the editor noted, "As an historical item, it might be well to mention that Mariano Autobees and Wild Bill, both acting as scouts and guides, had a slight misunderstanding which led to blows, and terminated by Wild Bill knocking down Mariano Autobees, and administering a severe castigation."

We are left with a confusion of fact and fiction. Carr's assessment of Hickok was influenced as much by hearsay as personal acquaintance. Although his admitted prejudice against Negroes was well known, he evidently regarded the Mexicans in a better light. Racial conflict was common, which led to friction between the American and Mexican scouts. But it is very significant that the two Mexican scouts Charles and Mariano Autobees should speak up on Hickok's behalf—evidence, if any was needed that there had been fault on both sides.

How did the real Hickok compare as a scout or courier with such characters as William Comstock, Edmund Guerrier, or indeed his own friend Cody? Undisputedly, Cody was a good scout, buffalo hunter and guide, and proved himself courageous in hand-to-hand encounters with Indians. But like Hickok, he had no affinity with the Indians (although in later years he came to admire and respect them). Neither scout was versed in the languages of the plains tribes, though Connelley claimed that Hickok could "speak the language of every Plains tribe. In the villages of some of the tribes he had friends as well as deadly enemies."[26]

This is nonsense. Had Hickok been anything of a linguist, his worth and reputation would have been enhanced considerably. Some indication of the importance attached to interpreters can be gleaned from a study of the Hancock Expedition, which was frequently frustrated both by evasion on the part of the Indians and a lack of communication. A key figure in this respect was Edmund Gassea Choteau Guerrier, the son of French trader William Guerrier and Tah-tah tois-neh, a full-blooded Cheyenne. Born on January 16, 1840, in a Cheyenne village on the Smoky Hill River in central Kansas, Guerrier (known by various names, among them "Ed Geary"), received some education, then roamed the West for several years. He eventually returned to his late mother's people and was present at the Sand Creek massacre of November 29, 1864. Col. John Chivington and a part of the Third Colorado Volunteers (aided and abetted by territorial governor John Evans) attacked the village on Sand Creek, Colorado Territory. The Indians were convinced that they were at peace with the United States. They even flew the Stars and Stripes in preparation for negotiations with Governor Evans. The attack took them completely by surprise. Guerrier and his brother-in-law George Bent managed to escape. Chivington's action was widely condemned, but he left the army before any charges could be laid against him. His action led to widespread war, and left Guerrier with a distrust of the whites.[27]

Guerrier's sympathy toward the Indians was never suspected, for he carried out his duties efficiently. He was present when Hancock interviewed several of the chiefs, among them White Horse, Tall Bear, Bull Bear, and the notorious Roman Nose, who

was married to Guerrier's cousin. Roman Nose had let it be known that he intended to kill Hancock, whom he regarded as his worst enemy, but he never attempted to carry out his threat. Guerrier once remarked that he was unsure if Hancock had "suspicioned trouble" or not. George Bent later claimed that Guerrier told him that he had connived in the Indians' decision to flee. He deliberately led Custer astray when ordered to find Indian villages, rather than endanger his kinsmen among the Sioux. These close family ties led him to serve two masters.[28]

When William A. Comstock (known as "Medicine Bill") was detached from Fort Wallace to accompany Custer's command, Guerrier realized that he could no longer sabotage the campaign, for Comstock would have soon discovered what he was up to. Comstock, believed by many to be part Indian, was in fact a white man and was related to James Fenimore Cooper, the novelist. Born on January 17, 1842, at Comstock Township, Michigan, he was orphaned as a child, spent periods of his youth with various relatives, and then fled west. In 1860 he was earning a living as an Indian trader at Cottonwood Springs, Nebraska Territory, and by 1867, he was considered one of the best scouts on the plains. Custer claimed that no "Indian knew the country more thoroughly than did Comstock. He was perfectly familiar with every divide, water-course, and strip of timber for hundreds of miles in either direction. He knew the dress and peculiarities of every Indian tribe, and spoke the language of many of them."[29]

Theodore Davis, a *Harper's Weekly* correspondent and artist, noted that his "qualifications as an interpreter and scout are said, by those best qualified to judge, to be unsurpassed by any white man on the plains." But Hickok, recalled Davis, writing from memory some thirty years later, was his "special aversion," an overdressed dandy with perfumed hair, "faultlessly clad under surprising circumstances." Davis also doubted Hickok's ability until he proved himself by venturing alone into a dugout occupied by deserters and convincing them that it was better for their health if they surrendered.[30]

Therefore, while Hickok, for whatever reason, may have been the "most prominent" of the white scouts on the Plains, there is no doubt that Comstock was, according to Custer, "the favorite scout, a host in himself." Indeed, the general felt the loss person-

William ("Medicine Bill") Comstock, possibly the greatest of all the plains scouts. (Courtesy Kansas State Historical Society)

ally when Comstock was murdered in August 1868. Comstock was leaving Chief Turkey Leg's Cheyenne encampment, where he and Sharp Grover had been sent to persuade the chief to bring his young men under control. As the scouts left the camp they were attacked, some believe because of the ivory-handled, silver-mounted Colt's revolver Comstock carried on his belt. Comstock was killed. Grover, badly wounded, feigned death until he was able to escape under darkness and reach the railroad twenty-five miles away. There he was picked up by a train and taken to Hays City.[31]

Today, Comstock is almost unknown to the public. He is remembered by some for his alleged 1868 buffalo hunting contest with Buffalo Bill for the title "Champion Buffalo Killer of the Plains." Cody claimed that the contest had been set up by officers at Fort Wallace who backed Comstock. According to Cody, the contest took place twenty miles east of Sheridan and was well advertised. Cody won the contest by killing sixty-nine buffalo to Comstock's forty-six. However, there is no evidence to support this story. Another reason to doubt it is the fact that Comstock was wanted for murder at the time. He had shot down one H. P. Wyatt at Fort Wallace, who reportedly owed him money and had also provoked him by claiming to have been a member of Quantrill's guerrillas. Therefore, it is highly unlikely that Comstock would wish to attract too much attention.[32]

Buffalo Bill Cody earned a tremendous reputation as a scout for the Fifth Cavalry and later earned worldwide acclaim for his Wild West Exhibition. But he often displayed surprising insecurity over his reputation, as in the case of John Crawford. John Wallace Crawford was an Irish immigrant, ex-coalminer, and would-be poet and actor. Without the benefit of being "born" either to the profession or in the West itself, he achieved a reputation as a scout and guide (he even succeeded Cody as chief of scouts to the Fifth Cavalry in 1876 when Cody returned East). When the press began eulogizing Jack as a scout, Buffalo Bill took exception to some of the comments. On August 23, 1885, he wrote Crawford to remind him that he had earned more money than any other scout he could name: "I have scouted for the Army more days than all of them put together. These are facts and can be proven in the Quarter Master department but mind you I don't say that they are not good men or frontiersmen [but] *I have done more scouting than all of them put together.*" Mr. Cody neglected to mention that a number of his rivals had either died in action or resigned. Curiously, he did not mention Wild Bill.[33]

To put Hickok into perspective with Comstock and Guerrier, the facts and not hearsay must be examined. As a scout and courier, he proved himself equal to the task. Despite Carr's allegations, his courage is not in doubt. When ordered by Custer to ride sixty miles through country known to be occupied by hostile Indians he did not hesitate, yet Carr implied that he hesitated at the very suggestion of Indians. The conclusion must be that

Carr, understandably angered by the loss of official documents, allowed his personal prejudice to color his later recollections.

General Custer's extraordinary, pointed reference to Hickok's presence during the Hancock Expedition played a major part in furthering Wild Bill's reputation as a plainsman and scout. Custer, however, was by no means the first or the last of Hickok's contemporaries to praise his abilities. Nichols referred to him as "the famous Scout of the Plains" at a time when he had no such reputation—unless Nichols was referring to Hickok's Civil War reputation as a scout and spy. And during the brief period that Hickok appeared on stage as a member of Buffalo Bill's Combination, he was described either as "Wild Bill, one of the greatest scouts of modern times" or as "the only member of the combination who is a real Indian-fighter." This latter comment seems ironic when one remembers that in 1872 Cody won the Medal of Honor for his actions against hostile Indians in Nebraska. Still, accolades of that nature went far toward establishing yet another facet of Hickok's legend—a point not lost on the more romantic of Hickok's biographers. Wilbert Eisele even made it a declaration:

> No man, probably, was better fitted for scouting than Wild Bill. Joined to his tremendous strength he was an unequaled horseman; he was a perfect marksman, he had a keen sight and a constitution which had no limit of endurance. . . . He was of a race of dare-devil fighting plainsmen, reared amid the hard conditions of western border life, a class of men who became mankillers from stern necessity.[34]

Again, it was thought necessary to bolster an already established reputation as a scout with that of mankiller—almost as if one could not exist without the other. But as one pioneer newspaper man recorded in 1879, Wild Bill was ideally suited for the role:

> He belonged to that class of men, justly termed "the link between civilization and savagery:" men who held their lives "but as a pin's fee," endured hardships and danger to protect the border from renegades and savages, and now travel to contrast city life with prairie existence, serving a purpose fitly illustrating to the uninitiated, who, like the youths at school, read histories of battles past to form a theory, without stopping to think that the Indian of

to-day is a more formidable foe to face than twenty times his number in the days of our forefathers.

It is rarely that one meets the frontiersman who does not prefer peace with the Indians. Even "Wild Bill," daring as he was, and as great a dread as it was his power to create in the camp of the savage, could not in all probability, have any especial love for these spasmodic outbreaks of uncivilized warfare; and it is due these hardy men to say that few can realize the outrages that they suffer at the hands of the redskins, before they reach for the trusty rifle which hangs in the antlers over the rude fire-place of the ranche, which is their home only so long as they are suffered by the Indians to occupy it.[35]

That description portrays both the real Hickok and the mythical character that was even then beginning to assume an identity of its own. But legend aside, and disregarding the powerful image created by Hickok's presence, looks, and bearing, the facts indicate that he may well have been the most prominent of the white scouts during the Indian wars of the late 1860s. Yet even he would admit that he was by no means the greatest. Legend has for so long obscured Hickok's real capability as a scout and guide that skeptics may be forgiven for doubting his genuine role as a Plainsman.

Five

"A Bad Man to Fool With"

I n an interview at Fort Zarah, Kansas, early in April 1867, Henry M. Stanley asked, "I say, Bill, or Mr. Hickok, how many white men have you killed to your certain knowledge?" After some deliberation but without batting an eyelid, Hickok replied, "I would be willing to take my oath on the Bible tomorrow that I have killed over a hundred, a long ways off." "What made you kill all those men; did you kill them without cause or provocation?" Stanley persisted. "No, by heaven!" said Hickok, "I never killed one man without good cause."[1]

That exchange was published less than two months after Col. Nichols wrote in his *Harper's* story that he believed "Wild Bill with his own hands has killed hundreds of men. Of that I have not a doubt. 'He shoots to kill,' as they say on the border." Nichols then asked Hickok how he felt about killing and Hickok replied: "As ter killing men, I never thought much about it. The most of the men I have killed it was one or t'other of us, and at sich times you don't stop to think, and what's the use after it's all over?" Later, when Stanley asked him how old he was when he killed his first man, Hickok replied that he was aged "twenty eight" (he was almost thirty at the time of the interview), and the victim was the "first white man" he had killed, a gambler who had tried to ambush him in his hotel room. "If ever a man deserved killing he did."[2]

Today, such colorful statements would be easily discounted, but at that time their impact was both dramatic and far-reaching. With the publication of the two interviews, Wild Bill became one of the foremost "mankillers" on the plains overnight. And Hickok's alleged reliance on the pistol to settle all his disputes became the mainstay of his legendary reputation. Therefore, to suggest that Hickok settled some of his differences in other ways may come as a surprise. It would have come as a surprise to Theodore Henry, a man who had known Wild Bill in Abilene. He declared in 1904 that Wild Bill without his guns would have been tame.

There is plenty of evidence to the contrary. In 1867, according to Francis Cragin, he thrashed a man at Monument Station for insulting the wife of Oliver Wiggins (who was absent at the time). Luther North in later years recalled that Hickok fought and thrashed a tough muleskinner. And in 1869, Wild Bill and the Mexican scout Mariano Autobees had reportedly fallen out, and in the subsequent brawl, Wild Bill severely "chastised" the Mexican. John Malone, who had known Wild Bill on the plains, even went so far as to suggest that Hickok was "the only frontiersman who would take his pistols off and fight a square fight with anyone who wanted to settle a dispute in that way." When the occasion demanded, Hickok was clearly capable of fighting without weapons. But this sort of fighting detracts from his reputation as a mankiller, which probably explains why his pugilistic exploits rarely get mentioned by those anxious to perpetuate his lethal reputation.[3]

However, the earliest newspaper references to Hickok were not devoted to his reputation as a mankiller, but to his prowess as a Union Army scout, and later articles also focused on his employment as a scout during the Indian wars of 1867 and 1868–1869. Indeed, one editor who met Hickok and other scouts on a train in October 1867 observed that it was a "pity that young men so brave and daring should lack the discretion to sheath their daggers forever when the war terminated! But such is the demoralizing effect of war upon those who engage in it and certainly upon all who love the vocation."[4]

The "killer instinct" more than anything else set the gunfighting fraternity apart from their fellow human beings. Some men looked upon the revolver as a crutch or an equalizer that gave them the courage they lacked without it. Once they got their hands on a pistol, all manner of characters were capable of murder. But the men who achieved or earned reputations as mankillers walked a mental tightrope and were constantly on guard, for death was only a trigger-pull away. A few, a very few, gloried in their reputation. Others tried to live it down. John Wesley Hardin, Texas's most famous gunfighter, in letters written while he was in prison and in his autobiography, boasted of the number of men he had killed in combat or from ambush. He showed no remorse for what he had done; rather, he attempted to justify the killings. And he was not alone. Ex-guerrillas were proud of the havoc they had wrought before and during the Civil War as their contribution toward the cause. Their deeds set them apart and made them men of reputation among those who had not fought. Only much later, when the smokescreen of romanticism had drifted and accountability was called for, did others question the guerrillas' motives. By then, of course, the men and their deeds were legendary.

It is apparent that Wild Bill's growing reputation as a mankiller was inspired by colorful and frequently inaccurate press reports. So it is understandable that his real and imaginary killings aroused controversy that continued long after his death. But historians who have branded Hickok a murderer on hearsay evidence seem to have overlooked the effect publicity had, and continues to have, upon his reputation. Some of Hickok's contemporaries intensified the effect. Through ignorance, admiration, or spite, they delighted in extolling his killer status. William Francis Hooker, who met Hickok in Cheyenne, had no doubts. In his opinion, "Hickok took advantage of his job as city marshal to kill a number of men; perhaps most of the men he killed deserved killing. I am sure he murdered some of the men he killed, marshal or no marshal."[5]

Few of Hickok's critics or eulogizers have considered that Wild Bill and his contemporaries might never have achieved either fame or infamy but for the appearance in the 1830s of the revolver. The significance of the revolver was soon appreciated by both law-abiding and lawless individuals—especially the latter. In California, by 1854 the "universal and cowardly practice of carrying revolvers" was blamed for more deaths than any other cause. Criminals anxious for gain used it freely, and during the Civil War it became the favored weapon of the guerrilla, scout, and spy. Some men carried as many as eight revolvers or extra loaded cylinders on their belts or in saddle bags or holsters. Its effectiveness as a weapon of both defense and offense encouraged its use in the settlement of personal disputes.

The character depicted today as the gunfighter (as opposed to the outlaw or gunman), really evolved during that turbulent period of frontier history when, in the absence of law and order, the six-shooter prevailed, a time when many relied on the pistol as a way of life and some perished by it. The man with a reputation for being a good shot or quick on the draw became the target for others who tried to "get the drop" on him in order to add yet another "notch" to their own reputations as fighting men.

Dueling, as practiced in Europe, followed a long tradition with its own etiquette or code. Young men of rank were expected to become expert with sword or pistol and to protect their own or another's honor, if necessary, in a fight to the death. On the Continent the sword was the principal weapon, but in England duelists favored the pistol. By the mid-nineteenth century, dueling was actively discouraged in England but not in Ireland, where it was almost a way of life. Well-bred young men were reared in the belief that training in their chosen profession should also include developing skill with a brace of dueling pistols. In 1777 the Irish Code Duello was adopted and with it strict rules governing the conduct of duelists and their seconds. The tradition was carried across the Atlantic and continued, particularly in the South. But when the sword gave way to the pistol and that in turn to the revolver, the Code Duello itself was largely ignored by the sinister "pistoleer," whose sole object was to "get the drop" on an opponent at a time when reputations were made or lost with the squeeze of a trigger.[6]

The men who inspired the gunfighter of fact and fiction came from a variety of places and professions. But they had one thing in common: they shot to kill. In the Southern states, where a man's honor took precedence over responsibility, men would fight over trivial matters—simply because someone "refused to drink with a gentleman" who, it transpired, was drunk and belligerent. Racial disputes were also common in a society that thrived on cheap labor, and some were only too anxious to squeeze the trigger and elevate some "heathen Chinee" or Mexican "Greaser" heavenwards. Efforts to restrict the carrying of revolvers, especially in the Southern states, proved fruitless. Louisiana, for instance, made it unlawful for people to carry weapons "concealed in the bosom, coat or other place," and permitted officers of the law to stop and search suspicious individuals. Freed blacks could carry arms if provided with a permit issued by a justice of the peace, but no slave was allowed near any kind of weapon.[7]

Out West, particularly in the more inaccessible regions where the law was, for all practical purposes, unenforceable, lawlessness was rife. Every man was expected to defend himself, his family, and his home. Few cared to be without some kind of weapon. By the time Hickok and Dave Tutt exchanged shots in 1865, a tradition of violence and a reliance upon weapons—particularly pistols—was well established. Newspapers and periodicals delighted in regaling their readership with gory tales of pistoliferous encounters out West.

The mankiller or gunfighter (the latter term was in use as early as 1874 but did not become common until the turn of the century) was no single type of man. In 1910, Edgar Beecher Bronson declared that "there were two types of man-killers" and proceeded to subdivide them into classes: outlaws whose bloodletting became a mania; those who killed in defense of spoils or their liberty or otherwise good men who had slain in the heat of a quarrel and fled rather than face the consequences. The second class included the peace officer who killed in the execution of his duty.

Allied to the second class of mankiller was an individual who had killed a man but was by no means a bad man or outlaw. Rather, his contemporaries would define him as a "bad man to fool with."[8] And here is where the definition of the "good bad man" becomes blurred. According to the editor of the Kansas City, Missouri, *Journal,* the "gentleman who has 'killed his man' is by no means a rara avis and could be found in church, on the street, driving a cab or indeed in almost any occupation and, if his homicidal talents had been employed in the enforcement of law and order, he would be ranked as a 'great Western civilizer.' "[9]

The hint of humor in the foregoing assessment of the mankillers was not lost upon contemporary readers. The vicious killer and incorrigible thief infuriated the masses, so the actions of those who curtailed or eradicated them met with popular approval. Public sentiment did not, of course, exempt lawmen from a coroner's court or other legal scrutiny, for then, as now, their actions were often highly controversial.

The public's infatuation with mankillers and their exploits prompted numerous journalists to expound on the subject. But probably the man best qualified to do so was himself the victim of fictioneers who credited him with "twenty-seven notches" by his early twenties. History records that he may have killed only one man, but William Bartholomew Masterson, alias Bat (he later changed his second Christian name to Barclay), had an impressive record as a peace officer and sheriff in Kansas long before he gave up the pistol and took up a pen. In 1907 he wrote a number of articles for *Human Life* in which he defined the mankillers of the Old West: "I have known so many courageous men in that vast territory lying west and south-west of the Missouri River— men who would when called upon face death with utter indifference as to consequences, that it would be manifestly unjust for me even to attempt to draw a comparison."[10]

Masterson claimed that courage "to step out and fight to the death with a pistol" was only one of the three qualities any man should possess who contemplated such an act. The other two were skill with weapons and deliberation. Hickok echoed the latter quality in 1865 when he remarked that he had seen "many a feller slip up for shootin' in a hurry."[11]

In essence, killing in self-defense or in the execution of one's duty had to be justified both in the eyes of the law and of the community. The so-called Code of the West never existed, but among men of reputation, both antagonists were expected to be armed and facing each other when they were provoked into an exchange of shots. In reality, few men with reputations as mankillers or gunfighters got into gunfights with each other. Instead they usually fought the tyro or reputation seekers. Since fist fights were uncommon in the West, "getting the drop" on an antagonist was essential. To some this suggested that the code of chivalry had degenerated to the point that gunfighters only fought smaller, unarmed men or shot them in the back. If the one who beat the other then "bit his ear or nose off as a memento," his "reputation as a fighting man is made." This eyewitness to the antics of "so-called dangerous characters" concluded that "such men as Wild Bill who fight with the weapons best adapted to the circumstances almost invariably carry the day, even in the face of immense odds."[12]

The importance of "getting the drop" was common knowledge. In 1873, a Leavenworth editor remarked that Wild Bill was "known as a good fellow, and one who will fight on the shortest provocation, provided he is on the right side and has the 'drop' on his opponent." He added, "That Bill fights discreetly, as well as effectively, is attested by the success he has achieved in various encounters."[13]

The noted mankillers were constantly vigilant and aware of the risks of their reputation. They had no doubt of their fate should they grow careless and expose themselves to attack from ambush or from behind by lesser individuals anxious for a reputation. And thanks to Colonel Nichols's article, Hickok's reputation as a pistol shot preceded him wherever he went. In his review of the *Harper's* story, the editor of the Springfield *Patriot* acknowledges Hickok's "superior skill with the pistol," but thought Nichols "cuts it very fat" when he describes his feats in arms. In Kansas, the editor of the *Atchison Daily Champion* agreed that Hickok was "a dead shot" with a pistol but placed more emphasis on Hickok's quiet manner and lack of a quarrelsome disposition. To their credit both editors sought to modify Hickok's mankiller image.[14]

Despite such denials and Hickok's established reputation as a scout and a guide, it was his growing mankiller status that attracted most attention. Even Custer, who employed him as a scout and courier in 1867, devoted some space to the subject:

> "His skill in the use of the rifle and pistol was unerring. . . . Wild Bill is anything but a quarrelsome man; yet no one but himself can enumerate the many conflicts in which he has been engaged, and which have almost invariably resulted in the death of his adversary. I have personal knowledge of at least half-a-dozen men whom he has at various times killed, one of these being at the time a member of my command."

Custer, although describing events that took place in 1867, did not write about them until 1872, which enabled him to include several individuals killed in the late 1860s and early 1870s. He also noted that on one occasion, Hickok paid for the funeral of one of his victims (Mike Williams), describing it as a "thoughtful" act.[15]

Contemporary and later recollections of the number of men Hickok killed in gunfights has increased with the telling. It was claimed that up to "the spring of '68, according to his own statement, Bill had slain twenty-six men."[16] By 1871, Coe and Williams, at Abilene, were added to the "long catalogue of those who have perished at his deadly hand."[17] This double killing prompted one Texas newspaper to dub him "Wild Bill, the terror of the West," and declare that the "gallows and penitentiary are the places to tame such blood thirsty wretches as 'Wild Bill.'"[18] Curiously, few contemporary accounts dwelt upon the necessity for Hickok to draw his pistols on another man. Instead, the emphasis was upon yet another "victim," thereby suggesting that Hickok was always the aggressor rather than exploring the reason for such drastic action. Adding to the confusion were comments by individuals who later sought to amend their original conclusions. Joseph G. McCoy, as Abilene's first elected mayor, hired Wild Bill as city marshal in 1871. During Hickok's lifetime, the closest McCoy got to any mention of him was an oblique reference to him in his book on the cattle trade published in 1872: "No quiet-turned man could or would care to take the office of marshal, which jeopardized his life; hence the necessity of employing a desperado—one who feared nothing and would as soon shoot an offending subject as to look at him." Forty years later, however, he was quoted as stating that Hickok had killed forty-three men prior to his appointment as town marshal, where he ruled "with a rod of iron."[19]

Hickok's actions when faced with a life or death situation have inspired some colorful reports, especially concerning the speed with which he got his pistol into action. Today's expression "fast draw" evokes an image of tied-down holsters and individuals crouched forward and facing each other about eight feet apart. On a given signal both men draw and fire and the fastest man is the winner. In Hickok's time, the scene was very different. The term "fast draw" was never used. But a man could be "quick as thought" in his reaction to danger, which caused many to confuse reaction time with speed. Hickok's reaction in a shoot-out inspired this contemporay comment:

> His arms were Colt's "Navies," and in the rapid and wonderfully accurate use of them it is admitted he had no equal in the West. They were handsome ivory-handled articles, and were always at that time swinging to his belt.
>
> The secret of Bill's success was his ability to draw and discharge his pistols, with a rapidity that was truly wonderful, and a peculiarity of his was that the two were presented and discharged simultaneously, being "out and off" before the average man had time to think about it. He never seemed to take any aim, yet he never missed.
>
> Bill never did things by halves. When he drew his pistols it was always to shoot, and it was a theory of his that every man did the same.[20]

Although Wild Bill did not always use guns in a fight, as we have seen, he usually did. However, most people easily understood why: fists cannot stop bullets. Even so, there was a great deal of feeling against violence among the settlers—especially the violence inspired by the free use of firearms. To control it, they needed both laws and a means of implementing them. Ironically, Westerners were prepared to tolerate the use of firearms if it led to control of violence. Therefore, Wild Bill, with his reputation as a pistol shot, a mankiller and an "utterly fearless" man, seemed the ideal choice for the role his contemporaries might have described as "civilizer."

The popular conception of the "two-gun" town marshal, or one man against the mob, is not confined to this century. Contemporary dime novels and newspapers also played their part. In 1874, the Boston press credited Hickok with the comment that there "was no Sunday west of Junction City, no law west of Hays City, and no God west of Carson City," thus suggesting that he was personally familiar with all forms of lawlessness and how to contain it., The press considered his comment accurate: "his remark bids fair to go into history as thoroughly representative of an epoch."[21]

Hickok's real and imaginary reputation as a mankiller was enhanced by oblique references as well as direct ones. In December

1869, it was reported that a Junction City prostitute "a brawny six-foot female American citizen of African descent, hideous to behold, and known as 'Black Sal,'" who between bouts in bed took in washing for a living, was aroused at 2:00 A.M. by about twelve troopers who demanded her services. In their drunken stupor they began throwing her irons about. Sal promptly pulled a pistol and opened fire, killing two men and wounding others. The boys promptly dubbed her "Wild Bill No. 2."[22]

Further speculation on Hickok's alleged killings was fueled when it was intimated in 1873 that between the publication of the original *Harper's* story and his appearance as Abilene's marshal, Hickok had "disappeared from public notice, and how many men he killed during his retirement is as yet unknown."[23] Such unwarranted publicity must have exasperated Hickok, but there was little that he could do. He was painfully aware that on hearsay evidence, he had been branded a "red-handed murderer." He also grew heated when others suggested that he and his kind "should all die with their boots on." In response, he demanded to know who the man was who could prophesy how men should die, or their class, "so the public may know who is right and who is wrong." He had never, he said, "insulted man or woman in my life." Later, he was to declare to a woman in Cheyenne: "That I have killed men I admit, but never unless in absolute self defence or in the performance of an official duty. I never, in all my life, took any mean advantage of an enemy. Yet understand, I never allowed a man to get the drop on me."[24]

Hickok's justification for his actions is important, because his awesome reputation clearly bothered him. Otherwise he would have dismissed such allegations without comment. In fact, the records of Hickok's career are filled with suggestions that violence was a last resort for him. One contemporary described him as a "creature of circumstances, for having acquired a reputation as a 'shot' and as a fearless man in early life, he was time and again called upon to defend himself by killing men against whom he had no ill will whatever," men whose ambition was simply to be "the man that killed 'Wild Bill.'" But "it can never be said of Bill that he was the unprovoked assailant of any man." Another recalled that Hickok "was not a demon who delighted in taking life, and even if in truth he was a desperado, he was so by force of circumstances."[25]

Many of Hickok's contemporaries conceded that provocation played a part in his actions. Some historians, however, made the mistake of judging his and others' actions in a modern context. One of them, Joe B. Frantz, with no attempt at explanation, stated that Wild Bill "shared a good many of the qualities of a mad dog." Such an unsupported conclusion is inexcusable. He later described John Wesley Hardin (whom some believe to have been a homicidal maniac, and others the victim of circumstance) as "the most prolific killer of them all," which implies that he found reason to excuse Hardin's homicidal tendencies but not Hickok's—perhaps because he felt Hardin had achieved folklore status.[26]

Unlike Hickok, Hardin's career is peppered with homicides, eight of them in 1871 when he came up the Chisholm Trail to Kansas and appeared at Abilene during the summer. And if accounts of his behavior in adolescence (when he killed his first man at the age of fifteen) and later during his involvement in the Sutton-Taylor feud are to be believed, his alleged "forty notches" may be true. However, it is his relationship with Hickok that is our concern. In his autobiography published after his death in 1895, Hardin claimed to have pulled the "road agent's spin" or "border roll" on Wild Bill when he tried to disarm him. Hardin claimed that at the time Hickok had two cocked pistols lined up on him, which suggests remarkable self-control on Hickok's part, or a tall tale on Hardin's. Yet, in a letter written from Huntsville prison to his wife dated June 24, 1888, Hardin made no mention of this exploit. Instead, he wrote that "no braver man [than Wild Bill] ever drew breath." In analyzing Hardin's behavior patterns, a psychiatrist, who has devoted some years to the subject, concluded that Hardin in fact idolized Wild Bill, whom he saw as a "selfobject." More recently, however, the same writer has indicated that Hardin was a very disturbed character, and one who shed tears and expressed a terror of the mob and of being lynched.[27]

Despite his belligerent reaction when threatened with extinction, Hickok seems to have regarded violence as a last resort. Charles Gross, Joe McCoy's bookkeeper, who knew Hickok well in Abilene, recalled that Wild Bill himself never used the word "killed" when referring to his gunfights. Instead, he spoke of having "shot" various individuals, adding, "Charlie, I hope you never have to shoot any man, but if you do[,] shoot him in the Guts near the Navel, you may not make a fatal shot, but he will get a shock that will paralize his brain and arm so much that the fight is all over."[28]

In assessing Hickok's real and imaginary reputation as a mankiller, we must remember that when he was provoked into action he did not hesitate to shoot to kill. And anyone who made it known that he was after Hickok, ran the risk of being hunted up. Consequently, the public's conception of a "two-gun Galahad" was not only erroneous but historically inaccurate. That Hickok was a killer is undeniable. But it is important to understand the circumstances that led him to kill other men. Wild Bill's involvement in the incident at Rock Creek, Nebraska Territory, when David C. McCanles and two others were killed, is still debated. He claimed to be defending company property. His fight with Dave Tutt was to settle a personal quarrel, and for that he was tried and acquitted. Mulvey, Strawhun, Coe, and the unfortunate Mike Williams all died when Hickok fired his pistols in an official capacity. Some may well question his motives and his actions, while others condone them. But in the final analysis we would be wise to remember that while opinions will always differ, only Hickok himself could provide the answers to many questions.

Allied with his mankilling reputation is Hickok's prowess as a gunfighter, which forms a large part of his legend. If even half of the stories concerning his alleged gunfights were true, then every day of Hickok's life would have been spent fighting for survival. Hearsay claims that he killed between thirty-six and over a hundred outlaws and others who dared to face him down. But such claims are soon discounted. The true figure is closer to ten. But people have always preferred their heroes and villains larger than life, and the likes of Wild Bill were tailor-made for such an image. Indeed, the image of the American gunfighter as a righter of wrongs and defender of the poor and helpless is as fictionalized as that of the knights of ancient Europe, except that in place of the battle ax, sword, or lance, the gunfighter wields a pair of

Colt's revolvers, and his dexterity and speed with his pistols are his armor against the forces of evil. But there the similarity ends, for unlike the knights of old, who could plead privilege, wealth, prestige, and religious motivation, the gunfighter had no such claim.

This oversimplification of the gunfighter has been exploited for generations. He has become established in folklore in a role that places him above the law even though his task is to preserve and maintain it. When he confronts his enemy and the inevitable roar of six-shooters announces to his public that yet another "bad man" has been dealt "justice," everyone sighs with relief. But however sympathetic one might feel toward such a character, the idea of an individual setting himself up as a walking "judge, jury and executioner" would not be tolerated in the real world. Yet to those frustrated by civilization's bureaucracy and a legal process that sometimes takes years to resolve problems, or fails on a technicality, the idea of an individual who can, at the squeeze of a trigger, provide instant "justice" arouses strong emotions. The gunfighter then is seen as a kind of superman, a person with no qualms about killing when preserving law and order.

By the mid-1860s, the enforcement of law and order on the frontier by the use of arms had become a way of life. With it came a grudging respect for individuals who could maintain or enforce the law at the point of a pistol. This attitude is apparent in the years following the Civil War, particularly in the Kansas cowtowns, Colorado and Nevada mining camps, and other places where large numbers of men congregated. But the anarchy of earlier times finally gave way to the establishment of civil and territorial law and local legislation against the carrying and use of firearms. But even when a lawman used his pistol in defense of himself or society, he still had to justify his actions. In the same manner, individuals who "shot it out" in a saloon, on the street or in a corral, were still subject to the law.

Hickok's status as a gunfighter has been magnified both by his contemporaries and by later generations. Of his seven authenticated shoot-outs, only one of them conforms to the accepted "duel" status beloved by Hollywood and novelists. The remainder were the result of provocation that led to a swift and lethal reaction. Yet the belief persisted that Hickok regularly engaged in pistol fights, and with each telling his tally of victims increased alarmingly.

One incident more than any other established Wild Bill's fame. This was the so-called McCanles Massacre, when he is reported to have single-handedly killed ten men in an encounter that must be one of the goriest fights of Western legend. Stories of individuals fighting against impossible odds are by no means uncommon, but in this instance the story was given credence in a highly respected magazine. According to Col. George Ward Nichols, Hickok said he had been visiting a friend, a Mrs. Waltman, when the cabin was attacked by McCanles and ten men. Noting that he was well aware of the story's "extreme improbability," Nichols related (in Hickok's words) how the scout was armed with only one pistol, with one chamber empty, when attacked. But he also had a rifle that belonged to Mrs. Waltman. He reloaded his empty chamber and prepared to fight to the death. Four men were shot with his pistol, and in the hand-to-hand skirmish that followed, others (including Hickok) were stabbed and battered with rifle butts. McCanles was shot through the heart. Hickok, badly wounded and carrying buckshot, was cut in thirteen places. He collapsed. All he could remember afterwards was that during the fight he had "got ugly" and "was wild."[29]

Although it was 1867 before this remarkable story received its nationwide publicity in *Harper's,* it had been well known locally for some time. Even then the number of men involved was disputed. The "McCanles gang" noted one paper, "consisted of only the leader and three others, and not of fourteen as stated in the magazine." According to this account, Wild Bill shot the leader with his rifle and two others with his revolver while the fourth man, only slightly wounded, fled and "was not heard of afterwards."[30]

The truth behind the fight at Rock Creek is as controversial as the *Harper's* version. David C. McCanles, a native of Watauga County, North Carolina, where he had served as county sheriff, had a local reputation as a hard man. He was married with children but had a mistress, Sarah Shull, daughter of a local mill owner. She bore him a child that died in infancy. In 1859, he fled west to escape disgrace, accompanied by Sarah and funds owed to the county. At Rock Creek, Nebraska Territory, he learned that the owner wished to sell a small overland station and corral. Discouraged by returning disillusioned goldseekers from proceeding west to seek gold, McCanles decided to settle at Rock Creek. He purchased the station, improved it, and later built a ranch close by. He then sent for his family. His wife was angered to find Sarah in residence but resigned herself to the fact.

Nichols and others have portrayed McCanles as the leader of a band of cutthroats and a Confederate sympathizer. He was neither, but some considered him a typical Border Ruffian. In April 1860, when Russell, Majors & Waddell organized their Pony Express, they also set up a series of relay stations along the route. One of these was at Rock Creek, in what later became known as the East-side ranch. The original intention of the firm was to rent the property, but later they negotiated a sale—one third down, the remainder in monthly installments spread over three months. A man named Horace Wellman was appointed stationkeeper, assisted by his common-law wife, Jane Holmes. Wellman assumed his duties early in May.

We have already noted that James Hickok probably arrived at Rock Creek at about the same time as the Wellmans. But we do not know for sure if he was employed by Russell, Majors & Waddell or was hired by Wellman. His duties at the station consisted of stock-tending and other tasks, and he was on hand late in June when Russell, Majors & Waddell was in serious financial trouble. Worried about the firm's delinquent payments, McCanles persuaded Wellman to go to Brownville to ask the company's line superintendent, Benjamin Ficklin, to explain the delay. Accompanying Wellman was McCanles' twelve-year-old son, William Monroe, who also had the task of obtaining supplies and identifying some of his father's stock and harness in possession of the Rocky Mountain Dispatch Company, which had left the station owing him money.

Wellman returned on the afternoon of July 11 to report that the company was bankrupt and that William H. Russell was in Washington for discussions with the government. Meantime, McCanles had been trying to persuade the people at the station to move out so that he could regain his property. They refused. McCanles had also accused Jane Wellman's father, who lived nearby, of theft and had given him a thrashing. Not surprisingly, Jane hated him for it.

On the afternoon of July 12, McCanles, his son William Monroe, and two employees, James Woods and James Gordon, arrived at the station and demanded its return. Wellman, who allegedly feared McCanles, told him that he had no such authority. He then retreated into the house while his wife continued to berate McCanles over his treatment of her father. Hickok then appeared on the scene and was advised to keep out of the way. Claims that McCanles was unarmed have been refuted. Some believe that he carried a shotgun and was usually armed with a pistol. During the heated discussion at the door of the house, McCanles suddenly asked for a drink of water. Hickok stepped inside to get it and moments later a shot was fired and McCanles fell dying. Other shots were fired at Woods and Gordon. Woods was killed just outside the house when a hoe smashed his skull (some claim the killer was Jane, and others blame her husband). Gordon fled into the brush, but his escape was thwarted by his own bloodhound, who ran after his master and thus led his killers to him. Gordon was killed with a blast from a shotgun. William Monroe, meanwhile, rushed to his father's side but was driven away by Jane Wellman. He escaped into the brush and ran home to report what had happened.

On July 15, Hickok, Wellman, and a Pony Express rider named James W. ("Doc") Brink were arrested on warrants sworn out by the McCanles family. Taken to Beatrice, Nebraska Territory, the trio had a preliminary hearing before T. M. Coulter, justice of the peace. Brink's role in the affair has never been defined. Jane Wellman was permitted to testify on behalf of the territory, while the defendants pleaded that they had been defending company property. William Monroe McCanles was not allowed to testify. Coulter, after listening to the evidence, decided that the charge of murder could not be sustained, and the defendants were discharged.

Some regarded the hearing as a sham, and Coulter's later exposure as an embezzler (he escaped before trial) did little to change local opinion. Sarah Shull claimed originally that she was some miles away when the shooting took place. Shortly before her death, however, she did admit that she was in the house. But she did not know who fired the fatal shot that killed McCanles, because she and another woman (Sarah Kelsey) were both bundled into the root cellar when it looked as if there might be trouble. Claims that Hickok and McCanles clashed over Sarah's charms were refuted by Sarah herself, though she admitted she was attracted to Hickok. Wild Bill, she recalled, was not a man to run from a fight, and "I came close to having an affair with Hickok."[31]

Did Hickok shoot McCanles, or was it Wellman? Opinion remains sharply divided. Both men were inside the house when the shot was fired. Wellman certainly had more reason than Hickok to kill McCanles. But without proof the question must remain unanswered. One thing is certain, however. The so-called McCanles Massacre, a minor event by frontier standards, propelled James Butler Hickok toward a notoriety that he may or may not have sought. Its impact upon his burgeoning legend was paramount.[32]

Hickok's reputation as a man of action was well established by 1865, but his notoriety as a gunfighter was yet to come. On July 21, on the public square in Springfield, Missouri, he and a fellow gambler named Davis K. Tutt fired one shot each and established a tradition—the walk and draw gunfight. Duels were common in the South, but the rules had changed in the West, and a duel there was very much a personal thing with no seconds or other third parties to consult. This fight would form the basis for the countless novels, articles, and films depicting individuals facing each other down in a shoot-to-kill situation.

Tutt, an Arkansan, was born in 1839. At an early age, he experienced the violence of the Tutt-Everett interfamily feud. He was mustered into the Confederate Army in 1862, but by late 1863 he had disappeared following detachment to the quartermaster's department as a brigade wagonmaster. Did he return to his home? Did he remain with the rebel forces, or did he, perhaps, change sides? This latter possibility must be considered, because at the time of his shoot-out with Wild Bill, Tutt had been in Springfield for a year. He had arrived there in 1864, accompanied by his widowed mother, a sister, a half-brother named Lewis, a former slave, and perhaps other family members. It was generally understood in Springfield that he and Hickok had been "intimate for years." Both had been in the "habit of appearing on the streets with two

revolvers strapped to their belts" and were "noted scouts, desperadoes and gamblers." It was gambling that led to their fatal
shoot-out.

Nichols cited "Captain Honesty" as the source of his background information on the fight. Honesty claimed that on the
evening before the fight, the pair played cards together and fell
out over an alleged debt owed by Hickok to Tutt from a horse
deal. Hickok paid the $40 Tutt asked for, but when Tutt claimed
another $35, Hickok said it was only $25. Tutt then picked up
Hickok's watch and said he would keep it until the debt was paid,
adding that he would pack the watch on the square next day.
Hickok warned him that it was a health hazard, but Tutt ignored
him.

According to contemporary and later versions, Tutt walked
onto the square from in front of the courthouse at 6 P.M. on Fri-
day, July 21, 1865. Hickok appeared from the southern side.
They advanced upon each other and, when about fifty yards
apart, drew their pistols and opened fire. Tutt missed, but Wild
Bill's ball struck him in the heart. Hickok then turned on his heel
and offered to fight Tutt's friends.

Controversy over this incident has raged for years, over both
the distance between the antagonists and the cause of the fight.
Only very recently have statements by eyewitnesses come to
light. The most publicized was that of Albert Barnitz, a colonel in
the Second Ohio Volunteer Cavalry and, at that time, military
commandant of the Post of Springfield. He wrote down his impression within hours of the event, confirming Honesty's version
of the fight and the dispute over the watch. He added that both
men "fired simultaneously, as it appeared to me, at the distance
of about 100 paces. 'Tut' [sic] was shot directly through the
chest."[33]

Barnitz had Hickok arrested and handed over to the civilian
authorities. He was first charged with murder, but the charge was
later reduced to manslaughter. Barnitz wrote that public opinion
was about equally divided between both characters. Hickok was
tried on August 5 and 6, 1865, and was acquitted. However, the
verdict aroused much controversy. It was welcomed by those
who had employed him or served with him during the late war.
Nichols's Captain Honesty, was, as mentioned earlier, actually

Richard Bentley Owen, a much respected quartermaster. Together with several others, he put up Hickok's bail. Two of the
jury members, J. P. Julian and John Foster, were reported to be
former officers who had served with Hickok under Gen. John B.
Sanborn.

As late as 1957 it was reported that the original trial transcript
was on file at the courthouse but that it disappeared when the
place was visited by a group of writers. It is now doubted that a
transcript of the trial ever existed. All the records that remained
were a number of subpoenas for witnesses and a few other trial
documents. However, in 1994–1995, when the records of the
Greene County Archives were recataloged and a number of
boxes that had remained untouched for more than a century
were opened, several important and startling documents relative
to the shoot-out came to light.

Within hours of the shooting, the coroner, J. F. Brown, had
summoned a jury of six to appear before him. After hearing the
evidence, they decided that "Davis K. Tutt came to his death by a
pistol shot and that the jury further find that the said violence
causing said death was committed by a certain James B. Hickock." The witnesses and most of the court documents, however,
referred to Hickok as "Bill Haycock." On the order of the court,
these references were later changed to James B. Hickock. Similarly, David Tutt was changed to Davis K. Tutt. These court records also revealed the information that in Springfield, Dave Tutt
was generally called Little Dave Tutt, presumably in reference to
his size.

Eight men gave evidence before the coroner. When their statements are examined, it becomes clear that much of the aggrava-
tion said to exist between Hickok and Tutt was untrue. Indeed,
the situation seems more tragic than confrontational. In essence,
the story of the card game in Hickok's room at the Lyon House
on the evening of July 20 was true. Hickok lost a game, and in set-
tling up was told by Tutt that he still owed him $35. Hickok dis-
agreed, saying it was only $25, and reminded Dave that he had
previously paid him $10 at "Oak Hall." Tutt insisted on $35.
Hickok removed his watch and laid it on the table. Tutt took it up
and said that once Hickok paid the remainder owing he could
have it back. Wild Bill then suggested that they go downstairs so

he could check his memorandum (or pocketbook). If he owed Tutt that much money, he would pay it. Tutt then demanded $45. J. W. Orr, under oath, declared that when Tutt walked out, Hickok turned to Orr and asked him to tell Tutt to bring his watch back in one hour and he would receive the $25. If he did not, "something else would be done."

Late the next afternoon, Hickok was on the public square where he, Tutt, and Orr sat discussing the difficulty. Wild Bill was obviously upset by Dave's refusal to meet him halfway. Eli J. Armstrong stated that at about 5:00 P.M. on July 21 he came upon "Haycock, Tutt & Orr sitting on the porch of the Lyon House." He realized there was a problem and asked, "Boys, what's up?" Hickok said nothing much, except that there was a little dispute between him and Tutt over some money. Armstrong then recommended that Tutt accept the $35 rather than create a "fuss." Hickok was still adamant that he did not owe Dave that much money. At that moment, Tutt pulled out Hickok's watch and declared that if he paid him $45 he could have it back. According to Armstrong: "Haycock remarked to Tutt that he would rather have a fuss with any man on earth than him for you have accommodated me more than any man in town for I have borrowed money from you time and again, and we have never had any dispute before in our settlement. Tutt said he knew that & did not want any difficulty himself." It was then decided to go for a drink. Tutt, however, soon left Hickok and Orr together and went first to a livery stable and then made his way back to the courthouse. John Tutt, one of Davis's brothers, walked up to Hickok and said that he was sorry that "there was a difficulty" between him and Dave, and if he would "come down" Dave would settle the matter. Hickok then started towards Crenshaw's store.

Tutt was reported to be wearing a "linen duster" when he returned to the courthouse. He was about thirty paces from it when Hickok, estimated to be "one hundred and twenty" paces across the other side of the public square, called out to Tutt warning him against carrying his watch onto the square. Tutt's reaction was to put his hand behind him, grasp his pistol and draw it. Hickok promptly drew his, and both men fired. Many of the witnesses thought only one shot had been fired. Ironically, they all claimed to have taken their eyes off the pair for an instant. One witness heard what he thought was one "report" but saw smoke coming from both pistols. Another saw the flash from Hickok's but was unsure about Tutt. A. L. Budlong, however, did state that he later saw Tutt's pistol at the courthouse with one chamber fired and the "exploded cap on the nipple."

Witnesses were agreed that when he was shot Tutt staggered or "ran" toward the courthouse before collapsing in front of it. F. W. Scholten stated that after the shooting he turned to Hickok and said "that is rather hard & Haycock said it was two [too] late now & he was not sorry."

Mr. Budlong further stated that "Dr James stepped in and opened his (Tutt's) vest and shirt [and] saw a wound in both sides back behind and below the nipple." Later, Dr. Edwin Ebert went before the coroner on July 22 and, after being sworn, stated:

> He made on evening [of] July 21st 1865 an examination of the body of David Tutt and found that a bullet had entered on the right side between the 5th and 7th rib and passed out on the left between the 5th and 7th rib[.] The examination being only super-ficial could not state the precise point from his sudden death[.] I am led to believe that some of the large blood vessels were wounded[.]

This evidence indicates that Tutt faced Hickok almost side on—dueling fashion—when he opened fire, which makes Hickok's shooting even more remarkable. Several of the witnesses reported that Hickok and Tutt made statements to each other that they could not hear or understand. None of them divulged what they had heard, which is unfortunate, since their statements might add credence to the oft-stated suspicion that there was something between the two men besides the dispute over cards.

However, truth was not served by the published report of the trial. Among the documents that came to light after the recent re-cataloging of county records was the original version of the judge's opinion, a list of witnesses for the defense and prosecution, and a case file involving Tutt that had apparently lain undis-turbed for 130 years. Sadly lacking are the statements made by the trial witnesses (there were twenty-two others besides the eight questioned by the coroner). These included R. B. Owen and Hickok's erstwhile scouting "mate" Thomas G. Martin. Curiously, Major Barnitz was not called to give evidence, despite the fact that he had witnessed the fight and ordered Hickok's arrest. After examining the evidence (that available in the press and the newly discovered documents), I find hints of a deeper rift between Hickok and Tutt than is apparent in the available statements.

Included among the documents is the original Indictment for Manslaughter against Hickok written in the old English legal style that reiterates each comment in order to avoid any misunderstanding. Of particular interest is the statement that Hickok with "a certain pistol of the value of five dollars then and there charged with gunpowder and leaden bullets" shot Tutt. The average Colt's Navy pistol (which Hickok is believed to have used on that occasion) sold for $15 to $25, which suggests that the clerk was in error when pricing the weapon.

When the *Weekly Missouri Patriot* reported the outcome of the trial, it included the judge's "instructions to the jury," but the paper neglected to include the most important comment, which was later filed as a separate document and is reproduced here in full:

> The Court instructs the jury
>
> That if they believe from the evidence that Tutt advanced on the Defendant with a pistol drawn & that he had previously made threats of violence to the Deft which had been communicated to the Deft & that Tutt was a fighting character & a dangerous man, there are circumstances from which the Deft may have had cause to believe Tutt intended to do to the Deft some great personal injury.
>
> That if they believe from the evidence that Tutt advanced on the Deft with a drawn pistol & that the conduct of Tutt on this occasion with his general character known to the Deft was such as to reasonably cause the Deft to apprehend a design on the part of Tutt to do the Deft some great personal injury & if they believe from the evidence the Deft had reasonable cause to apprehend immediate danger of such design being accomplished at the time he shot Tutt, they will acquit the Deft.
>
> That when danger is threatened and impending a man is not compelled to stand with his arms folded until it is too late to offer successful resistance & if the jury believe from the evidence that

Tutt was a fighting character & a dangerous man & that Deft was aware such was his character & that Tutt at the time he was shot by the Deft was advancing on him with a drawn pistol & that Tutt had previously made threats of personal injury to Deft & that Deft had been informed of such threats & that Deft shot Tutt to prevent the threatened impending injury & that at the time the Deft shot Tutt the Deft had reasonable cause to apprehend Tutt intended to do Deft great personal injury & that the danger to Deft was imminent & of such design being accomplished the jury will acquit.

That if the jury from the evidence have reasonable doubt of the guilt of the Deft they will acquit.

The remainder of the judge's comments were published in the paper. He made it clear that if Hickok had willingly engaged in a fight with Tutt, he was guilty as charged. But if he had fired in self-defense, then he should be acquitted. The jury obviously accepted the unpublicized version of the fight and regarded Tutt as the aggressor.

The recently discovered court documents that throw new light on the Hickok-Tutt fight also reveal a previously unknown charge against Tutt involving a horse trade and indicate that Hickok, too, was charged with illegal gambling. In July 1864 Dave Tutt was charged with a gambling offense and late in December was charged with resisting arrest. Then, in March 1865, S. M. Crews alleged that Tutt was in possession of an iron gray horse that he claimed was his. Tutt was ordered to appear in court in the July term, but the outcome of that case is unknown. However, on July 20 he appeared in court to answer the charge that in December 1864 he had resisted arrest by a sheriff's deputy. He was fined $100 and costs. Unable to pay, Tutt was jailed, but Thomas G. Martin, Hickok's former scouting "mate," came to his rescue and he was released. Much later, Martin was called to account for money still owed to the court from Tutt's estate, which might explain why Tutt was so anxious to obtain money that he risked his relationship with Wild Bill to get it.

The illicit gambling charges leveled against Hickok cover a similar period to those of Tutt. One charged Hickok with engaging in a game called "Heads and Tails." Some of the documents name him as Wm. Haycock, and others refer to him as J. B. Hickock. Nowhere in the documents so far examined does the name "Wild Bill" appear.

Some of the men who witnessed the Hickok-Tutt fight are among those whose names regularly appeared in court records on gambling and other charges. Levi Armstrong, John Mills, and John Orr were well known to each other. Mills was also charged with selling liquor without a license, and on one occasion he sold a quart of whiskey (for 25 cents) to Hickok.

Wild Bill, so far as available records indicate, did not attend court when charged with illegal gambling. Every time he was ordered to appear, Sheriff Patterson (and his predecessor in 1864) reported back that "the defendant is not to be found in my county." Prior to June 1865, Hickok's excuse would have been that he was scouting for the Union; but how he managed to avoid later appearances is a mystery. However, it says much for the civil authorities that they, despite the exigencies of the Civil War, were able to root out would-be miscreants engaged in such wicked pursuits as gambling.[34]

But possible causes of the fight soon seemed unimportant, since Wild Bill's reputation as a "dead shot" was now firmly established. Soon, thanks to *Harper's,* he would be elevated from regional to nationwide notoriety. The fight was also significant as the prototype of the classic Western gunfight and would inspire more fiction than any other facet of the frontier experience. It was unusual for yet another reason: apart from the McCanles affair and an incident in Hays City when Hickok was attacked by two troopers from the Seventh Cavalry, it was one of the few personal fights Hickok was involved in. Most of his altercations occurred in the line of duty as a peace officer.

Four years passed before Hickok killed another man in a gunfight—four years during which he was employed as an army scout or a deputy U.S. marshal. But thanks to the press, he developed a growing reputation as a mankiller.

Hickok's presence in and around Fort Hays and Hays City between 1867 and 1869 inspired a number of highly colored newspaper reports. Hays City at that time was the headquarters of buffalo hunters, skinners and teamsters, and its small resident population was boosted further by troopers from nearby Fort Hays. Between 1867 and 1868, workers on the Union Pacific

Railway Company's Eastern Division (the U.P.E.D.) also made the place their headquarters until a new railhead was established at Sheridan. Hays City's transient population and the number of men killed in gunfights or lynched by the vigilantes gave the city a bad reputation. On October 28, 1867, State Governor Samuel Crawford organized Ellis County, and Hays City became the temporary county seat. Elections followed, and on December 5, Thomas Gannon was elected the first sheriff of the county. William L. Totten and Peter Carroll were elected constables of Big Creek Township, but as far as the populace was concerned, Gannon was the law in Hays City, where he made his headquarters. But by April 1868, he had disappeared. Following a petition to the probate judge to incorporate Hays City, which was granted on February 6, 1868, a number of additional constables were appointed. J. V. Macintosh, a druggist, was appointed sheriff by the district judge and served until January 1869, when Isaac Thayer assumed the office. He, too, disappeared, to emerge later as a gambler at Wichita. Once again, Hays City was without any law enforcement. A petition to the governor in July to appoint one R. A. Eccles was ignored. So in August the county commissioners held an election, and Hickok was elected acting sheriff pending the November elections. The governor later disputed Hickok's status, but to the residents of the city and surrounding area, Hickok's new role was recognized and welcomed by many.

Wild Bill's growing reputation as a gunfighter and mankiller doubtless puzzled him and his close acquaintances, for it had little basis in fact. Yet mention of his name was sufficient to make rowdies think twice. And it is evident that when it suited him, Hickok himself relied on his reputation to scare the most persistent trouble makers. He was not alone; fact and fiction played a large part in any gunfighter's reputation. For Hickok, it meant that when he pulled a pistol he was expected to use it.

On August 22, soon after his election, Wild Bill was called upon to preserve the peace. Bill Mulvey (or Melvin) and some drunken companions raised a ruckus and "while attempting to preserve peace" among the "party of intoxicated roughs, or 'wolves,'" Hickok shot Mulvey "through the neck and lungs." He died some hours later. Mulvey, it was reported, had attempted to shoot several citizens but without success.[35]

The killing of Mulvey had far-reaching consequences, both for Hickok's legend and for Western legend as a whole. Buel's fictionalized version tells us that when Hickok came upon Mulvey, the trouble maker had two six-shooters pointed at him. Hickok ordered him to put up his pistols as he was under arrest. Mulvey refused. Hickok backed off and called out, "Don't hit him boys, he's only in fun." Mulvey turned. Hickok pulled a pistol and "shot Mulvey in the head, killing him with that rare skill for which he was remarkable."[36]

Buel's fiction merely gilded the lily, but he credits Hickok with a presence of mind that even under stress worked to his advantage. Today's historians may dismiss the story of Hickok's ruse as fiction, for it is a trick long employed in Hollywood Westerns. But it is important to remember that it reportedly occurred years before movies were even thought of. Eulogizers like to cite such ploys to establish Hickok's supremacy over his opponents. Others, however, infer that he used every dirty trick in the book to gain an unfair advantage. This is nonsense. Faced with sudden death, anyone can be excused for seeking a means of survival. A similar situation occurred less than a month later, when Samuel Strawhun and friends set about wrecking a saloon and removing all the glasses outside to prevent anyone purchasing beer. When Hickok was sent for and started to bring some glasses back, he was threatened by Strawhun—some suggest he used a pistol, and others allege that he smashed a glass and threatened Hickok with it. Wild Bill shot him dead. Contemporary accounts favored Hickok, but some recent writers have sought to condemn Hickok on the grounds that Strawhun's action was not life-threatening— ignoring the terrible damage inflicted when a jagged beer glass is thrust into someone's face.[37]

Writing in 1929, A. D. Bellport, who had been working on a government beef contract at Hays City in 1869, claimed that he had witnessed the murders of three men by Hickok: an unnamed youth known only as Tenderfoot who worked in a grocery store was shot by Wild Bill because he would not stop singing; later, Hickok shot a complete stranger in the back as he walked along the street and Hickok gave no reason. Both of these vague accounts reek of hearsay. However, Bellport did name the third man: Samuel Strawhun. According to Bellport, Hickok shot

Samuel O. Strawhun, known as "Stranghan" and other variants, was shot by Hickok during the night of September 27, 1869, when Sam raised a ruckus in John Bitter's Beer Saloon at Hays City. (Courtesy Mrs. Jean Fisherkeller)

Strawhun as "he was drinking a glass of beer at the bar. Sam was shot in the back of the head without having been given a chance for his life." As for the character of Wild Bill, he was "feared and hated but no one interfered with his meting out death instead of justice unless they were personally concerned. He was a coward and always shot from behind. To those who knew him, 'Wild Bill' was in no way the hero for which he is given credit in later writings." This sort of comment serves no useful purpose unless it is backed up by facts, and the suggestion that everyone in Hays City was terrified of Wild Bill is nonsense.[38]

In 1909, Captain John Ryan, a sergeant in the Seventh Cavalry in 1870, published the best account extant of a fight between Hickok and some troopers. He also summed up Hickok as a man and perhaps unwittingly included a hearsay account of an alleged shooting:

> Bill Hickock, better known as Wild Bill, was a noted scout who was connected a good deal with Custer's command, who, according to my estimation, was able to hold his own among the tough element in that city [Hays]. In front of a saloon kept by a German, named John Bitters, was one of those old-fashioned bucket windlasses used for drawing water. Wild Bill would sit on the railroad track, draw his pistol and fire and the bullet would cut the rope and the bucket would drop into the well, then Bill would pay Bitters to get it out. One day a party of men were sitting around the table gambling, others were watching the game, while more were drinking at the bar, when Bill walked in, whipped out a pistol, reached over one man's shoulder and shot another, who fell to the floor dead. Wild Bill whipped out another pistol and asked if anybody wanted satisfaction. Nobody seemed in great haste to answer, and the game went on. There was a vigilance committee in the place and the next morning they got together and pronounced the shooting justifiable. They paid a colored man $1.50 to take the dead man away and bury him. Shortly afterwards a cemetery was laid out about half a mile north of the city. On another occasion Wild Bill had a dispute in the temporary post office with another man named Strawhorn, and when Bill had played his hand there was another murder added to the list. I have often talked with Wild Bill, and always found him to be a sociable kind of man; nevertheless he had a reputation as an all-round bad man, with whom it was best to have nothing to do.[39]

Hickok's critics have also alleged that since his appointment as acting sheriff had been sponsored by the vigilance committee, he was beholden to them. Strawhun and Joseph Weiss, a deputy U.S. marshal and former inmate of the state penitentiary, had been ordered out of town by the vigilance committee in July 1869. Alonzo B. Webster (who later became mayor of Dodge City) was postal clerk at the time, and his was the unenviable task of advising the pair that they should leave. Weiss and Strawhun entered his post office and attacked him. In desperation he pulled a pistol and shot Weiss through the bowels. Weiss died soon afterward. Strawhun fled. A number of Weiss's friends then invaded the building vowing revenge. They were confronted by Wild Bill, seated on the counter, who remarked that he would take over the fight. They all left. Evidently, feelings among Strawhun and his companions against the vigilance committee ran high, and the appointment of a coroner's jury composed of men presumably loyal to the vigilance committee only increased tension. Ignoring any vigilance involvement, the press considered Hickok's actions in enforcing law and order to be justifiable.[40]

In Buel's version of the killing, Strawhun strolls into the saloon hoping to take Hickok unawares. But at the last moment, Hickok turns and places one shot through Strawhun's left eye. Hickok hardly waits until the body hits the floor before inviting everyone for a drink. Later writers placed Wild Bill at a bar facing a large mirror. He watched Strawhun's every movement in the mirror until at the last moment, he drew his pistol and pushed the barrel over his left shoulder and shot Sam dead.[41]

Buel's attempt to create a superhuman reaction on Hickok's part suggests that his hero treated the matter with callous indifference. This suggestion conflicts not only with his image, but suggests Wild Bill was above the law. In fact, the killing of Strawhun, controversial though it was, reemphasizes how anxious some writers were to elevate Hickok's known pistol prowess to the bounds of improbability. They wanted a superman, a deadly pistoleer whose every shot counted and every pull of the trigger meant one less "bad man" to worry about.

On November 2, 1869, the county elections took place, and Hickok, who hid his Republican sympathies in the guise of an "Independent," was defeated by his deputy, Peter Lanahan, a Democrat in a largely democratic locality. Between January and July 1870, Hickok spent much of his time visiting friends in places as far apart as Jefferson City and Warrensburg, Missouri, and serving subpoenas as a deputy U.S. marshal. On July 17 he was back in Hays City, Kansas. Whether he had returned on official business or for personal reasons is unclear. He was attacked in Paddy Welche's saloon by two drunken Seventh Cavalry troopers named Jeremiah Lonergan and John Kile. Kile had won the

Medal of Honor during service with the Fifth Cavalry but had later deserted. A few months prior to the saloon fight he had re-enlisted in the Seventh. He had probably never met Hickok, whereas Lonergan is reported to have had a dispute with him some time before. The pair made their move as Hickok stood talking to the bartender with his back to them. Lonergan rushed up, threw his arms around Hickok and pulled him back to the floor. As Hickok struggled to get at his pistols, Kile pulled his .44 Remington from beneath his shirt, thrust the barrel into Hickok's ear, and pulled the trigger. The pistol misfired. But before he could recock it, Wild Bill managed to get a pistol out, cock it, and thrust the muzzle against Lonergan's knee. The shock of the wound forced Lonergan to let go. Hickok then turned the pistol on Kile and shot him twice, once in the arm and once in the body. The threat of attack by their drunken companions prompted Hickok to leap through the saloon window, taking the sash with him, and head for his hotel room where he grabbed his Winchester and some ammunition. He then hid out on Boot Hill, prepared to sell his life dearly. But the troopers' drunken friends did not find him.

John Kile died in the post hospital next day. Because he received his wound in a "drunken row" and not in the line of duty, no further action was taken. Lonergan recovered some weeks later and was himself killed in a brawl some time afterwards. As for Hickok, his escape was little short of miraculous. Had Kile been armed with a Colt Army pistol instead of the Remington (which was notorious for misfires and, on occasion, blowing up), the outcome might have been different.[42] The citizens of Hays City greeted the fight with mixed reactions. Some wanted to lynch Hickok, while others conceded that alcohol played a large part in the proceedings. But once Wild Bill had left the area, no further action was taken.

The story of that shoot-out was to become the military equivalent of the so-called McCanles Massacre, for within a very short time, the two troopers became as many as fifteen. Buel thoroughly enjoyed himself in retelling that encounter. He even managed to change the date to February 12, 1870. According to his version, the troopers were led by a sergeant with a great reputation for a fight. Buel claimed that Hickok was still the law in Hays

City at the time and had gone to arrest the group for disturbing the peace. The sergeant then offered to fight Hickok man-to-man. The offer was accepted, both men leaving their weapons with Paddy Welche, owner of the saloon. The two launched into a tremendous fight. But when the circle of soldiers saw that the sergeant was not getting things all his own way, they attacked Wild Bill. Welche then rushed in and returned Hickok's pistols. Shooting then commenced. Hickok downed three men and was himself wounded seven times before escaping. General Sheridan ordered him brought in "dead or alive." Other accounts state that it was Custer who gave the order, unaware that Custer's own brother, Tom, had led a revenge-seeking force once he learned about the shoot-out.[43]

Wild Bill's alleged ability to fight anyone at any time despite the odds was a key factor in this fantastic version of the shoot-out. This tale persists, as do many of the fables recounted about Hickok. The suggestion that Hickok might have been the worse for liquor, and perhaps bore some responsibility for the fight with Lonergan and Kile gets little attention. Instead, it is the soldiers who are the aggressors, simply because they were soldiers.

Hickok's final, yet most significant, gunfight took place more than a year later at Abilene. He had been appointed marshal there in April 1871, succeeding the legendary Thomas J. Smith, who had been killed in the line of duty on November 2, 1870. A succession of fill-in appointments had carried the town through the winter of 1870–1871, but with the cattle shipping season due to start in May, the city needed a strong police force. Hickok's appointment was welcomed by those anxious to avoid the confrontations with Texans that had occurred regularly before Smith's appointment. It was hoped that Hickok's reputation as a mankiller would prove a bonus and not a liability. As it turned out, Hickok was able to maintain law and order (aided by a succession of deputies) without bloodshed until the season ended.

The reputation of the Texas cowboy at that time was very low. It would be another twelve years before Buffalo Bill's Wild West Exhibition would see him reborn as a "Knight Chivalric of the Plains." Fear of the Texans was not groundless, for their behavior in most Kansas cowtowns gave cause for concern. And, inevitably, their actions were magnified in myth. One editor, in reviewing the poor reputation of the cowboy and cowboy life in general, claimed that cowboys invaded Abilene and took possession of the place until "Wild Bill, the Indian fighter and scout, became marshal of the town. Wild Bill killed six of the most desperate cowboys of Abilene in a single night. Thereafter he was respected and feared by the cowboy element."[44]

Despite its inaccuracies, that brief comment sums up both the reputation of the cowboy and Hickok's alleged role in taming them. His reputation as both a killer and a civilizer received a boost on October 5, when a number of Texans were celebrating the end of the cattle season and their intended return home. Rain had prevented many of them from visiting the Dickinson County fair, so they wandered from saloon to saloon. Hickok was not popular with the Texans. He represented the Yankees who had fought against them during the war, and (on the orders of the city council) he had curtailed many of their pleasures when he and his police cleared out the brothel district in September. Many of them thought him overbearing, but few were prepared to attack him face-to-face. One who did was Philip Coe, a Texas gambler of some repute who owned the Bull's Head Tavern. Rumor had it that the pair had fallen out over the favors of a prostitute, but that was never proved. The press, however, did note that Coe swore to get Hickok "before the frost."

On October 5, at about 9 P.M., a number of the Texans wandered the streets demanding that citizens buy drinks. Hickok warned them against carrying arms. When he heard a shot fired outside the Alamo Saloon, he hurried over to find out who fired it. He was confronted by Coe, pistol in hand, who said that he had shot at a stray dog. He then pulled another pistol and fired twice at Hickok, one ball going through his coat and the other hitting the floor between his legs. Wild Bill "as quick as thought" then pulled two pistols and shot Coe twice in the stomach. At that moment, Michael Williams, a personal friend of Hickok's and one-time city jailer, appeared brandishing a pistol. Hickok fired instinctively and shot him dead. He carried Williams into the Alamo, laid him down on a billiard table, then swept into the crowd and drove the Texans out of town.

Press reports following the shooting were bizarre. Some claimed that Hickok went berserk and killed two of his police-

*Philip Coe, who shot it out
with Wild Bill at Abilene
on October 5, 1871, and
died three days later.
(Courtesy Chuck Parsons)*

men; others alleged that Williams had fired at him and Hickok was forced to defend himself. V. P. Wilson, editor of the *Abilene Chronicle* and no fan of either the marshal or the mayor, reported that during the shooting "one or two others in the crowd were hit, but none seriously." This is the only report I have found that suggests anyone but Hickok and Coe actually opened fire. Considering that more than fifty armed and drunken Texans were present, the lack of further victims is as "truly marvelous," as was, according to the editor, the marshal's own escape.

Other reports of the affair either corroborated the *Chronicle's* version or suggested that Hickok caught Coe unawares—a view held in Texas. But Coe either lost his nerve or simply was not in the same class as Hickok, for the men were less than eight feet apart when they opened fire. Later claims that Hickok thought he had fired too low do not make sense, for like most men who engaged in gunfights, he aimed for the navel rather than a tricky head or heart shot. As noted earlier, Hickok had once advised Charles Gross that one should aim for the navel: "You may not make a fatal shot, but he will get a shock that will paralize his brain and arm so much that the fight is all over."[45]

The real victim of that encounter was, of course, Michael Williams. Williams, a former Kansas City bartender employed as a bouncer by the Novelty Theater in Abilene, had come to town presumably to make some extra money. He was due to return home that very night. Instead he was shipped home to his wife in a box. Hickok paid for his funeral, and it was later reported that he visited Mrs. Williams and explained to her what had happened.[46]

The Coe fight had a great effect upon Hickok: it proved to be his last gunfight. He declared that he regretted Coe's death, but one suspects that it was the death of Williams that really disturbed him—there are stories of him weeping as he laid his friend on the billiard table. The next day he procured a sawed-off shotgun, which he carried under his coat. A month later Hickok personally "circumvented" an attempt upon his life by five Texans on a train en route from Abilene to Topeka. When the train reached Topeka he faced them with drawn pistols and forced them to remain on board when it left. The local press commended his actions and then praised his peace-keeping role in Abilene. On December 13, however, the council dismissed Wild Bill and his deputies. The cattle season was over, and plans were already afoot to ban cattle trade altogether, which meant that there was no further need of his expensive services.[47]

There were many gunfighters or mankillers whose personal tally far exceeded Wild Bill's. But for whatever reason—lack of publicity, personality, presence, or public appeal—they failed to generate the interest, adulation or hatred that dogged Hickok during his lifetime and even after his death. Though his reputation as a mankiller and gunfighter has fascinated generations, Hickok himself found it abhorrent. Perhaps it is best left to Hickok to sum up his real and imaginary gunfighting reputation: "If you knew what a wholesome regard I have for damn liars and rascals they would be liable to keep out of my way."[48]

Six

"A Terror to Evil-Doers"

W herever he went, Wild Bill Hickok created a stir, especially when he assumed an official peace-keeping role. For the press, Hickok's presence meant the possibility—or threat—of some future shooting scrape. Others viewed his presence with relief; even though he may have been a "desperado," he was well able to keep the unruly element under control. And the consensus of opinion was that once committed to the task, Hickok was indeed a "terror to evil-doers."

James Butler Hickok's involvement in law enforcement began in 1858 when he was one of four constables elected to serve the magistrates of Johnson County, Kansas. His name appears regularly in the territorial court records, either as J. or William Hickok. On August 16, 1858, he advised his family that he had "been and served three summonses this morning," and then noted that horse thieves were at work in the area and if they were caught they ran the risk of being "run up awfull soon to the top of Some hill." By 1859, however, James had left the area to become a teamster. As late as 1860, a warrant issued on March 4, 1859, for the arrest of one "J. Hickox," who had failed to appear as a juror at the Second Judicial Court at Lecompton in October 1857, had not been served. If this was James Hickok, it seems odd that he was not "apprehended" during routine appearances at the courthouse in 1858.[1]

As noted earlier, Hickok served for a short period in 1864 on the provost marshal's staff at Springfield, Missouri, before being hired as a scout and spy at the request of Gen. John B. Sanborn. Following the war and his much publicized duel with Dave Tutt at Springfield, Missouri, Hickok was a candidate for marshal in the Springfield city elections held in September 1865. But he was beaten into second place by Charles C. Moss. Several months later, in January 1866, Hickok was ordered to Fort Riley, Kansas, where his former quartermaster, R. B. Owen (at that time assistant post quartermaster), appointed him as a "government detective" to "hunt up public property," for which Hickok was paid $125 a month. For several months he was active in the apprehension of mule thieves, and court records disclose that in January 1867, he and his partner, Jack Harvey, arrested two men for possession of stolen mules.[2]

Following service with the Seventh Cavalry from May to August 1867, Hickok was appointed deputy U. S. marshal, a position he held intermittently until 1870. In July Wild Bill reportedly had stood as a candidate for city marshal of the newly founded city of Ellsworth, but he evidently withdrew. In the November election, however, he did stand for county sheriff and received more votes from within city limits (155) than any other candidate. He received little support, however, from the outlying settlements.[3]

In August 1869, the Ellis County commissioners held a special election at Hays City, Kansas, and Hickok was elected acting sheriff, pending the upcoming November elections. When the Ellis County elections did take place, on November 2, Hickok stood as an Independent, and his deputy, Peter Lanahan, as a Democrat. Lanahan won. Hickok perhaps sowed the seeds of his own defeat. In March 1868 the "Republicans of Ellis County" had met at Lawrence, Kansas, "indorsing Congress and ratifying their action in impeaching Andrew Johnson." At the meeting, Hickok was elected one of the vice presidents and was one of those who spoke in support of the motion. It was later reported that "one thousand men" had offered themselves to Congress "if it should be necessary to quell resistance to the measures taken against the President."[4]

Wild Bill's final service for law enforcement was to be his most famous—as marshal of Abilene from April 15 to December 13, 1871. It was this appointment more than any other that would boost his real and fictional reputation as peacekeeper.

Hickok's role as a law enforcer was sporadic. But in each position he held he aroused controversy and inspired some remarkable tales of heroism in fights against "bad men" hell-bent on anarchy. His alleged heroics in keeping the peace played an important part in establishing his reputation as a civilizer.

The belief that Wild Bill Hickok was a Western civilizer has been fostered for generations, although one finds no suggestion of it during his own lifetime. The word "civilizer" seems to have crept into use by the late 1870s, when the term "gunfighter" was rarely used. "Shootist" or "mankiller" was too explicit. "Civilizer," however, had an air of authority that at least suggested a legal purpose. Nevertheless, it was used tongue-in-cheek by an editor writing several years after Hickok's death. No one, it seems, dared to dispute the legend of the law-and-order man who "executed a violator of the law without waiting for the silly formalities of a judge and jury," yet lived as a respected citizen and went to church and prayed with a "regularity, grace and precision only equalled by his unerring aim with a revolver, the great Western civilizer."[5]

It was not Wild Bill who saw himself as a "civilizer," but his eulogizers. Some of them still believe that Hickok single-handedly tamed Abilene and Hays City. No wonder historians continue to question Hickok's status. Hickok was employed to keep the peace by upholding the laws of the state and local ordinances, and performing whatever other official duties were imposed upon him. There his responsibility ended. It was the task of others to sort out the questions of morality and its place in civilization. But writers were faced with an eastern audience that demanded more of its heroes. Those who had known Wild Bill and were familiar with his peace-keeping activities were probably amazed to learn, within a generation, of his role as a "civilizer."

The tradition of the law-and-order man goes back a long way. Americans based their legal process on the old English common law, which existed long before the American Revolution. In England, the individual has the right to defend himself using reasonable force. But if his actions lead to a killing, only extenuating circumstances will save him from the gallows or a prison sentence. This rule also applies in Canadian law. In the United States the common law tradition underwent subtle changes. Students still compare the English ruling with the more permissive American version.

The influence of the frontier has survived into the present day. People living in the more remote areas of the West still tend to take care of their own problems, while in the more populated eastern states, people are more willing to rely upon available law enforcement or legal advice. Today's Westerner is no less law-abiding than his Eastern counterpart, but in the West, the individual is expected to assume some responsibility for his own and others' welfare rather than leaving everything to legislation. And in the middle nineteenth century, when decisions were often made in a hurry, there was little time to worry about legal technicalities. In effect, Westerners had little sympathy for their Eastern cousins.

On a purely technical level, most Western acts of "justice" might today be deemed unlawful, and sometimes overhasty decisions were made that in hindsight might best have been deferred. A modern historian has suggested, when reviewing the number of hangings credited to Judge Isaac Parker's court at Fort Smith, that by "current standards the hangings themselves would have been invitations to violence," presumably because of the present lenient attitude toward crime and criminals. Nevertheless, he seems contemptuous of the attitudes of some of those devoted to law and order who he concludes were themselves "as closely associated with violence as the outlaw." Hickok, for instance, is described as a violent man "who is supposed to have quelled violence on the frontier and to have brought the blessings of organized law and order to our Western civilization. But he was ever ready to kill, on either side of the law." This opinion, although obviously based upon hearsay, does highlight the conflicting opinions then current concerning the likes of Wild Bill and many of his contemporaries.[6]

There was also a curious attitude toward the better-known members of the outlaw fraternity. Jesse James remains the most potent of these, and the love-hate relationship that existed between him and the people of Missouri during the latter part of his life is exemplified by comments in the press. On September 26, 1872, when he and his gang robbed the gate of the Kansas City fair of an amount thought to be less than a thousand dollars, and in shooting their way out, the outlaws wounded a little girl, reaction was mixed. The *Times* seemed to regard the action as "diabolically daring" and the perpetrators were to be admired. Two days later the editor waxed lyrical on the event and compared the James boys with the knights of King Arthur. Later, one normally reliable individual was to state that the raid on the gate was in fact frustrated by "Wild Bill, a pistol in each hand, in such a way as to cause them to make themselves scarce instanter." Hickok was indeed at the fair, but his moment of glory came a day later when a gang of drunken Texans ordered the bandmaster to play "Dixie," and Hickok, ignoring their pistols, stopped the music.[7]

But following the murder of Jesse James, the *Times,* in its issue of April 12, 1882, published the following comment from the *New York Herald.* It puts the "bad man" into perspective by robbing the dead outlaw of some of his romance:

Apparently the outlaw James is regarded in some quarters as a first class hero, and his relative [*sic*] who killed him as a dastard and a traitor of the vilest sort; and this view seems to be held by persons who were not brought up on dime novels. Indeed, to practice the industry of a highwayman on so large a scale as to stop a railway train where the old fashioned gentlemen of the road used to rob a coach or an individual wayfarer imposes upon the imagination and deceives the reason. It is easier to stop a train than a coach, for the coach may struggle on down a road and fight its way through a running fire, while if two or three rails are removed from their places the train must stop upon the alternative of a grand smash up. And the train once stopped, it is not, after all so grand an achievement for a well organized body of bravoes with firearms to do the rest, for they come suddenly upon peaceful travelers not prepared for such emergencies and commonly accompanied by women and children. In such a case all the "heroic robber" does is to plunder men whose hands are tied by restraints of humanity and tenderness that the bravo can not feel. The most cowardly killing of such a fellow is not more cowardly than his daily life.

The romanticism surrounding Jesse James has been attributed by some to the fact that unlike many of his contemporaries who fought as Rebel guerrillas, Jesse James did not receive a pardon because he had fought with Quantrill. The James family claimed that his troubles began at that time. Perhaps, but that does not seem reason enough to start robbing banks, trains, and organizing gangs of criminals. Nor did the claim that he was protesting against the robber barons of the railroads excuse his crimes. Nevertheless, flimsy excuses are sometimes put forward that gloss over the violent side of such men and suggest that they were on the side of the people. Although there is some evidence to support the claim that Jesse and Frank James did try to get back at the railroad barons, the government did eventually legislate against such speculators. By the late 1870s there was no longer any excuse for the James brothers' actions. Public sympathy, however, was extended to the James brothers when the Pinkerton Detective Agency used a government-issued bomb containing what some described as 'Greek fire' against the James family. The bomb was tossed into the family home in January 1875, and as a result, Jesse's young half brother was killed and his mother lost an arm. The Pinkertons denied that they used a bomb. Its actual type only came to light in recent years when Ordnance Department records were discovered authorizing its issue.

Western violence, then, existed in many forms. The so-called "bad man" was as much a part of society as was the law-abiding individual, a situation that exists in any society. But thanks to newspaper and dime novel publicity, the Western "bad man" assumed a higher status than the common criminal. Westerners, too, succumbed to the romanticism associated with such characters. On October 12, 1880, the Sacramento *Daily Bee* satirized the "Bad Man from Bodie" (Bodie was one of Nevada's more notorious mining camps) in a manner that could have applied to almost any location. Emphasizing his profanity, violence, and determination to kill, the bad man was reported to have said: "I was born in a powder house and raised in a gun factory. I am bad from the bottom up and clear grit plumb through . . . I'm chief of Murdertown, and I'm dry. Whose treat is it? Don't all speak at once, or I'll turn loose and scatter death and destruction full bent for the next election." In hindsight such an individual (like the character "Cemetery Sam," who proclaimed himself a "gunfighter" as early as 1874 and got knocked down for his trouble) is amusing, but in his own time, he rarely was.

The legend of the gunfighter exemplifies the romanticized "bad man" more than any other. He is as instantly recognizable as is the cowboy (in whose image he is often depicted), but he is not as easily defined. A complex character, he was considered to be a man apart, a "lone wolf" with few friends and a reputation as a killer when provoked. Some gunfighters, though, killed just to "see a man kick." Tradition separates the good from the bad by describing the men who fought on the side of the law as "gunfighters" and the others as "gunmen," a subtlety preserved in Western movies when the "good guys" wore white hats and the "bad men" wore black.

One of the problems faced by any researcher into the origin and true status of the gunfighter as a character is the tendency of writers to set him apart from his fellow beings. One facet of the character that attracts today's audiences is his reluctance to form any long-term emotional or physical relationships. He has no visible means of support. His presence is felt to be providential, but once his task is over, the gunfighter rides off into the sunset. This lack of commitment betrays, to most people, a basic immaturity and fear of responsibility. The gunfighter of legend, however, is not a normal person. Rather, he is the principal character in the modern "morality play," and for him to succumb to normal human needs and desires would defeat his purpose. Therefore, his audiences are prepared to ignore his weaknesses, because they know that his strength lies in his ability with a gun and his courage in fighting evil so that good can prevail. Gunfighters (on both sides of the law) were tolerated as a part of Western society, though, and the stories of the men whose exploits have been told and retold now form a part of the Western myth. The gunfighters who fought on the side of law and order have long been depicted as the Old West's civilizers, and it is difficult to convince people otherwise. But history and legend have always gone hand in hand. If, in order to keep history alive, a certain laxity in factual reporting is permissible, then the gunfighter will always have his niche in history.

One eminent historian, who later expanded his comments into a formal social study, succinctly summed up both the gunfighter and the legal implication of his acts:

The West was "tamed" (as was Australia, South Africa, etc.) by a burgeoning, irrepressible Anglo-Saxon impulse toward expansion and exploitation. No one set of individuals (unless one were to single out the Army) suppressed lawlessness and disorder. Gun-fighters as a rule blossomed where there was no law and order; the researcher finds them existing in their classical form only in the mining communities, where their anti-social behavior was toler-ated because the predominantly male society was too busy dig-ging gold or silver to bother about establishing local government. Once in a while, as in the Kansas cowtown, a throwback took place, wherein in spite of the march of Anglo-Saxon civilization a temporary condition of real or threatened lawlessness was thrust upon a community. Community leaders then might call upon the temporary services of a specialist. Such specialists need not be liked or even respected by the townspeople, and often it was felt that the town was simply hiring a thief to suppress other thieves. As soon as the specialist's services were no longer needed, he was discharged and a local man became city marshal again at a greatly reduced salary.[8]

But early Western communities probably did not think too much about old English law or the parasitic side of so-called gun-fighters who, when unemployed, tended to linger, doing little ex-cept adorning brothels, gaming halls or saloons. Rather, they were concerned with keeping the peace and were generally able to do so until places such as Abilene, Wichita, Ellsworth, and Dodge City got into the cattle business. At that point, the existing police force could not cope with the sudden influx of Texas cow-boys and thousands of long-horned cattle. The city fathers found it necessary to employ the sort of individual whose reputation alone might deter trouble makers. It was this practice that in-spired the "civilizing" part of the Hickok myth.

Western communities were prepared to go to almost any lengths to curtail violence. The early efforts by the vigilante com-mittees in California and later efforts in Montana proved to be re-markably effective. California's situation was unique. It was ceded by Mexico as a part of the Guadalupe Hidalgo Treaty early in 1848. The discovery of gold led to such an influx of people that California was granted statehood before its residents had ad-justed to territorial status. As a result, law and order was nonexis-tent in some areas. In San Francisco the law-abiding citizens formed committees or courts to resolve civil disagreements over

mining or land claims. By 1851, however, the increasing numbers of criminals anxious to rob men of their claims and "dust"
prompted the establishment of vigilance committees. Formed on
democratic lines, the committee elected juries. Early crimes concerned claim jumping, or sluice-box robbing, which usually resulted in a flogging and the suggestion that the miscreants leave
town. When murder was committed, the punishment was death.
Appeals were useless and the sentence was generally carried out
soon after the verdict. Outsiders tended to equate the vigilance
committees with the Committee of Public Safety of the French
Revolution; others described them as little more than mobs. Unlike the mob, however, with its hotheaded, often irrational reaction, vigilantes were properly organized, and for those who lived
during the days of mob rule when the revolver was freely used,
the vigilantes were a godsend.[9]

Following the Civil War and the growth of the Texas cattle
trade, vigilante committees were rarely needed or encouraged
(although the one at Hays City was quite active in 1869). For the
most part, city, state and federal law had been established, and
district courts were kept busy. Mining and cattle communities
were the exceptions. There the large influx of people not only
overstretched the existing police forces, but conflict arose between the local people over the economic advantages of the cattle trade and the violence that accompanied it. At this point, the
townsfolk accepted the need to increase the police force and hire
someone of reputation to head it. So began the myth of the
"two-gun city marshal."

The era of the cowtowns spanned about twenty years, a period that witnessed many social and economic changes. Abilene
became the first of the so-called Kansas cowtowns. Established as
a stagecoach stop in the early 1860s, it lay beside the route of the
Union Pacific Railway Company, Eastern Division (the U.P.E.D.)
then building West toward Denver. Joseph G. McCoy, a partner in
the firm of William K. McCoy and Brothers, realized its potential.
In negotiations with the company president, he agreed to a price
of $5 for every car shipped east loaded with cattle and made ar-
rangements to accommodate the animals. On June 18, 1867, he
purchased 250 acres of land at the northeastern side of Abilene,
and within three months he had built shipping pens large

enough to hold one thousand head of cattle. He also had various other buildings constructed, and the U.P.E.D., as a part of its agreement, put in a one-hundred-car switch to handle McCoy's Great Western Stockyard output of forty freight cars in two hours. The first shipment of cattle eastwards occurred on September 5, following extensive advertising by McCoy to persuade the Texas drovers to bring their herds as far as Abilene.

The route the cattlemen followed was directly north from Texas, up through Indian Territory and as far as Wichita. This trail had been established by the half-breed Indian trader, Jesse Chisholm. Although Chisholm's Trail officially ended at Wichita, there was no railroad at the time, so McCoy established the Abilene Trail or McCoy's Extension to reach the shipping point. Soon other trails branched off or crossed the Chisholm Trail to Newton, Ellsworth, and later Dodge City and Caldwell, as well as places farther north or west.[10]

Abilene was unique as the first of the Kansas cowtowns and in another respect as well: it had no police force. But in 1869 its citizens petitioned for third-class city status, which would enable them to elect a city council and a police force. Until that time they had relied on the Dickinson County sheriff and a couple of constables from Grant Township. Thomas J. Smith, the first marshal, was appointed in May 1870. When the other towns later took on the cattle trade, all had established police forces and experience of dealing with violence. So, through trial and error the citizens of Abilene learned how to tackle violence. They also inspired, through their venture into law and order, the myth of the lone marshal facing down the mob—a situation that never really existed in any of the cowtowns.

The ordinances of every cowtown outlawed the use and carrying of firearms within city limits, but they were not easy to enforce. Tom Smith tried, with reasonable success, in 1870. In July 1871, his successor, Wild Bill, even had notices posted advising visitors that the ordinance against the carrying of firearms would be strictly enforced. This prohibition was also underlined by the prevailing state laws against the carrying of firearms by former rebels or Confederates. No one really believed that these rules could be enforced, but people hoped that the violence could be contained. In 1871, the city of Wichita, fearful of the threat of so

many armed men, ordered city marshal Michael Meagher to erect
two hand-painted notices advising all persons that the carrying
of firearms or "other dangerous weapons within the city limits of
Wichita" was banned "under penalty of fine and imprisonment." Later, in 1872, the Chisholm Trail Bridge tollkeepers were
sworn in as special police and authorized to relieve individuals of
their pistols in exchange for a metal token. This strategy was
abandoned in 1873 in favor of a notice to visitors: "Leave your
revolvers at Police Headquarters and get a check."[11]

The city police usually consisted of a marshal or chief of police and several deputies or policemen. During the winter
months the force was reduced, as were their salaries, to be increased again at the beginning of the cattle season. Some towns
hired as many as five policemen, whose duties included street
cleaning, the disposal (by shooting) of stray dogs, and other
mundane tasks. But their prime responsibility was to uphold the
law. Each policeman was armed and his weapon was openly displayed. Some residents objected to so many armed police, but
with a transient population known to be armed, the policeman
had no choice. Ironically, on August 14, 1873, the Ellsworth *Reporter* protested that the police were overarmed, that one six-
shooter should be enough: "It is too much to have to see double
armed men walking our peaceful streets." The next day, Ben
Thompson's homicidal brother Billy, in a drunken rage, shot
down Sheriff Chauncey B. Whitney with his brother's shotgun
and escaped. When he was eventually brought back for trial in
1877, he was acquitted on a technicality.

The task of policing the cowtowns was, therefore, fraught
with problems. But the myth of a lone man handling such an environment is nonsense. In reality, an individual courageous
enough to face down the opposition was backed by a strong
force of officers and, when necessary, the additional assistance of
townsfolk. It is in this context that Wild Bill's role as a city marshal or "civilizer" must be viewed.

Wild Bill's relationship with law and order has been interpreted as an ongoing involvement that began in his early years in
Kansas. There he witnessed some of the violence that beset Kansas in the territorial period. In an undated comment found

among other letters written home in 1858, he refers to a fight that is thought to have taken place at Monticello:

It was the first time in my life that I ever saw a fight and did not go to see it out[,] and I am glad of it now[.] you don['t] [k]now what a Country this is for drinking and fighting[,] but I hope it will be different some time and I [k]no[w] in reason that it will when the Law is put in force[.] there is no Common Law here now hardly at all[.] a man Can do what he pleases without fear of the law or any thing els[e.] thare has been two awful fights in town this week[,] you don[']t [k]no[w] anything about sutch fighting at home as I speak of[,] this is no place for women and children yet[,] all though they all say it is so quiet here[.] . . . if a man fites in kansas and gets whip[p]ed he never says anything more About it[,] if he does he will get whipt for his trouble.[12]

It is clear from that statement that Hickok did indeed have a sense of justice, and at various times during his lifetime and later, contemporaries recalled that he was always a law-and-order man. The emphasis on his peace-keeping role and his reputation as a "town tamer" or "civilizer" played a key role in the growth of his legend. This image was heightened further by comments made in the press and believed by members of his family. Writing to his mother from Fort Lyon, Colorado Territory, on December 2, 1867, Lorenzo Hickok bemoaned the fact that neither he nor the family had heard much from James for some time. James, he revealed, was too involved with his hectic activities. For James, writing letters was a bore. However, James did keep in touch with his brother by word of mouth. Lorenzo then disclosed that James "is now Stationed at Ellsworth, Kansas[,] and is Deputy U.S. Marshall for Kansas as the Marshall lives at Leavenworth, Mr. [Charles C.] Whiting is his Name."[13] Unwittingly, Lorenzo had glorified his brother's position, for James was in fact one of perhaps fifty deputies spread across the state. But Lorenzo was not alone in misunderstanding his brother's status, as can be gleaned from this comment in the Springfield, Massachusetts, *Republican* of February 21, 1874. At the time, Hickok was a member of Buffalo Bill's theatrical Combination touring the Eastern states: "Wild Bill . . . has served as United States marshal for the state of Kansas, where his very name has been a terror to evil-doers.

Reckless characters, whom no other man dared to tackle, have been consigned to his tender mercy, and in no case has he failed to make the desired arrest."

Hickok's attitude toward so-called "evil-doers" was a favorite theme in the Kansas press. In November 1871, when Hickok foiled an attempt on his life on a train bound for Topeka, the Junction City *Union* on December 2 remarked that "he still lives and moves, a terror to evil doers."

Such comments, whether true or flights of fancy, boosted an already snowballing reputation and enhanced his reputation as a law and order man who, if need be, would enforce the law at the point of a gun. In a society that had endured four years of civil war and was still trying to adjust to the experience, the likes of a Wild Bill must have seemed an ideal means of subduing some of the more dangerous characters. Hearsay played a great part both in promoting reports of violence and in the efforts to contain it.

Lorenzo Hickok's reference to his brother's presence as deputy U.S. marshal at Ellsworth in 1867 focuses attention on the reputation for violence the town had earned within months of its founding in January. Fort Ellsworth, named in honor of 2d Lt. Allen Ellsworth, who had established it on November 11, 1866, was later renamed Fort Harker after Brig. Gen. Charles G. Harker, killed in the Civil War. It was located on the Smoky Hill River where it crossed the Santa Fe stage road. It served the role of protecting both travelers and workers engaged in the construction of the Union Pacific Railway Company, Eastern Division. The post was relocated in January 1867, three-quarters of a mile northeast of the old one. On January 23, the embryonic settlement that would eventually become the town of Ellsworth was laid out about one mile from the fort. On June 8, however, the Smoky Hill River rose in flood and Ellsworth was quickly relocated on firmer ground to the northwest. In July the new site was legalized and city elections were planned.

The Junction City *Union* of July 6 (and a number of other statewide papers) carried a report of Indian attacks and riots among teamsters. And during the following months, Ellsworth's reputation for murder and mayhem was given wide publicity. An outbreak of cholera at Fort Harker (according to one report, it even claimed the life of Hickok) did little to attract settlement.

However, the city's first election, a special election, was held on August 10. E. W. Kingsbury ran for county sheriff and was elected, pending the November elections when he beat Hickok and several other candidates. Wild Bill, however, remained in and around the place for some months as an army scout or deputy U.S. marshal.[14]

An examination of official records indicates that Wild Bill was active in his official capacity during the latter part of 1867, early 1868 and again in the latter part of 1869–1870. He apprehended army deserters, mule and horse thieves, and illegal timbercutters (for railroad ties) on government lands. These activities inspired many of the tall tales concerning his official duties. Then as now, many people did not realize that U.S. marshals and their deputies were appointed officials acting within the law and not "judge, jury and executioner."[15]

Similarly, when Hickok became acting sheriff of Ellis County in 1869 and was headquartered at Hays City, some vested him with a status that bordered upon the absurd. His election, as we have noted, was disputed by the governor, James W. Harvey, who claimed that he alone was empowered to appoint individuals to fill vacancies occurring between elections. That claim was disputed by the county commissioners who relied on Kansas statutes for guidance. And it appears that they were right, for according to the Junction City Union of January 8, 1870, the governor recommended to the legislature that "where vacancies occur in the office of sheriff, no under sheriff having been appointed, as required by law, authority be given for the Governor to appoint a sheriff to fill the vacancy until an election can be held in pursuance of law."

This official wrangling meant little to the ordinary citizen, who believed that establishment of law and order was of paramount importance. Election of Hickok was welcomed by the majority of them. Contemporary accounts suggest that Hickok did what was required of him and that his presence did deter some of the more hardened characters from violence. On one occasion, he won the praise of the post commander at Fort Hays, Maj. George Gibson, when he stopped a lynching in Hays City.[16]

Writing in 1877, the editor of the Hays City Sentinel admitted on February 2 that stories of Hickok's exploits were subject to fabrication. And some of them displayed a "refreshing stupidity," claiming that "while a resident of Hays, Bill had killed twelve men, and wounded and maimed whole battalions and regiments." He went on: "Bill was not a demon who delighted in taking life, and even if in truth a desperado, he was so by force of circumstances." He then added that during Hickok's residence in Hays, "Bill killed only three men; and a coroner's jury exonerated him from blame—partly through a reverence and fear of his prowess, and partly because he was blameless." This latter comment indicates a genuine regard for a man whom he felt deserved a better fate but was a product of his time. He also intimated that much of the violence Hickok was reportedly involved in was due to his reputation. Indeed, the enigmatic side of Hickok's character inspired this kind of mixed reaction.

Despite the enormous amount of outside publicity he received during his period as marshal of Abilene, the *Chronicle* gave scant mention of him. Even when his death was announced, the paper chose to print an obituary published elsewhere. Only in later years, when old-timers reminisced about the early days, were pro- and anti-Hickok comments aired. One explanation for the delay may be that by 1876 Abilene was determined to put its past behind it and forget the cattle trade. If this hunch is correct, then in hindsight the decision was very shortsighted. For despite its violent overtones, Abilene owed its growth and prosperity to the cattle trade.

In the years that followed Hickok's brief period as marshal of Abilene, and for some time after his death, little was published locally concerning his service as marshal. Even Buffalo Bill failed to mention it in his autobiography published in 1879. It was left to the popular writer J. W. Buel to publicize and fictionalize the events. Typically, he asserted that Abilene was

> running over and bursting out at the side with the very double distilled essence of depravity. The town, with less than one thousand permanent residents, was filled with so much vileness that the very atmosphere appeared impregnated with the odor of abomination; murder ran riot, drunkenness was the rule, gambling a universal pastime, fighting a recreation, and the mischief to pay generally the engrossing occupation.

That description was worthy of a Sunday morning sermon, and warming to his theme, Buel went on to infer that the townsfolk were helpless in the face of such wickedness, and overwhelmed by the "great herds of cattle" and "scores of reckless cow-boys and owners who arrived every day."[17]

Buel made no mention of the part played in the "taming" of Abilene by Marshal Thomas ("Bear River Tom") Smith prior to his murder by two settlers in November 1870—perhaps because it might have detracted from Wild Bill's glory. For Smith's period as marshal or "Chief of Police" heralded a new beginning for Abilene. The lawlessness that had marked the place from 1867 until his appointment in May 1870 was gone. But in order to keep it at bay, a strong police force was needed. Hickok's arrival in the wake of Smith's earlier efforts was something of an anticlimax. But the city council was in no mood to take chances with the Texans, who were unpredictable at the best of times and homicidal when under the influence of liquor.

When T. C. Henry appointed Tom Smith as the city's first marshal, he was paid $150 per month, a salary that was later raised to $225, making him probably the most highly paid city marshal in frontier history. Hickok, on the other hand, was paid $150 and a percentage of court fines. By August 1871, when Hickok's policing of the city had kept a lid on most of the violence for some time, there was a move to reduce expenditure. On August 2 the council reviewed a citizens' petition asking that the four-man police force be reduced by half. The petition was not acted upon. Similarly, on the tenth a new ordinance lowered Hickok's salary to $100, and that of his police to $75 per month. But surviving records indicate that not all of the provisions of this ordinance were enforced. The November minutes disclose that on the fourth Hickok was allowed one month's salary of $150, but his two policemen received only $50 each. On September 2, James H. McDonald and James Gauthie were dismissed from the force. By November, Hickok's deputies were J. W. ("Brocky Jack") Norton, a newcomer to the team, and Thomas Carson.[18]

The council's matter-of-fact approach to finance is at variance with tradition that asserts that Hickok was paid as much as $1,000 a month to pacify Abilene. Ridiculous though that may appear, it does indicate that vast sums of money and hordes of dead "bad men" were important ingredients in the process of Western hero-making.

Buel left the impression that Hickok fought a lone battle against crime, a myth that was to remain in the public eye for almost fifty years, boosted by local accounts, most of them fictional. One tale that contained elements of both fact and fiction was a much publicized story by E. C. Little, a local businessman whose "A Son of the Border," first published in *Everybody's Magazine,* was later reprinted in the Topeka *Mail and Breeze* on September 13, 1901. Little played down some of the wickedness described by others, but not the violence. His account of Hickok's shoot out with Phil Coe received a lot of attention. Little was followed in 1904 by Arthur Chapman, who claimed that Hickok's reputation as a revolver shot did not convince the Doubting Thomases, so "Hickok's guns seldom saw a week of silence. Quarrels were picked with him with the intention of encompassing his death, but he dropped his man so invariably that finally none but methods of assassination were employed." Evidently, Chapman was familiar with the basic facts of Hickok's Abilene days, for he retold the story of an attempt on Hickok's life on a train and his habit of carrying a sawed-off shotgun.[19]

The distinguished novelist Emerson Hough also found Wild Bill a character worthy of his attention. In *The Story of the Outlaw,* he made a point of extolling Hickok's virtue as a typical town marshal, according him "an honorable place in American history." Yet he, too, relied upon Buel and others for his background material. Hough left his readers with the impression that the citizens of Abilene were proud of their marshal, who had increased his personal tally to 81. And there were others similarly devoted to the task of promoting or perpetuating Wild Bill's mankiller myth.[20]

Any suggestion that Wild Bill was somehow responsible for Abilene's moral welfare as well as keeping the town law-abiding is nonsense. Hickok was elected for the specific purpose of upholding the law as the following oath he swore when elected makes clear:

I James B. Hickok do Solemnly swear that I will support the Constitution of the United States, the Constitution of the State of Kansas, and faithfully discharge the duties of the Office of Marshal of the City of Abilene, to the best of my ability, so help me God.[21]

Some people did not think that Hickok lived up to the oath, among them Stuart Henry, younger brother of Theodore C. Henry, leader of the town's original trustees and the man who had appointed Tom Smith as city marshal. Although Henry was only ten years old in 1871, in hindsight he credited Hickok with courage and a reputation that was second to none. But he was critical of Hickok's peace-keeping methods. He claimed that unlike Smith, who kept up a continuous patrol of Texas Street on horseback or occasionally on foot, Wild Bill did not venture far, leaving such leg work to his deputies while he held court in the Alamo Saloon. He also asserted that Hickok was "ready to shoot down, to kill outright, instead of avoiding assassination when possible as the higher duty of a marshal. Such a policy of taking over justice into his own hands exemplified, of course, but a form of lawlessness." Henry did, however, note that Hickok's personal feuds were not the affair of the city, since men followed him there in the hope of wreaking personal vengeance or revenge for a "pard."[22]

Hickok never trusted the Texans. Their habit of ambushing people who had upset them was well known, and both Smith and Hickok avoided places where a potential assassin could hide out. But their reputation did not stop Hickok from confronting them. Early in August 1871, it was reported that Wild Bill had a "spite" at a Texas drover and hit him over the head with his revolver. According to the Kansas City *Journal* of August 13, he also "stamped him in the face with his boot heel, inflicting a severe wound." The fellow's companions then told Hickok that he would not be safe overnight. But they "mistook their man, as 'Wild Bill' is the last man to be driven away by such threats. At last accounts he was still there and unharmed. Such a marshal might do for such a place as Abilene, but for Kansas City we don't want him." At this late date, the cause of the fracas is unknown; and the paper's correspondent seems to have been ignorant of the frontier tradition of "marking" an enemy—a tradition that goes back to the mountain men and keeled riverboats when eye-gouging and ear-chewing as marks of victory were common. It is important to note that Hickok's alleged behavior on that occasion was not criticized locally, which suggests a tacit acceptance of his methods by the council. Mayor McCoy hinted at this acceptance in his book published in 1872, though he softened his view thirty years later and joined the hero-worshipers. Still, McCoy's meaning is plain: it takes fire to fight fire.[23]

Despite the contradictions in its retelling—or perhaps because of them—Hickok's time as marshal of Abilene did more than anything else to perpetuate his legend, and contemporary press reports indicate that his presence within the city was appreciated. Even the Abilene *Chronicle* that campaigned so spiritedly against the cattle trade was to state on October 12, 1871 (in its report of the shooting of Phil Coe by Wild Bill) that there "is no use in trying to override Wild Bill, the Marshal. His arrangements for policing the city are complete, and attempts to kill police officers or in any way create disturbance, must result in loss of life on the part of violators of the law. We hope that all, strangers as well as citizens, will aid by word and deed in maintaining peace and quietness." To this statement should be added the Junction City *Union's* comment of October 7 that "the verdict of the citizens seemed to be unanimously in support of the Marshal, who bravely did his duty." That Wild Bill did not aspire to the role of "judge, jury and executioner" meant little to the writers who based their accounts upon sensationalism and half-truths. Small wonder then, that when such as J. W. Buel produced semifictional works like *Heroes of the Plains,* few would question his veracity. Those that did rarely expressed their opinions publicly.

Writing in 1883, A. T. Andreas stated that as marshal of Abilene

> Hickok was a bold, bad man, and had no respect whatever for human life. He could draw a revolver in less time, and fire with surer aim than any other man in the West. Nor did he stand long upon the order of drawing. He was a terror to the cow-boys, he having caused several of them to bite the dust on short notice, and thought no more of killing a man than he would a dog.[24]

Andreas relied upon hearsay when assessing both Hickok's character and his dealings with the Texans, but in debunking the man and his myth, Andreas unwittingly perpetuated the widely

held belief that Wild Bill had six-shooter skills superior to anyone else. Similarly, the claim that Wild Bill killed several cowboys
is not only inaccurate but reiterates the belief that Hickok was a
killing machine. But his assertions are based on nothing more
than mischievous reporting.

Even a cursory examination of material devoted to Wild Bill's
real and imaginary exploits as a policeman reveals a demigod-like
figure, immune to normal constrictions and allowed to roam free
through the ranks of the ungodly. Invested with a code of chivalry that shields him from harm, he rights the wrongs of society
in the guise of the civilizer or gunfighter. This concept totally dis-
torts both the character of Wild Bill and his true place in Western
history. And it annoyed some historians when the late Dwight D.
Eisenhower, whose boyhood was spent in Abilene some years after Hickok's departure, stated publicly in 1953 that he had been
raised in "a famous place" called Abilene where "we had as our
marshal for a long time a man named Wild Bill Hickok." He
added that the town had a code which was: "Meet anyone face to
face with whom you disagree. . . . If you meet him face to face
and took the same risks he did, you could get away with almost
anything, as long as the bullet was in the front." Reaction by historians was swift: some applauded the president's remarks while
others, who failed to see Hickok or his contemporaries in an heroic light, criticized them. Hickok's reputation was so well entrenched that even presidents admired him. To be fair to President Eisenhower, during his boyhood in turn-of-the-century
Abilene, there were still people around who had known Hickok.
Some mothers were even reported to have quieted disobedient
offspring by threatening to send for Wild Bill—a reminder of the
awe in which he was held by many of the citizens who knew him
only by reputation. Indeed, it is easy to appreciate why the cry
"Wild Bill is on the street!" that so impressed the Texans could
be interpreted in later years to describe a kind of bogey man.[25]

Wild Bill Hickok's fictional exploits as a civilizer have tran-
scended his actual role as a peace officer in both a civil and federal capacity. His status as a renowned pistol shot and a character
tough enough to control others served only to enhance an already escalating reputation. That he never tamed any of the
places associated with him, or indeed influenced their moral

character, is ignored. History may rate his presence as timely and acknowledge that his efforts to keep the peace were appreciated by those involved. But it will also note that he did not influence the nation's destiny in the manner of a Washington or a Lincoln. Rather, he happened to be in the right place at the right time. Tradition, folklore, and oral history, however, would have it otherwise.

The mythical Wild Bill remains a larger-than-life "civilizer," a role that defies facts and reason. Perhaps he represents a facet of American civilization that needs heroes in an environment where the individual is no longer the master of his own destiny. Individualists are considered dangerous by the establishment, which prefers a person to be a "team player" who will conform to their standards rather than living by his own principles.

Seven

A Blood and Thunder Hero

The advance of "civilization" across the West inspired many myths, for the place was rugged, hostile, and vast. But a myth should be treated with caution, since it is just what it implies—a tale that is not what it seems. Many myths are complete fabrications, while others have a factual basis—a grain of truth that has been either deliberately distorted or enhanced far beyond its origin. And in this respect, the world of the frontier hero was very much a mixture of fact and myth. With constant telling and retelling, myth became accepted as historical fact. Because history itself is an interpretation of the facts or events and is based upon witnesses' accounts or written sources that are frequently in dispute, it is necessary for the historian to adopt a cynical, objective approach.[1]

The elevation of frontier characters to folklore heroes was a common practice. Daniel Boone, one of Kentucky's most famous pioneers, was renowned in fact and fiction, and many believe that he was the first real Western hero. Many of the deeds credited to him are easily verified. In 1784 he was featured in John Filson's *The Discovery, Settlement, and Present State of Kentucky,* and in 1813 his own nephew, Daniel Bryan published a poem entitled *The Adventures of Daniel Boone.* It is also claimed that in 1819 Lord Byron immortalized him in *Don Juan.* However, it was the publication in 1833 of *Daniel Boone, The First Settler of Kentucky,* by Timothy Flint that established him as a legendary hero, and one that symbolized the pioneering urge to civilize a wilderness.

Another character who also symbolized the explorer cum Indian fighter was Christopher Houston Carson, immortalized as

Kit Carson. He epitomized that tough breed of men who populated the West during the early and middle years of the nineteenth century, notably the fur trappers and mountain men, although he is best remembered as a scout and guide. In 1858 he
was the subject of a biography by DeWitt C. Peters that helped
establish his present day image.[2]

The frontier hero served as a role model, someone to be admired and perhaps emulated. And what better means of emphasizing the hero's exploits and strength of character than the humble dime novel? True, they left much to be desired among
educational purists and those anxious to dispel childish ambition
of a "free" existence in a beckoning wilderness. Yet for all their
faults, dime novels did inspire a sense of right and wrong, and
despite the "blood, guts and gore," they were strong on morality.

The dime novel era spawned a host of characters, not all of
them based upon real people. It was genre that reached a vast audience during the middle and later years of last century. Some
have suggested that although others had written novels exploit-
ing the Western experience, James Fenimore Cooper's novels had
most influence. His classic *Leatherstocking Tales* found a ready
audience. As early as 1823, his *The Pioneers* established a formula for what was to become a frontier theme. Others soon followed, and by the 1830s Cooper's much loved Natty Bumppo, a
character equally at home among the whites and the Indians, had
numerous rivals. But where Cooper portrayed a spirit of harmony between the whites and the Indians, many of his succes-
sors preferred to depict the Indian as a blood-thirsty savage. The
heroes of these sagas became household names, and they all
shared one basic trait: they were heroic in the Robin Hood tradition, totally devoted to the rights of the underdog. The public
adored them, as it later did their modern counterparts, Western
heroes of "B" movies. Unlike the movie heroes, however, dime
novel characters occasionally underwent character changes that
must have confused their public. Wild Bill Hickok survived several transformations, particularly at the hands of Ned Buntline.
Having killed him off in his first Buffalo Bill yarn, the redoubt-
able Buntline then resurrected him and featured him both as a
hero and, later, as a creature obsessed by the death of one of his
victims—each time he saw the man's sister he dropped down in a

dead faint. Fortunately for Wild Bill, others were not so erratic, among them Prentiss Ingraham, who wrote several Wild Bill stories that were well received and appeared in several editions.

Wild Bill Hickok's elevation to folk hero was a gradual process that by 1873 had him established in the role. Unfortunately, few clues exist to show how Hickok himself viewed his legendary status. In effect, he was a man living on a reputation—but which one? He had several: there was Wild Bill the frontier scout, a man of action and a figure, as Custer had perceived, that a "novelist might gloat over." Then there was Hickok as peace-keeper, as "terror to evil-doers." Allied to that was the more sinister tag of mankiller, insatiable slayer of innumerable "bad men." The mankiller version of his colorful past, in particular, seems to have displeased Hickok. In fact, his few published statements suggest that his "red-handed" murderer status infuriated him. So by the summer of 1873, Wild Bill, who had been in the public eye for almost ten years and the subject of much idle gossip, speculation, or downright mischief-making, was plagued by an awesome reputation.

Apart from the original Nichols interview, which in itself had contained a lot of fiction, and a brief conversation with Henry M. Stanley, Hickok refused to talk frankly about himself or express his own views on his controversial reputation. This reticence prompted some reporters to put words in his mouth, and the results both amused and irritated him. One such "interview" was published in the Springfield, Missouri, *Weekly Patriot* of October 9, 1873. The editor claimed that the paper had purchased the story from a young correspondent for a New York paper who was short of funds. Dated August 23, it recounts an alleged interview with Hickok on the subject of "Caesarism," a subject that was under discussion because someone had suggested that President Grant's status be elevated to that of Emperor. The article was generally humorous but, in parts, pointed. In describing Hickok to his readers, the writer noted:

> Perhaps the minions of civilization do not all know who Wild Bill is, though, there are not a few who will recollect him as the most daring scout and one of the best hunters of the west. For twenty years he has served the government in peace and war, and

though hated intensely by most of his profession, yet he is acknowledged to be a man of skill in his craft, and one of dauntless
courage. . . . Early in his life he betrayed a fondness for a wild life,
which eventually led him to the plains and made him what he is.

After crediting Hickok with some unkind comments on Buffalo Bill and his scouting accomplishments, the writer then
launched into a lengthy and amusing discussion with Wild Bill in
an attempt to elicit his views on "Caesarism." It was finally
agreed that if Grant were made king or emperor, Wild Bill would
expect to become U.S. marshal for the Indian Territory: "I will
get it or I'll take it. If anyone else gets it I'll go down there, and
then there'll be hell. There will be Caesarism there for a certainty." The interview (frequently interrupted by a sip of "something" at the bar) ended with Hickok threatening to boot the
luckless reporter into the street.

The obvious fiction of the foregoing "interview" highlights
the fact that Hickok had achieved a status that lay somewhere between the "Great Statesman of the Plains" (a subheading in the
article) or a living legend that inspired either adulation or trepi-
dation. In short, Hickok was larger than life, ideally suited for his
role as a dime novel hero and actor.

Hickok's dime novel career began in 1867 within weeks of his
appearance in *Harper's New Monthly Magazine.* Widely publicized, Nichols's story of Wild Bill attracted much attention. In
July, the third of DeWitt's Ten Cent Romances featured *Wild Bill
the Indian Slayer.* This issue reproduced as its cover the woodcut used in *Harper's* to depict the so-called McCanles Massacre.
Some months later, issue number ten was devoted to *Wild Bill's
First Trail,* and aroused some comment. On November 28, the
editor of the Leavenworth *Daily Conservative* wrote that a "pro-
spectus of the book" about the "well known scout" had been received, "as told by himself." The editor proceeded to cite the
publisher's blurb for *Wild Bill's First Trail* verbatim. At Hays
City, the *Railway Advance* of November 9 noted that Hickok,
then a deputy U.S. marshal, had lingered when the U.S. marshal,
Charles C. Whiting, and some companions, among them Hickok's "partner" Jack Harvey, had departed. Tongue-in-cheek, the

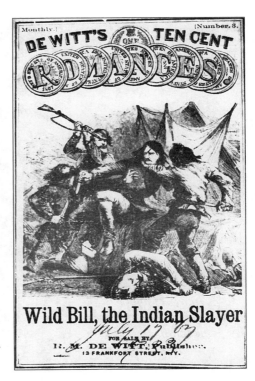

Wild Bill's first appearance as a dime novel hero in July 1867. (Courtesy Library of Congress)

Wild Bill, the Indian Slayer

FOR SALE BY
R. M. DE WITT, Publisher.
13 FRANKFORT STREET, N.Y.

editor remarked that he was "probably engaged in preparing his *LIFE* for DeWitt."

The two DeWitt novels followed closely the established formula of the time. *Indian Slayer* (credited to "Paul Preston" and thought by some to be a pseudonym either for Charles Morris, a noted dime novelist of the time, or Thomas Picton, a well known journalist) described Wild Bill's rescue of a white woman from the hands of a renegade named Jack Harris, who led a band of Sioux. *First Trail,* was purported to be based upon Wild Bill's life (as told by himself), but it is obvious from the blurb that it was just another "blood and thunder" yarn.

The DeWitt novels are important, however, because they established Wild Bill as a bona fide dime novel hero at a time when his real-life adventures were also receiving much publicity. Despite DeWitt's efforts, it was nearly two years before Wild Bill again came to the attention of the public as a dime novel hero. This time he was a supporting character in Ned Buntline's *Buffalo Bill, The King of the Border Men,* which was serialized in

Wild Bill's First Trail *was purported to have been based on Hickok's life "as he told it." (Courtesy Library of Congress)*

the *New York Weekly* in December 1869. (The first chapter was also published in other periodicals, but it was the *New York Weekly* that had the most impact.) Unfortunately for Hickok, Ned decided to kill him off. To add insult to injury, his demise was at the hands of a woman. The story included several factual characters who had been involved with Wild Bill and were now depicted in totally fictional surroundings. The plot demanded that because Wild Bill had killed her lover Dave Tutt, "Ruby Blazes" plunged her dagger into his heart.

Buntline's yarn formed the basis for Cody's early stage appearances, and it has been republished a number of times. In more recent years, one enterprising individual even credited the authorship to Cody. At the time of its original publication in the United States, *Buffalo Bill, The King of the Border Men* reached a wide readership. Within months it was also published in England in *Boys of England,* described as "A Journal of Sport, Travel, Fun & Instruction for the Youths of all Nations." Buntline was not credited as its author, but the editor did note that "in presenting this Tale to our readers, it is only fair to state that we do not wish to

PORTRAIT OF WILD BILL.

pass it off as an original composition. The story was written by an American author, and has already appeared in an illustrated weekly periodical, published in New York, called the '*New York Weekly.*'" Copyright being rather lax at the time, it is doubtful that Buntline received any English royalties for his efforts. But it

Wild Bill (top) and Buffalo Bill Cody (bottom) as depicted in Boys of England, *published in London in 1870. Buffalo Bill looks like a Swiss mountain guide, and Wild Bill appears to be modeled upon Italian brigands of the time. Without photographs to guide him, the artist did his best.*
(Author's collection)

PORTRAIT OF BUFFALO BILL.

was probably the first time that either Buffalo Bill or Wild Bill
were publicized outside the United States.[3]

Perhaps because of his early death in 1876, Hickok did not receive the same dime novel attention that was meted out to Buffalo Bill. Nevertheless, his dime novel appearances—either as the
central character or one of Buffalo Bill's "pards"—was impressive. Paul Preston's *Indian Slayer* was republished or revised by
Street & Smith as *Wild Bill's Trail; or, the Bluecoat Scouts of the
Prairie: A Remarkable Story of the West* in the Campfire Library,
together with *Wild Bill's First War Trail: A Stirring Tale of Real
Life on the Border,* by "William Hickok," which appears to have
been identical to the original DeWitt yarn. A number of Wild Bill
novels were published by Street & Smith in their Nugget Library
series and later as part of the Diamond Dick Library. Some of the
best known of these were written by Ned Buntline and Col. Prentiss Ingraham.[4]

Edward Zane Carroll Judson, to give Ned Buntline his real name,
was probably one of the most prolific dime novelists of his day. Tradition has it that he became aware of Wild Bill via *Harper's* and
later appreciated his potential when he saw him featured in DeWitt
and, perhaps, read some of the newspaper stories about his frontier
exploits. In 1869 he went West to find Wild Bill. According to
Hiram Robbins, who contributed material and a play or two to Buffalo Bill's Combination (as well as acting for a period as its man-
ager), Ned found Wild Bill in a saloon. The location was not disclosed. But since Texas Jack Omohundro, one of the characters
mentioned by Robbins, was running a saloon at North Platte at the
time, we may assume that was the place. Buntline, however, ruined
his chance of an interview by rushing up to Hickok and declaring,
"There's my man," adding, "I want you!" Hickok's reaction to this
was to draw his Navy pistol in preparation for a fight. Ned, realizing
his error, backed off and hastily announced who he was and that he
regarded Wild Bill as his ideal Indian-fighting hero. Hickok was not
impressed and gave him twenty-four hours to leave town. Learning
that Hickok did not bluff, a despondent Ned was consoled by Buffalo Bill and Texas Jack, who regaled him with stories about Wild
Bill which he translated into deeds about Cody. In revenge for
Hickok's dismissal, Ned killed him off.[5]

Robbins, who perhaps knew more about the Hickok-Cody-

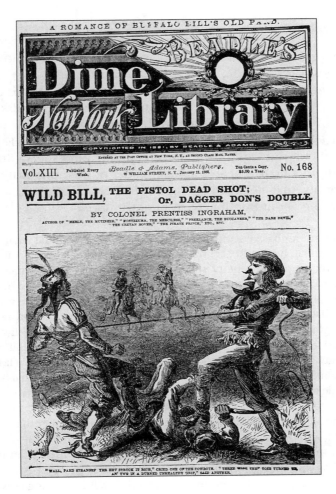

BEADLE'S
Dime
New York Library

COPYRIGHTED IN 1881, BY BEADLE & ADAMS.

ENTERED AT THE POST OFFICE AT NEW YORK, N.Y., AT SECOND CLASS MAIL RATES.

Vol. XIII. Published Every Week. *Beadle & Adams, Publishers,* 98 WILLIAM STREET, N.Y., January 11, 1882. Ten Cents a Copy. $5.00 a Year. No. 168

WILD BILL, THE PISTOL DEAD SHOT;
Or, DAGGER DON'S DOUBLE.

BY COLONEL PRENTISS INGRAHAM,

AUTHOR OF "MERLE, THE MUTINEER," "MONTEZUMA, THE MERCILESS," "FREELANCE, THE BUCCANEER," "THE DARE DEVIL,"
"THE CRETAN ROVER," "THE PIRATE PRINCE," ETC., ETC.

"WALL, PARD STRANGER THE HEV STRUCK IT RICH," CRIED ONE OF THE COWBOYS. "THERE WERE THE TOES TURNED UP, AN' TWO IN A DURNED UNHEALTHY GRIP," SAID ANOTHER.

Col. Prentiss Ingraham found Wild Bill a favorite subject for his dime novel romances. (Author's collection)

Buntline connection than most, probably had good reason for such a yarn. In truth, though, there is no evidence that Buntline ever met Hickok. Buffalo Bill first met Buntline at Fort McPherson in July 1869 (Hickok was in Hays City at the time). Ned was supplementing his earnings by a series of temperance lectures (an ironic subject, since his drinking habits were notorious). After Fort McPherson he was due to appear at Fort Sedgwick. After a word in the post commander's ear, he was allowed to accompany a detachment of the Fifth Cavalry en route to the fort. He soon latched onto

Cody and questioned him about his own and others' exploits. The result was *Buffalo Bill, The King of the Border Men.*[6]

Buntline's apparent love-hate relationship with Hickok manifested itself again in 1880. His yarn "On the Death-Trail; or, The Last of Wild Bill," published in the *New York Weekly,* incensed the Hickok family. Writing from Troy Grove, Illinois, on February 24, 1880, Horace Hickok informed the publishers (Street & Smith) that he had been a regular reader of their publications for years but that he was "taking the liberty" on this occasion to complain about Buntline's latest contribution:

> The author basely slanders the dead, and says of Wild Bill what, I do not think, he would dare publish if Wild Bill were living: and all, as I think, to gratify a petty spite. He says Wild Bill had separated or parted from his wife. That was not true. They were on the best of terms, and she intended to join Bill in the Hills as soon as he was established there. He (Ned) also makes Bill say that he once had a sister disgraced, or words to that effect, and that she was dead. Bill never said it. Furthermore, Buntline seems to be trying to make Bill out a regular desperado, with all that that word implies, and (in that last instalment of the story that I have read) a cowardly one at that—I allude to the fainting scene and the attack made upon a woman.
>
> Now, I have just this to say: Wild Bill was my youngest brother, and I have two older brothers, and two sisters, younger than Wild Bill, and they are now living, and they comprise the whole family, six in all. My mother died two years ago, and there are hundreds of people living here that have known James, or Wild Bill, from his boyhood, and when any one says that Wild Bill was a coward, or that he ever once in his life picked a quarrel with anyone, is either mistaken, or wilfully says that which is not true. . . . As an officer he did his duty, no matter what the odds against him were. He had a pleasant, good disposition; was slow to anger, but when aroused and obliged to fight he fought to the death. Bill Cody (Buffalo Bill) and James Hickok (Wild Bill) were friends, and Cody knows what I say is true; and I know, and Ned Buntline knows, he has not written the truth of my brother. I do not expect a work of fiction to be true in every respect, but it ought to have a faint resemblance to it, and not to be slanderous.

In a postscript, Horace noted that had he had Buntline's address he would have written to him directly, adding: "You can do what you please with this, but I would like to have Ned see it at least." To their credit, the publishers printed Horace's letter; Buntline's reaction is not known. On March 23, 1880, writing from the Metropolitan Hotel in Boston, Cody was quick to assure Horace of his own reaction:

My dear Sir,

Seeing your letter to Messrs Street & Smith regarding your brother and my friend, I write to say that I am glad indeed that you have written correcting the statements which have gone before the public through the story of Ned Buntline, an author so well informed generally that it is a surprise to me he should make such mistakes of the character of Wild Bill, and which I intend to refute in a serial for the *Saturday Star Journal,* and of which romance I intend making your brother the hero.

My long and intimate association with Wild Bill will enable me to found my story on solid facts, and correcting errors regarding his life and character, is a pleasure to me, as well as a duty I owe to his memory, for he was ever in good or evil times a tried and true friend of mine.

With kind wishes

Sincerely Yrs.
[Signed] W. F. Cody
"Buffalo Bill"[7]

Despite his assurances to the contrary, Cody made little or no attempt either then or in later years to correct some of the lies that Buntline and others continued to promote concerning his "true friend." Buntline himself died in 1886, and Cody was powerless to prevent reprints of some of the more lurid tales, among them the notorious *Wild Bill's Last Trail* that had so upset Horace, which was republished in 1896 as number 191 in the Diamond Dick Library. Horace's anger was understandable. Buntline described Hickok as a death-dealing desperado who had "killed at least one man for every year of his life." When it finally came time for him to die at McCall's hand, Buntline had Wild Bill gasp, "Jack McCall, I'm thankful to you, even though you've killed me. Wild Bill does not die by the hand of a *woman.*" The

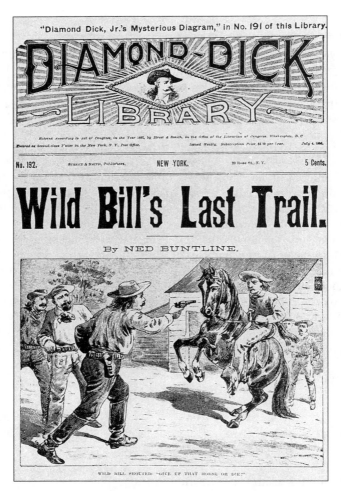

DIAMOND-DICK LIBRARY

Entered According to Act of Congress, in the Year 1897, by Street & Smith, in the Office of the Librarian of Congress, Washington, D. C.

Entered as Second-class Matter in the New York, N. Y., Post Office.   Issued Weekly.   Subscription Price, $2.50 per Year.   July 4, 1896.

No. 192.   Street & Smith, Publishers,   NEW YORK.   29 Rose St., N. Y.   5 Cents.

Wild Bill's Last Trail.

By NED BUNTLINE.

WILD BILL SHOUTED "GIVE UP THAT HORSE OR DIE!"

Ned Buntline upset the Hickok family with Wild Bill's Last Trail, *which led to a spirited attack from Horace Hickok. (Author's collection)*

lady in question, however, was furious with Jack, calling him a "villain" for spoiling her revenge. Buntline, it will be noted, had ignored the fact that he had already disposed of Wild Bill at the hands of a woman twenty years before.

Prentiss Ingraham's approach to Hickok was to intersperse fact with fiction and thereby create a believable character. For his best-known story, *Wild Bill, the Pistol Prince,* published in Beadle's Pocket Library on May 13, 1891, he evidently engaged in

Copyrighted, 1891, by BEADLE AND ADAMS. Entered as Second Class Matter at the New York, N. Y., Post Office. May 12, 1891.

No. 383. $2.50 a Year. Published Weekly by Beadle and Adams, No. 98 WILLIAM ST. NEW YORK. Price Five Cents. VOL. XXX.

WILD BILL, the Pistol Prince.

BY COLONEL PRENTISS INGRAHAM.

BOLDLY HE RAN AFTER THE BRUTE, CAME WITHIN PISTOL RANGE, AND, CONFIDENT IN HIS UNERRING AIM, FIRED.

It is probable that Hickok's post-1900 title "Prince of Pistoleers" was based on the title of perhaps Ingraham's most famous Wild Bill story. (Author's collection)

some research, for he tried to present the relationship between Wild Bill and Agnes Lake in a factual manner. Of additional interest is his assessment of Hickok's show career.

Wild Bill's dime novel adventures were not limited to the United States, for by the turn of the century he had appeared in several European publications. The British market was led in the early years of this century by the Aldine Publishing Company, which put out what it claimed was the "Original Buffalo Bill Library." As late as the 1940s copies of these stories were still being published in England. Hickok, however, rarely appeared as the lead character, since the series was, after all, devoted to Buffalo Bill. As early as 1895, however, the Budget Story Books published by James Henderson, London, devoted number 220 to Wild Bill. Texas Jack was the hero of number 216, while Buffalo Bill appeared in several yarns. (Sadly, despite some intensive research in various libraries, including the British Museum, I have not been able to find a copy of the Wild Bill volume.)

Hickok's career as both a dime novel hero and as a real live hero in Buffalo Bill's Combination was limited. But of the two, the theatrical exposure was the most potent. Here one finds evidence of his nationwide reputation, and even before he appeared on stage himself, the character of "Wild Bill" had been portrayed in a Western drama; Cody had led the way.

Buffalo Bill paid his first visit to New York in 1872, where he was the guest of a number of prominent individuals. There he again met Buntline, who persuaded him to visit the Bowery Theater where Fred G. Maeder's melodrama based on *Buffalo Bill, The King of the Border Men* attracted large audiences. As "Buffalo Bill," the actor J. B. Studley was impressive. But once it was learned that the "original" was in the house, his presence was soon requested on stage, and a bemused and shy Cody was persuaded to take a bow before making a hasty retreat. Offers of $500 a week to play himself failed to persuade the scout to quit the West and venture on stage.

On his return to Nebraska, Buffalo Bill was involved in a skirmish with Indians and so distinguished himself that on May 22, 1872, he was awarded the Congressional Medal of Honor. Later, he ventured into politics, but failed to claim his seat. He next spent a short period as a justice of the peace before he and Texas Jack Omohundro finally decided to take a chance and join Buntline's show. They were paid off as scouts on November 30, and by December 12 the pair were in Chicago. From then until June 1873, when the season ended at Port Jervis, New York, Cody and Texas Jack reaped the benefits of dubious fame as members of Buntline's theatrical combination. Once the season ended, however, they split with Buntline over money, claiming that he had not been fair with them. Cody was all for returning to the West, but Omohundro persuaded him that they could carry on on their own.[8]

Following a brief return West to visit his family and engage in some hunting expeditions, Cody announced in the Omaha *Daily Bee* of July 28 that his new play would be *Buffalo Bill and Alexis on the Plains,* to be based upon his own role as scout for the expedition organized early in 1872 by General Sheridan to entertain Grand Duke Alexis, third son of Czar Alexander I. Following the Alexis play, Cody proposed to tour Europe, "accompanied by James B. Hickok, the original 'Wild Bill.' " Neither the Alexis play nor the European tour took place; but Cody was able to persuade Wild Bill to join his Combination.[9]

Hickok was living at Springfield, Missouri, where he had been since the early fall of 1872. His income was derived from gambling, a hazardous occupation at best—especially with city ordinances against it. So Cody's offer of "a large salary if he would play with us that winter" was tempting. Cody noted in his 1879 autobiography that Hickok was "doing nothing at the time, and we thought that he would like to take a trip through the States, as he had never been East." This was not quite correct, for only the previous year Wild Bill had appeared at Niagara Falls in a "Grand Buffalo Hunt" organized by Col. Sidney Barnett. It was not a financial success, but Wild Bill's presence as Master of Ceremonies attracted the public. The exposure he would receive, and Cody's offer of a "large salary," doubtless influenced Hickok's decision join him.[10]

Cody recalled that Hickok arrived in New York with a flourish: he beat up a cab driver who tried to cheat him and told Cody that he would never make an actor. Buffalo Bill assured him that the important thing was to impress the public and persuade them to buy tickets. On August 25, Cody was playing himself at the Bowery Theater while Texas Jack was in Rochester, New York, preparing for his wedding to Guiseppina Morlacchi on August 31. Hickok probably arrived very late in the month and spent some days being tutored in the fine art of acting. Cody realized he would have problems, because although Hickok "had a fine stage appearance and was a handsome fellow, and possessed a good strong voice, yet when he went upon the stage before an audience, it was almost impossible for him to utter a word. He in-

Advertisement for Wild Bill's first appearance before the public, as the master of ceremonies in Sidney Barnett's "Grand Buffalo Hunt" at Niagara Falls in 1872. (Author's collection) sisted that we were making a set of fools of ourselves, and that we were the laughing-stock of the people." Cody, however, was not discouraged. As a preliminary introduction, according to the *New York Clipper* of September 15, 1873, Hickok walked on stage one night and "gave an exhibition of rapid pistol-shooting and fancy shots." Its impact must have been impressive, for Hickok's nationwide reputation had been built up around his ability with pistols and the number of "bad men" he was credited with putting away in the interest of law and order. Consequently, the sight of Wild Bill suddenly drawing a pair of Colt's Navy revolvers and opening fire "Gatling gun fashion" (despite the cloud of powder smoke engulfing the first three rows) must have thrilled an already captivated audience. Texas Jack's appearance a day later exhibiting his roping skills seems tame by comparison.[11]

Wild Bill's name and reputation were well known to the public, thanks to *Harper's* and his appearance in two dime novels and newspaper exposure. Indeed, as early as 1872, one J. T. Vegiard had copyrighted *Wild Bill, or The Scout of the West*. He was followed by Hiram Robbins, who wrote and copyrighted a five-act drama entitled *Wild Bill, or Life on the Border* in 1873. Copies of the manuscripts of either play are unknown today. Robbins knew a great deal about Cody, and following Robbins's death on January 21, 1899, it was reported that his

"Scouts of the Border" and "Life on the Plains" were peculiarly successful. W. F. Cody, familiarly known as "Buffalo Bill," appreciated their money-making possibilities and put them on the road. For a year or more Robbins traveled with Cody and assisted in the production of his plays, which scored a financial triumph. It may be said by way of parenthesis that these two plays are still money-makers in Europe, although credited to another man. While with Cody, Robbins became intimate with many border celebrities, among whom were 'Texas Jack,' 'Wild Bill' Hickok and Jack Crawford.[12]

Hickok's intention of joining the Combination had been announced by the *New York Clipper* on August 16, which also noted that "his duties on the plains will only permit him to travel during one season." We suspect this meant that his contract with

Cody was based upon a mutual agreement: if things did not work out, he would be free to return West.

According to the New Brunswick, New Jersey, *Times* of September 9, Cody's new Combination made its first appearance at Green's Hall on the evening of the eighth, where it was described as a great success. Although Hickok's name appeared on the program, no mention was made of him in the review. The Combination then moved on to West Chester, Pennsylvania, where Cody had installed his family. After that, the troupe set course for Columbus, Ohio, where it appeared on September 15 before beginning a tour of several Eastern states. Newspaper reactions to the troupe were mixed, but most of them agreed that it was not the performers' acting abilities that made the show work, but the spectacle of continuous action and the presence of the "real heroes."[13]

Buntline had realized his error in allowing Cody to venture out on his own. The *New York Clipper* on August 16 had also carried an advertisement for Buntline's "Scouts of the West," featuring one "Dashing Charley," and "Arizona Frank." It transpired that "Dashing Charley" was Charles E. Emmet, known "on the plains as Dashing Charley the Scout." The cast was reported to include a troupe of "Wild Comanche and Kiowa Indians." The fact that neither Buntline nor Cody used real Indians in their troupes did not deter their audiences. They were there to see "blood and thunder" heroics. By October, however, Buntline's venture was in a shambles. His constant drinking and public rows (on one occasion he had appeared in public armed with a brace of pistols and had insulted a man, who then came close to shooting him) finally led to the closure of the show. In order to retrieve their trunks from a hotel, the cast put on a special farewell performance before departing for New York. The *New York Clipper* on November 1 noted that "Indians" formerly employed by Buntline were now members of Cody's Combination. Ironically, Cody's troupe and Buntline's missed each other by one week in Indianapolis, so a possible confrontation between Wild Bill and Buntline was avoided.[14] At Jamestown, New York, on November 7, the *Daily Journal* did not appear impressed by the Combination, urging that "those in need of a jolly laugh had better attend."

One of the few surviving cheaply printed programs handed out at each performance of "Scouts of the Plains." (Courtesy the late Ethel Hickok)

Buffalo Bill, whose ego fed upon the adulation of his fans, was probably irked at times by the attention paid to Wild Bill by the press. On October 11 the Titusville, Pennsylvania, *Herald* remarked that "the great plainsman, humble scout, and law-preserver, Wild Bill, created a decided sensation in the drama, and gave a realistic rendition of scenes in the Western wilds." Another reviewer described Hickok as "one of the greatest scouts of modern times," while the Meadville, Pennsylvania, *Evening Republican* of November 4 said that the drama "had been especially adapted to him." Custer's description of Hickok in *Galaxy* for April 1872 (which he later included in his book *My Life on the Plains*) was widely quoted and also appeared on some of the programs issued to audiences. But the critics also noticed that despite his stage presence, Wild Bill was no actor. He was probably grateful when at Easton, Pennsylvania, according to the *Daily Express* of December 16, he "was suffering last evening, with so severe a cold, that most of his lines were necessarily omitted." The Troy, New York, *Times* on February 25, 1874, however, declared that Wild Bill was "said to be the only member of the combination who is a real Indian fighter," which must have further annoyed Buffalo Bill.

Cody's later comment that Hickok had been a "difficult man to deal with" was hinted at in an amusing story published by the Longview, Texas, *Democrat* of September 28, 1881:

> Wild Bill, it was noted, was one of the "genuine Indian scouts" of General Custer. Some years ago he had shot a desperado in Missouri following "particular aggravation." Years afterward, Bill became a member of Buffalo Bill's droll theatrical company, and, in compliance with the story of the play, had to repeat every night upon the stage the killing which, as a reality had made him famous. Bill watched the first rehearsal patiently, then he went to the stage manager. "I can't kill that chap, no how," quote Bill. "Why not?" inquired the manager. "Well," said Bill, tranquilly, "Buffalo slings him around in the first act, and Maeder clips him in the ear in the second act, and Mrs. Maeder drives him out of the ranch with a broom in the third act. Then I've got to kill him after all in the fourth act. Why, I never killed such a coyote as that in my life! It's all wrong, pardner! It's all wrong making him out such a

"The Scouts of the Plains," ca. 1874. Left to right: Elisha Green, Wild Bill, Buffalo Bill Cody, Texas Jack Omohundro, and Eugene Overton. (Courtesy Buffalo Bill Historical Center)

squaw-man as all that. By golly, sir, he was the biggest gentleman, I ever shot!

The *Chicago Inter Ocean Magazine* of October 15, 1911, cited Buffalo Bill's recollection of further problems with Hickok:

> "Wild Bill was a bad actor most anywhere, but he was an especially bad actor on the stage. Jack Omohundro, known as Texas Jack, was with the show, and when the curtain fell at the close of the first act he and I and Wild Bill were supposed to stand out near the front of the stage clasping rescued maidens to our breasts in the white glare of the calcium. But Wild Bill was never out there where he belonged. He invariably hung back in the shadows at the rear or remained half-hidden behind a painted tree or rock. He was a poor hand to pose or show off and hated to have a lot of people staring at him. One night when the spot light found him leaning against a gnarled oak in the background, it made him mad, and he took a shot at the spot light machine in the central aisle of the balcony, shattered the bull's eye and broke the machine. The show had to go on to the end without the usual calcium effects.
>
> If Wild Bill was not a star on the stage, he was a sensation off it.

Crowds followed him about everywhere. I didn't wonder at it, for aside from his picturesque Western garb, he was one of the handsomest men I ever knew.

During his tour as a member of Cody's Combination Hickok became aware, perhaps for the first time, that he was a living legend. That he did not care for such a status seems obvious, for at the first opportunity he returned to the West. The Springfield, Massachusetts, *Republican* on February 21, 1874, was particularly impressed by Hickok's record as a cool and desperate "spy during the rebellion." Also his service as "United States marshal for the state of Kansas," where his name was a "terror to evil-doers" was something to be reckoned with.

Hickok's appearance with Cody was fraught with problems. Buffalo Bill later recalled that his constant pranks (that amused and irritated Cody at the same time) were annoying. Wild Bill delighted in shooting his pistols close to the legs of the "supers" dressed up as Indians. This made them jump about and howl instead of dropping dead on cue like a "good Injun" of the period should. But the truth was that Hickok, already painfully aware that he was no actor, also disliked living out of a suitcase, and public attention bored and annoyed him. About 1900, Capt. Jack Crawford, writing in the New York *Journalist,* stated what many believed to be true: "He hated hypocrisy and fraud and that was why he said he would rather go back to the West and get killed than accept $500 per week and play in a dime novel melodrama which was a libel on the West and destined only to ruin credulous boys." Despite his own venture into the limelight, Crawford himself expressed this view on many occasions, and it formed the basis for many of his lectures. Cody reacted to an audience—it was food and drink to him—but Hickok did not share that view.

Things finally came to a head at Rochester, New York, on March 12, 1874. Hickok quit the Combination despite pleas from Cody and Omohundro to stay. As parting gifts the two men each gave him $500, and they also presented him with a pair of .44-caliber Smith & Wesson "American" revolvers. The Rochester *Democrat and Chronicle* reported on March 14 that Hickok had received a call to return to the frontier where the Sioux were

Wild Bill photographed with Eugene Overton. From a plate made by Gurney & Son, New York, ca. 1874. (Courtesy Buffalo Bill Historical Center)

The most familiar of several portraits of Wild Bill made during his time with Cody's Combination, ca. 1873–1874. (Author's collection)

preparing to go on the warpath. The reporter probably summed up Hickok's true vocation when he described him as a "child of nature," hinting that he really did belong to the wide open spaces, one jump ahead of civilization. If the real Wild Bill was no longer around to play himself, then there were others anxious to do so. It was reported that Hickok discovered one such characterization, broke up the performance, and threw the luckless actor off the stage—for which Hickok was arrested and fined. By

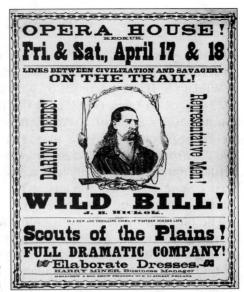

By the time this poster appeared in April 1874, Wild Bill had quit Cody's Combination and returned west. (Author's collection)

1875, however, the character of "Wild Bill" was established on stage. He was portrayed by Julian Kent that year in a play ironically titled *Wild Bill, King of the Border Men,* a role he apparently played at least until April 1881.[15]

In spite of his assurances to the Hickok family that Wild Bill was his "true friend," Cody thought fit to include him among others he regarded as disloyal. In a letter to Sam Hall, seeking to discourage him from obtaining employment on stage, he wrote:

> I would never again have another Scout or western man with me. That is one whom I would work up. For just as soon as they see their names in print a few times they git the big head and want to start a company of their own. I will name a few. Wild Bill[,] Texas Jack[,] John Nelson[,] Oregon Bill[,] Kit Carson[,] Capt. Jack[,] all busted flat before they were out a month and wanted to come back. Because I would not take them then they talked about me.[16]

By the early 1900s, motion pictures were beginning to make an impression on the public. One of the earliest pictures to tell a story was a Western *The Great Train Robbery,* filmed in the wilds of New Jersey in 1903. It hinted at things to come. The movie Western was a natural successor to the earlier dime novels and stage melodramas. Buffalo Bill Cody, then in his early sixties, appeared in several, including *The Indian Wars,* a historic depiction of the West. (Sadly, it is no longer available in its entirety.) He must have wished the medium had existed thirty years earlier.

William S. Hart's portrayal of Wild Bill in *Wild Bill Hickok* in 1923 has often been considered the first. However, in 1988 an antique dealer in South Dakota offered for sale an early seven-reel silent film made in 1915 titled *In the Days of '75 and '76, or The Thrilling Lives of Wild Bill and Calamity Jane.* The film was virtually unknown, but diligent research by the staff of the Nebraska State Historical Society, which purchased the film, revealed an interesting if bizarre story.

The film was made on location in Nebraska and South Dakota by residents of the frontier town of Chadron, Nebraska. The script was written by Mary Hartzell, who played Calamity Jane's mother in the film. Her own daughter Freeda played Jane, partly because it was very much a family project and partly because Freeda was a good horsewoman and a good shot. Local business-man A. L. Johnson, a very large, broad-shouldered individual who bore a slight resemblance to Wild Bill, played the lead. In many respects the production was a first in that it used tech-niques that were copied and bettered by others. In an effort to be authentic, the film's director recruited the troops at nearby Fort Robinson (dressed in their khaki uniforms of the period). They participated with the approval of Col. H. H. Sickel—he and his Twelfth Cavalrymen had also been involved in Buffalo Bill's 1913 epic, *The Indian Wars.*

The story itself had no basis in fact. Rather, it perpetuated al-ready established myths. Its most important contribution to the Hickok story is the fact that in the plot Hickok and Jane were married, and that it was her desire for revenge that saw Jack Mc-Call, Wild Bill's murderer, hanged at Yankton. As the title sug-gests, the film takes place over two years and gives the impres-sion that it was two years after Hickok's assassination that McCall was brought to justice. Nevertheless, the film is an important contribution to the Hickok myth.[17]

William S. Hart's version of the Hickok story was predictable. Hart, a former Shakespearian actor well known on Broadway, had made the transition from stage to screen and established himself as one of the earliest cowboy stars. His Hickok portrayal was well received by an adoring public, but not all critics were impressed, particularly those who were aware that Hart himself wrote the screenplay. His interpretation of Hickok's life amused and irritated the Hickok family. Wyatt Earp's sister, Adelia Earp Edwards, recalled in 1934 that Hickok was a nationwide hero when she was a child. She was in Dodge City when news of his death reached the Earps. "They [the Earps] all admired him," she said, and Luke Short and the Mastersons shared that view. Wyatt remarked that he never knew Hickok personally but saw him once at Abilene. When Hart's movie came out, the whole family went to see it.[18]

Other viewers found the film thrilling but far-fetched. Carl Sandburg, at that time the film columnist for the Chicago *Daily News,* took the opportunity to review both the actor and his subject:

> There was a time when Bill Hart wore Lincoln green tights and was the wrestling hero in a music-haunted drama of William Shakespeare's known as "As You Like It." That was years ago on Broadway. Since then Bill Hart has been up, and Bill Hart has been down—up as a two-gun westerner in the movies, living the life as he said, "of the old west as I knew it," and down on account of real life blackmailers and hysterical rattlebrains. Now he is back as the two-gun Westerner reliving the hero days of the old west as he knew it. . . . This lapse may account for the sometimes rusty story Bill Hart has written. This lapse has not hurt Bill Hart's particular brand of acting.
>
> He is "Wild Bill Hickok" at McVickers this week, and thousands of little boys are there wishing that they were him; thousands of men are there feeling the call of the ranges stir in them, and thousands of women are there wishing now and then that William wouldn't make up so that he looks so much like his horse in the face.
>
> "Wild Bill Hickok" was a real character in the west. He killed and loved and did things of great bravery. He was rough and adventurous. If he lived today, he would probably be a beer-runner on the Lemond road, and be called "Wild Bill Hick-Up," but the West was the West, and there is downright thrill in "Wild Bill" as Bill Hart plays him.
>
> It may be far fetched to send your horse for help while you stand off stage coach robbers for hours, with two guns, but it is

entertaining as the old dime novel Buffalo Bill stories were behind the barn years ago.[19]

In 1924 the character of Hickok was introduced into *The Iron Horse*, and he was also featured in *The Last Frontier.* Like Hart's version, the subsequent portrayals of Hickok paid little attention to historical fact. The name alone attracted audiences and writers of screenplays. By the early 1930s Hickok had been featured in a number of films, but in 1936, the announcement that Cecil B. DeMille was to make a movie based upon his life aroused considerable interest. His sources for the story, however, did not inspire confidence. Frank J. Wilstach's 1926 book and some additional material from Courtney Riley Cooper were chosen as "factual" backgrounds. The late Jean MacPherson, who had researched and gathered material for the screenplay, soon discovered that the real Hickok was as controversial as the film's sources. She also pointed out to DeMille that his intention to claim that Calamity Jane was Hickok's sweetheart would provoke a storm of protest. Once a hint got into the press that Jane was to be featured, the response from Hickok's family in Troy Grove was predictable. Howard L. Hickok recalled his own anger at the suggestion:

> William S. Hart's portrayal of J. B. Hickok; DeMille's Plainsman both brought my pressure to the boiling point. Imagine how our family felt, the uncle whose memory we loved and revered, portrayed on the nation's screen as the lover of Calamity Jane; married to a grand good woman, our aunt Agnes [Lake]. . . . and mixed up with Calamity (whose shortcomings had been known to us for years) a few short months later. Letters to Hart, to DeMille; the response: the public demands pictures like theirs they said. I say character assassins; money hungry men.

Howard was angered further by a telegram from DeMille that advised him that it was too late to remove Calamity Jane from the script because the program was already prepared for a Lux Radio broadcast.[20]

J. B. Edwards of Abilene, who had known Wild Bill intimately, was also disturbed by the proposed characterization. He sent DeMille a copy of his own prized photograph of Wild Bill and some suggestions concerning how he should be portrayed. Jean Mac-

Pherson, later discussed the furor with the late Col. Paul King, and told him that as a result of the uproar, DeMille toyed with several plot changes and endings to the film. The Hickok family's resistance to Calamity Jane ruled out an envisaged marriage, as well as the suggestion that Hickok, Cody, and Jane should ride off into the sunset together. Eventually, as a compromise, the film portrayed the relationship between the pair as one of love-hate, with Jane planting a final kiss on Wild Bill's lips as he lay dead in Saloon No. 10. It was left to the 1953 movie *Calamity Jane* starring Doris Day as Calamity Jane and Howard Keel as Hickok to distort history still further and marry the pair off—again much to the anger and despair of the Hickok family.[21]

As history, *The Plainsman* was a failure. As a Hollywood spectacle, *The Plainsman* was a great success, even though DeMille directed most of the outdoor scenes, with the aid of a landscape model, via telephone from his Hollywood office. Gary Cooper's performance was both convincing and sensitive. More important, perhaps, was the impact the film made upon other studios. Columbia Pictures followed it up in 1938 with *The Great Adventures of Wild Bill Hickok,* whose star, Gordon Elliott, then continued to play the part in other epics. Eventually he was billed as "Wild Bill Elliott."

In 1941, Bruce Cabot starred in *Wild Bill Hickok Rides,* memorable for a brief scene at the beginning when Wild Bill foiled a train robbery by hiding his pistol inside a doll's dress and then shooting one of the robbers as he grabbed for the doll. That same year Richard Dix, one of the film colony's more distinguished actors, portrayed Hickok in *Badlands of Dakota.* Unlike anyone else who has played the part, Dix bore a likeness to Hickok. But by 1952, when Gary Cooper had the unusual experience of being "shot" by Hickok (played by Reed Hadley) in *Dallas,* the character of Wild Bill had ceased to attract "epic" attention. In fact, a turning point in the character's fortunes came in 1953 when Columbia Pictures put out *Jack McCall Desperado.* In this film George Montgomery played a heroic Jack pitted against a villainous Hickok (Douglas Kennedy) who was shot between the eyes by McCall in the final reel. This travesty of fact led to a spate of magazine articles written by so-called experts who condemned the real Hickok. Hickok's screen appearances since then have been few and far between.

If Howard Keel as Wild Bill in *Calamity Jane* seems out of place, and the antics of Douglas Kennedy in *Jack McCall Desperado* equally absurd, then consider the bizarre appearance of Charles Bronson as Hickok in *The White Buffalo* in 1976. Mr. Bronson was quite diminutive in comparison with the giant figure of Clint Walker, who played the "heavy." He competed with Bronson and an out-of-place Crazy Horse, who had joined Hickok in a hunt for the white buffalo. For Crazy Horse, its robe would be a burial blanket for his daughter, and for Hickok a rare prize. Due to the height disparity between the actors, most of their close-encounter scenes were shot with Bronson seated and Walker standing. The story, inspired in part by Mari Sandoz's book, *The Buffalo Hunters,* was ridiculous. But one writer accepted verbatim Mari Sandoz's version of Hickok and declared that Bronson portrayed Hickok "pretty much as he must have been, which is to say a haunted, nearly psychotic killer."[22]

An equally preposterous and macabre scenario was presented in Thomas Babe's play *Fathers and Sons.* The plot centers around the appearance in Deadwood of Hickok's son, the result of his love affair with Susannah Moore. The son is Jack McCall, determined to avenge his mother, whom Wild Bill had treated badly. Produced in the early 1970s by the New York Shakespeare Festival, the play starred Richard Chamberlain. Historically, the play is worthless, but it indicates that Hickok continues to fascinate audiences and motivate sometimes weird interpretations of his character.

By the 1990s, however, Hollywood historians had rethought Hickok, and he has again emerged in a heroic light. The first of the crop was *Wild Bill,* directed by Walter Hill and featuring Jeff Bridges as Hickok. (His father, Lloyd Bridges, played Hickok in a television film in the late 1960s.) Hill's script was based upon hearsay and fiction, the main source being the novel *Deadwood* by Pete Dexter, who also wrote the original screenplay. The story also includes material from Babe's play "Fathers and Sons." Hill said: "I took Dexter's script and put it into my Wild Bill script, and it fit nicely. But the core material is really the play." Predictably, Calamity Jane is also a star player. "We posit an ongoing relationship with Calamity Jane, which is of course part of the legend but under much dispute by most historians of Hickok and the time,"Hill added later. He claimed that the film was concerned with character rather than incident and also revealed why Hickok fascinated him: "It's his personality, his sense of humor about himself. He seemed to understand his own legend. He both fueled it and was a prisoner of it; it was his *raison d'etre,* and at the same time he felt himself very constrained by it." That statement at least suggests that Hill was more concerned with the real Hickok than most of his predecessors.[23]

An enduring facet of the Hickok legend—which filmmakers were quick to take advantage of—is Wild Bill's remarkable horse, Black Nell. In his *Harper's* article, Colonel Nichols described the horse as a gallant mare that saved her stellar boss from certain death and had been prepared to sacrifice her own existence for him. Overnight Hickok joined the ranks of other superheroes who owed their lives to their horses and whose devotion to the animals ensured the adulation of their public. Harrison Ainsworth was well aware of readers' fondness for the hero-and-his-horse scenario when he immortalized Britain's most infamous highwayman, Richard ("Dick") Turpin, and his faithful mare Black Bess (a story that may well have inspired Nichols). She gave her life in a celebrated ride to York in 1739 that presaged some of the celebrated feats credited to Pony Express riders. It was this affinity between man and beast that formed a major part of the cowboy myth. Once Hollywood's "B" Westerns hit their stride, the hero's horse also became a star, and the feats credited to Wild Bill's Black Nell became commonplace. Back in 1867, though, to an audience still unused to such a relationship between man and horse, the effect of the story was electric. But even a cursory examination of some of Hickok's plains exploits revealed that in place of a prancing black mare (or the "one-eyed" stallion that was a "goer" recalled by the press of the time), Hickok made most of his scouting expeditions on the back of a government mule.

In assessing Hickok's role as both a dime novel and movie hero, we must bear in mind that he had initially had a great impact upon the imaginations of the people who read the printed word. But when transferred to moving film, the images were given the life and form of the person playing the part at the time. Gary Cooper is the best remembered Hickok, and Richard Dix the most lifelike; but to this day, no one has produced a film about Wild Bill that even remotely portrays the real character, which is unfortunate. Instead, Hickok continues to be overshadowed by his myth.

Eight

"The Deadman's Hand"

By 1876, James Butler Hickok was facing an uncertain future. The West he had known and loved since childhood was fast disappearing as civilization crept along the expanding railroads. Scouting for the army no longer attracted him; gambling, for so long a passion, was no long-term occupation; and the tragic incident at Abilene in 1871, when he shot Mike Williams by accident, very likely put him off any future peace-keeping role. So the gold strike in the Black Hills following Custer's 1874 expedition must have seemed like a lifeline.

When Hickok left Cody's Combination in March 1874, and eventually found his way to Cheyenne, Wyoming, he probably had no plans for the future. Some reports suggest that he rented a room over a saloon; others suggest that during 1874 and 1875 he lived at 421 West 27th Street, a house that was torn down during the early years of this century. In June 1875, the city fathers deemed him a vagrant and had him arrested and bailed to appear in the November term. Court records disclose a number of continuances, the last one dated June 12, 1876. It was followed by the comment that the defendant was dead and that the case had been dismissed.

A welter of fact and fiction surrounds Wild Bill's so-called vagrant status. The continuances suggest that as long as he kept out of the city, or was at least gainfully employed, the court would not bother him. His friends claimed that there was no real cause for the charge in the first place, whereas others described him as a "worthless bummer." William Francis Hooker even claimed that a printed notice was posted ordering Hickok and other undesirables out of town. Wild Bill calmly destroyed it with his Bowie knife. Hooker's opinion of Wild Bill is interesting:

> If my estimate of Wild Bill Hickok is worth anything, I am willing, in the interest of history and to help straighten out the record, to give it.
>
> It is this. He was a man of nerve, and had, as city marshal of Abilene, kept the town in fairly good order for those times; and in doing it he was obliged to scatter quite a bit of lead among the garroters, then the pest of every camp along the K. P.
>
> Of course, he killed a number of men, and when he blew into Cheyenne on the big stampede to the "Hills," . . . he was just a plain gambler and, I believe, not a very successful one, and with but little money. I doubt if he owned a horse, something nearly every one had in those days (and blankets), although I have a faint recollection of seeing him emerge from Tracey's corral a-straddle a fine-looking sorrel and gallop off toward Fort A. D. Russell. Tracey's Corral and barn were located on the outskirts of Cheyenne on the Loraine Trail, and our camp was on Crow Creek, not far away, in plain sight of Fort Russel[l] and Camp Carlin. For all I know Bill was then headed for Custer.

In 1918, Hooker disclosed his own experience with Hickok: One night in the Gold Room in Cheyenne, Hickok pulled Hooker's chair away from him so Hickok could sit at a table. Infuriated, Hooker grabbed "his gun, got his knife out and picked up a chair. Then he started for Hickok." Terrified, Hickok begged for his life. Hooker never made it plain whether he was gifted with three arms (which might explain Hickok's terror of him) or if the description of his actions was a misprint. By 1936 the story had changed: Hooker left the room without causing any fuss, but soon was back:

> When I showed up an hour or so later with a Winchester [and] twelve of my friends from the [John] Hunton camp were scattered along 16th street, and I guess Bill knew it, for as soon as he saw me approaching, nearly a block away, he threw up both arms; I shifted my rifle to the crook of my left arm and walked fast toward

him, and we shook hands, went into a saloon and had a drink, and
he told me this:

"I'm not afraid of any living thing with two feet or four feet—
EXCEPT a man who is nothing but a boy who is foolish to do
what you have done." And he laughed all the time. So did I, and
my friends in the Hunton outfit were satisfied that I had kept up
the reputation (and pledge) of the Hunton train, which was not to
allow anyone to do dirt to any one of us. We always traveled together whether at Cheyenne, Medicine Bow, Fetterman or (Fort)
Laramie or anywhere else.

If Hickok had made a false move—just a slight one—that
looked as if he intended to bore a hole in me, he would have been
riddled—and he knew it—by my friends, and I wouldn't have had
a chance to shoot, perhaps; so, I admit, what I did do was not
brave or anything like it.

Hooker claimed to have had long chats with Wild Bill, who
fascinated him, though Hooker regarded him as a "really bad
man." He said that Hickok told him many tales of his Kansas
days, but when he "told me about an assault he made on Mor-
man women on the old Salt Lake trail I took a strong dislike to
him."

Nothing has yet come to light to suggest that Hickok ever had
any dealings with the Mormons whatsoever. Hooker, and perhaps others, may have confused Hickok with the notorious William ("Bill") Hickman, who was actively engaged in the Mormon
War of 1857–1858, where he was reported to have murdered a
number of people. In more recent years, he has been called
"Wild Bill" Hickman—a sobriquet invented by the publisher of a
book on the subject.[1]

Hickok's image during his intermittent appearances in Cheyenne, where he was remembered chiefly as a quiet, gentlemanly
fellow who liked to gamble, belies that suggested by Hooker. The
late Russell Thorp told me that he was acquainted with many of
the men who knew Hickok during his stay in Cheyenne. "I am
sure that Hickok was never known as a vagabond and vagrant.
Had he ever been so classed, I surely would have known of it."
Thorp's own father and many of the early shotgun guards on the
Cheyenne and Black Hills Stage and Express line were well acquainted with Wild Bill and respected him. "Bill was always

classed as a law and order man,"concluded Thorp. Nevertheless, it was reported that the city marshal, John N. Slaughter, had ordered Hickok out of the city on several occasions. But Slaughter himself denied this account. In any event, Hickok did disappear from the city for some months before reappearing at St. Louis early in 1876. Some sources suggest that the intervening months had been spent at Kansas City, Missouri, where he underwent treatment by Dr. Joshua Thorne for eye problems. They have been described as both "opthalmia" (induced by exposure to the elements in the hills) and glaucoma (incurable, quickly causing blindness). But the consensus of opinion among present-day experts is that Hickok, like others of the time, may have suffered from trachoma, a painful disease that without treatment led to blindness. This might account for press references to "powerful mineral drugs" used to treat him. Buel noted the eye problems but also suggested that Hickok and several companions had spent time in the Black Hills from about April 1875. There is evidence to suggest that prior to his final trip to Deadwood, Wild Bill did visit the Hills.[2]

Hickok returned to Cheyenne early in 1876. He was on hand when Agnes Lake arrived to stay with Minnie Moyer, her friend from circus days. When Hickok learned of her presence, he hastened to visit her. They were married on March 5 and honeymooned in St. Louis and her home town of Cincinnati, Ohio. Two weeks later, he returned West to Cheyenne to organize a Black Hills expedition. A perusal of the St. Louis press has revealed some interesting comments. A report dispatched to the *Republican* by a correspondent in Cheyenne, published on March 27, noted that Wild Bill was staying at the "Miners' Home," a popular rendezvous spot for all new arrivals preparing to visit the Hills. Hickok had made the place his headquarters. The writer claimed that Hickok was "forty-six years old" and had spent nearly all of his life in the far West. He noted that Hickok was well dressed, but stated, "I think he has a cold, gray eye that, were his passion aroused, might resemble that of the tiger." He added: "He is a trifle pale now, because of a recent illness. He is the observer of all, and believes in the Black Hills, especially the Big Horn country. I had a private conversation with him, and he

Perhaps one of the last photographs of Wild Bill, this tintype (reproduced in reverse to correct the mirror image) is thought to have been made on March 5, 1876, prior to his marriage to Agnes Lake Thatcher at Cheyenne. Standing is S. L. Moyer, one of the witnesses. (Courtesy Wyoming State Archives)

spoke favorably of the prospects in the new El Dorado as soon as the weather permits."

Wild Bill was soon on the move, and on April 21, the St. Louis *Times* noted that he could be found at the Old Pacific Depot where he had "just returned from the Black Hills country, and will cheerfully tell you all about it." By April 29, he had begun organizing his own expedition to the Hills. He dispatched letters to the Cheyenne press announcing his intentions, intimating that every man should have "one good rifle each, and 200 rounds of ammunition, one tent for two, four or seven men; camp supplies; one rubber blanket, two woolen blankets, and four to six months' provisions." Problems with the route and competitors, notably "Idaho Bill" and C. C. Carpenter, engaged in similar pursuits, eventually led to a consolidation of the two outfits.[3] Hickok advised his wife that he had put off his own plans until June. During that month he was back in Cheyenne, where he teamed up with Colorado Charlie Utter. Utter was keen to oversee his recently established Black Hills transportation line, and together they organized a group bound for the Black Hills. About June 27 the Hickok-Utter party left for Deadwood and arrived about July 12. The only extant letter written by Hickok from Deadwood suggests that he was busily engaged in prospecting and had hopes for the future:

Dead Wood Black Hills, Dacota July, 17th 1876

My own darling wife Agnes. I have but a few moments left before this letter Starts I never was as well in my life but you would laughf to see me now Just got in from Prospecting will go a way again to morrow will write In the morning but god nowse when It will start my friend will take this to Cheyenne if he lives I dont expect to hear from you but it is all the same I no my Agnes and only live to love hur never mind Pet we will have a home yet then we will be so happy I am all most shure I will do well hear the man is huring me Good by Dear wife love to Emma

J B Hickok
Wild Bill[4]

During his short period in Deadwood, Wild Bill was reportedly "trying the best he knew how to be respectable. He shunned all disturbance, and took every means in his power to lead a quiet and inoffensive life."[5] Nevertheless, his presence in the place aroused considerable interest, even though most people were more concerned with gold than reputations. But during much of the time he was in Deadwood, Hickok was left alone to prospect (as he claimed) or play poker (as others asserted). In any event, Wild Bill kept out of trouble until the eve-

ning of August 1, when he played cards with John ("Jack") Mc-
Call. McCall lost and Hickok gave him money for his breakfast,
advising him not to play unless he could cover his losses.[6]

On the afternoon of Wednesday, August 2, 1876, as he sat
playing poker with friends in Nuttall & Mann's No. 10 saloon,
Wild Bill was shot through the back of the head by McCall. He
died instantly. McCall, once he realized that Hickok was dead,
tried to escape, snapping his pistol at anyone who came near
him. It failed to go off.[7] He tried to mount a horse, but the saddle
turned over (its owner had eased off the cinch straps because of
the heat). He then ran into a butcher's shop, where he was arrested at the point of a Sharps' rifle and placed under heavy
guard to await trial.

Hickok's assassination inspired many tall yarns. Some claimed
that the very moment McCall fired his fatal shot, Hickok's re-
flexes were still so good that he pulled both pistols before slump-
ing sideways to the floor. Those who witnessed his death swiftly
discredited those stories. The truth was that Hickok was taken
completely unaware. The ball struck him just behind his right ear
at the "base of the brain, a little to the right of center, passing
through in a straight line, making its exit through the right cheek
between the upper and lower jaw bones, loosening several of the
molar teeth in its passage, and carrying a portion of the cerebel-
lum through the wound. From the nature of the wound death
must necessarily have been instantaneous." Hickok's head jerked
forward, and for some moments he sat perfectly still. His body
then slumped sideways and fell from the stool to the floor, his
poker hand spilling from his fingers, still crimped from holding
his cards. Ellis T. ("Doc") Peirce recalled that when Hickok was
"shot through the head he bled out quickly, and when he was
laid out he looked like a wax figure. I have seen many dead men
on the field of battle and in civil life, but Wild Bill was the pret-
tiest corpse I have ever seen. His long moustache was attractive,
even in death, and his long tapering fingers looked like marble."[8]

A split second after it killed Wild Bill, the bullet then embed-
ded itself in the wrist of one of the other poker players, Capt.
William R. Massie. Massie was a former Mississippi and Missouri
riverboat pilot. His first reaction was to think that Hickok had
shot at him because he had just "beaten him on his hand." But

when he looked up, he saw Hickok slump sideways and the pistol in McCall's fist. He realized the truth. Accounts differ concerning Massie's wound. Some say that a doctor removed the bullet and Massie carried it around for years; others claim it remained in his wrist until his death. On July 30, 1885, the Cheyenne *Democratic Leader* reported:

The Ball That Killed Wild Bill

The Bismarck *Tribune* says: The ball that killed Wild Bill arrived in the city yesterday. It is in the wrist of Bill Massey, an old time steamboat pilot, who arrived from below yesterday. Massey is well known to all Bismarckers, and those who have read the history of Wild Bill are familiar with his name. He was playing cards with him in Deadwood when the latter was shot; the ball passed through Wild Bill's head, lodging in Massey's wrist where it now remains.[9]

Another widely believed and much publicized story asserts that Hickok never sat in on a game of cards unless his back was to a wall. In its later account of the shooting, the Deadwood *Black Hills Pioneer* on August 10 remarked: "For some unexplained reason, he was not sitting with his back to a wall. This has been his rule for many years, since his career of law enforcement had developed a long list of men who swore they would shoot him at the first opportunity." On that occasion, Hickok lost the wall seat to Charlie Rich, who refused to give it up. Grudgingly, Hickok took the seat that placed his back to the door and the bar.

Despite some intensive research, no contemporary reference has been found to the hand of cards Hickok was holding when he was shot. In later years, however, the hand was to become immortalized as the "Deadman's Hand" and was reputed to consist of the ace of spades, the ace of clubs, two black eights, clubs and spades, and the jack of diamonds. But the last card is disputed— some sources suggest that it was the queen of diamonds. In any event, the value of that hand depended on whether the "two pair" were held before the draw, in which case he was on the way to a full house (that is three of a kind plus a pair). But if that hand followed the draw, then it was of little value.[10]

The so-called Deadman's Hand has now become a part of

Hickok's legend, but it has yet to be established just when the term was attributed to Wild Bill. Buel, who was quite accurate in his description of Wild Bill's murder, simply recorded that when the shot was fired, the "cards fell from his relaxing grasp." The origin of Hickok's Deadman's Hand may be found in the correspondence between Ellis T. Peirce and Frank J. Wilstach. According to Pierce, "Bill's hand read 'aces and eights'—two pair, and since that day aces and eights have been known as 'the deadman's hand in the Western country.'"[11]

Further research into the legend of the Deadman's Hand, has revealed an ongoing argument between vested interests in the Black Hills and others interested in perpetuating an air of "destiny" or "fate" concerning Hickok's poker hand. To add to the confusion, a poem titled "Jacks and Eights—The Dead Man's Hand" was discovered in an undated issue of *The Rocky Mountain News*. It concerned the demise of an ailing rancher known as the "Parson" in a game with his friend "Gambler Jim." The Parson was gambling away his possessions, until on the final night, near death, he played his last hand, and Jim called:

> Now, watcher got? I'll call yer bluff
> Mine's deuces say ain't them enough?
> But the "Parson's" soul had passed away.
> He had cashed in his chips, as the gamblers say,
> So they turned up his cards to see what he had
> Jim scowled as he said, "Say, I feel kinder bad,
> But I'm glad that he won, for he made a good stand."
> There were jacks and eights in the dead man's hand.

"Gambler Jim," rather than profit from his friend's death gave up the receipts for cattle and land:

> All the wealth that was won by the dead man's hand.
> This is the tale from beginning to end,
> The story as told by the deadman's friend.[12]

The superstition associated with the Deadman's Hand is matched by the rumors that circulated after Wild Bill's death, claiming he had several times stated that Deadwood would be his last camp. Indeed, as early as August 26, 1876, the Cheyenne *Daily Leader* published this telling comment:

Wild Bill's Presentiment

A week before Wild Bill's death he was heard to remark to a friend, "I feel that my days are numbered; my sun is sinking fast; I know I shall be killed here, something tells me I shall never leave these hills alive; somebody is going to kill me. But I don't know who it is or why he is going to do it. I have killed many men in my day, but I never killed a man yet but what it was kill or get killed with me. But I have two trusty friends, one is my six-shooter and the other is California Joe.

It could be argued that such a hindsight prophesy is valueless. But others also mentioned Hickok's preoccupation with death. And the content of the last letter he wrote to his wife also suggests that he did indeed have a premonition of his impending demise:

[Deadwood, Black Hills, Dakota, August 1st 1876]

Agnes Darling, if such should be we never meet again, while firing my last shot, I will gently breathe the name of my wife—Agnes— and with wishes even for my enemies I will make the plunge and try to swim to the other shore.

[J. B. Hickok, Wild Bill][13]

When word got around Deadwood that a number of men were anxious to kill him, Wild Bill refused to be intimidated. Many have since dismissed the suggestion that he was murdered because he was considered to be a threat to the lawless element who feared that he might become city marshal. On August 10, however, the editor of the *Pioneer* stated that Hickok was probably "the only man we have yet had in our midst who had the courage and other qualifications to bring some semblance of order to the lawless element of our camp. The fact that he was killed by one of the sorriest specimens of humanity to be found in the Hills is significant." Leander P. Richardson, who met Wild Bill only a day or so before his murder and later wrote several contradictory accounts of the event and Hickok's character, was credited in 1876 with the remark: "There were a dozen or more men in Deadwood who wanted to kill Wild Bill because he would not 'stand-in' with them on any 'dead-beat' games, but not one man among them all dared to pick a quarrel with him. They were all waiting to get a chance to shoot him in the back." This "clique," according to Richardson put McCall up to the killing and ensured that he got off.[14]

The belief that Hickok's presence in the gold camp could have led to his appointment as a city marshal was long-lived. Fifty years later, Henry Onsgard, when describing the desperadoes who frequented the Black Hills, thought it "necessary to clothe some man, conspicuous for his courage and honesty, with the power of marshal and direct him to clean up the town." He went on:

> Such a man was James B. Hickock, better known through out the entire land as Wild Bill. He spent but a small part of his turbulent career in the Hills but he was a product of the west, denoting the transition from the wild chaotic days of frontier life to the more settled life of organized society. Wild Bill probably sent more men prematurely to the shades of hell than any man that ever lived. During the Civil War he killed many men with his own hand, a fact that is vouched for by authoritative witnesses. Of course, that is what war is for and he excelled in that field. Outside the army he shot many men either in self-defense or to uphold the dignity of the law. Such was the unsavory record of James B. Hickock! Yet a closer intimacy with the man would have belied the opinion you have already conceived of him. His manner was gentle and unobtrusive. Annie Tallent said he had the appearance of a minister; another contemporary maintained that the woman nature with its tender emotion was strong in him; Major Coursey ascribes to him the melancholy of Shakespeare's Jacques. Such a man he truly was but underneath this placid and gentle exterior lay concealed the dormant ferocity of a savage tiger, which, if it could be awakened was governed by a clear intellect and a steady nerve. . . .
>
> I once met an elderly gentleman in the Hills who declared that though he lived in eastern Canada, he had always felt a strong desire to visit Deadwood merely to see the grave of Wild Bill and to view Mount Roosevelt. Both of these names though so different had this in common; that they represented the great American ex-

ponents of an active and strenuous life. Wild Bill was a true type of those men on the frontier that drove out one age and made possible a new and better one. Whatever Wild Bill's personal character may have been, his claims to the gratitude of his country are many and great.[15]

Whatever the truth of Hickok's premonitions, his poker hand, and the motive behind his killing, the dominant fact is that he was murdered by an individual who, it was generally agreed, was too cowardly to face him like a man. But in many respects, Jack McCall is as much an enigma as the man he killed to gain a reputation and a dubious immortality.

Jack McCall had several aliases. When he shot Wild Bill he was calling himself Bill Sutherland, but it was soon established that McCall was his real name. He was about twenty-five-years old and is believed to have been born in Jefferson County, near Jefferson Town, Kentucky (other reports suggested New Orleans and elsewhere). His boyhood and adolescence are shrouded in mystery. He is thought to have left his home about 1869 or 1870 and drifted west into the Republican River country on the border between Nebraska and Kansas. Some have claimed that he was known locally as "Buffalo Curly" and was a buffalo hunter with a mean streak. The date of his arrival in the Black Hills is not recorded, although it has been suggested that he probably arrived some weeks or perhaps months before Hickok.[16]

The events that led up to the afternoon of August 2 have bemused, baffled, and fascinated historians and students for generations. The evidence disclosed at both the Deadwood and Yankton trials indicates that McCall may have had a grudge against Wild Bill or was bribed to kill him. But a more bizarre reason has been offered: that McCall was a cousin of Samuel Strawhun, killed by Hickok at Hays City, Kansas, on September 27, 1869. According to this story, Jack set out to find and kill Wild Bill in revenge for his "kin" in true mountain folk tradition. Yet another reason put forward was an alleged incident in Tim Dyer's Road House near Fort Sydney, Nebraska, in which Hickok, unrecognized and treated like a greenhorn, was attacked by one "Big Jack," said to be McCall's hide-hunting foreman, and two others. When the smoke cleared all three were dead. Deprived of his principal means of support, McCall swore vengeance. Unfortunately, a search of local court records and surviving newspapers has found no mention of what would, by frontier standards, be news. The conclusion is that it was another version either of Hickok's fracas in the Gold Room at Cheyenne or Buel's yarn in which he claims that in December 1869 in Nebraska he had a shoot-out with four cowboys, killing three of them and seriously wounding the fourth. The only fault with this latter story is that Wild Bill was in Hays City at the time, employed as a deputy U.S. marshal.[17]

On August 3, 1876, a hastily arranged trial was convened. Riders had been dispatched to all the diggings to bring in men to witness the trial. The names of twenty men from each of the three mining districts were written on pieces of paper and shaken in a hat. The twelve chosen names became the jury. As their foreman they chose Charles Whitehead, a Kansas City, Missouri, newspaperman. Judge W. L. Kuykendall, a former president of the Wyoming Stock Growers' Association, was selected as judge or "chairman." Col. George May was the prosecutor, and a "Judge Miller" handled the defense.[18]

The trial opened at McDaniels' Theater at 9 A.M. Everyone, except McCall, of course, was armed, and there was an air of the theatrical about the whole proceeding. The correspondent for the Chicago *Inter-Ocean,* in his report published on August 18, made his feelings toward the defendant very clear:

> Never did a more forbidding countenance face a court than that of Jack McCall. His head, which is covered by a thick crop of chestnut hair, is very narrow as to the parts occupied by the intellectual portion of the brain, while the animal development is exceedingly large. A small, sandy mustache covers a sensual mouth. The nose is what is commonly called "snub," cross eyes, and a florid complexion, and the picture is finished. He was clad in a blue flannel shirt, brown overalls, heavy shoes, and as he sat in a stooping position with his arms folded across his breast, he evidently assumed a nonchalance, and bravado which was foreign to his feelings and betrayed by the spasmodic heavings of his heart.

A number of witnesses were called, including all the men who had sat at Hickok's table. Each of them testified that McCall had fired at an unaware Hickok while shouting, "Damn you, take that!" Harry Young (both he and Anson Tipple were serving as bartenders at the time) testified that he had handed Hickok fifteen dollars' worth of checks moments before the shooting. When questioned, Captain Massie remarked that he presumed that the ball that had killed Hickok and entered his arm was still there, because a careful examination of the floor and wall had failed to find it.

Various witnesses testified to McCall's character as a "quiet peaceable" individual, but Hickok was described as a noted "shootist" who always got his man. McCall, in his own defense, and in a "harsh, loud, and repulsive voice," declared that Hickok had killed his brother and he had killed Wild Bill in revenge and would "do the same thing over again." Colonel May summed up by declaring that Hickok was a much abused man who had never imposed upon anybody, and every killing attributed to him had been the result of self defense or in the line of duty. But when questioned about Hickok's gambling, he agreed that his reputation as "a gambler was bad."

Despite the overwhelming evidence of murder, the jury brought in a verdict of "not guilty" which was condemned by Colonel May and later by the editor of the *Black Hills Pioneer.* Frowning upon citizens courts, he recommended that any future homicides be dealt with by the resident deputy U.S. marshal: "He will take the offender to Yankton, where he will have justice meted out to him in proportion to the crime." That comment is important, because it underlines another equally important fact—Dakota Territory, at least the part of it that encompassed the Black Hills, was still part of lands ceded to the Sioux Nation in 1868. Therefore, any trials held in Deadwood were illegal.[19]

Once he was released, McCall chose to hang around, though Colorado Charlie Utter and others made it known that they were after his scalp. The only person, however, who actually approached him and suggested that the "air thereabouts" might be bad for his health was California Joe (Moses E. Milner). Jack took the hint and left the Black Hills.[20]

Meanwhile, Col. George May, furious at the verdict, was determined to bring McCall to justice. He followed McCall to Laramie, where he heard him boast publicly that he had got away with

Hickok's murder. May acted quickly. A bench warrant was obtained and on August 29, Deputy U.S. Marshal Balcombe arrested him. Following a hearing before U.S. Commissioner Bruner, McCall was remanded to Yankton on a charge of murder. But the colonel was unable to see the matter through; taken ill early in November, he died in Yankton on November 21. The local bar association paid for his funeral two days later.[21]

On November 9, McCall and his cellmate, a man named McCarty, also charged with murder, made a dramatic bid for freedom. They attacked their jailer but were prevented from escaping by the timely arrival of U.S. Marshal J. H. Burdick and an assistant. McCall then decided to turn state's evidence. He alleged that a gambler named John Varnes had hired him to kill Hickok in reprisal for a row the pair had in Denver that was continued in the Senate saloon in Deadwood. A deputy U.S. marshal and a posse went to Deadwood but found no trace of Varnes, who remains a shadowy figure.[22]

McCall's trial opened at Yankton on December 1 and ended on the evening of December 6. During that time a number of witnesses were called both for the defense and prosecution. The evidence disclosed was overwhelming: McCall was guilty of murder. All through the proceedings Lorenzo Butler Hickok, who had traveled from his Illinois home, sat and stared at McCall. At one point, either during the trial or following it, he was allowed to visit McCall's cell, where he learned first hand that McCall had been paid to kill his brother.[23]

McCall was found guilty and later sentenced to death on January 3, 1877. There were several attempts to have the sentence commuted. One ploy was to suggest that Hickok was a desperate and dangerous character, and that McCall's actions had been in self-defense. This accusation brought forth a spirited denial from the prosecuting counsel, William Pound, who declared:

> The murder having been a deliberate assassination, of the most cowardly character, an effort seems to be made now again, as it was on the trial, to excuse or palliate the act by a reference to the peculiar condition of society as then existed in the Black Hills. In the same connection, while conceding that this is scarcely an excuse for assassinating him, counsel find it convenient to refer to

the deceased as a "notorious character," and as one whose real
name was only disclosed by the evidence. A reference to the indictment will show that both his real name and the alias of "Wild
Bill" were used in it. But the name "Wild Bill" had been given to
him and fastened upon him so that he was really better known by
that than by an other, and without any discredit to himself . . . and
he certainly had no reason, during his life to be ashamed of it. . . .
[In the] Black Hills, his old enemies . . . [gave him] . . . a bad name
whenever and wherever they dared to do it.[24]

McCall's sentence was confirmed, and he was hanged at Yankton
on March 1, 1877.

News of Wild Bill's murder had been slow to reach the outside
world. When Custer and his men were annihilated at the Little
Big Horn, the news was telegraphed to London, where it was announced in *The Times* on July 8, some days before the news
broke in many American cities. But that was not unusual. The
telegraph service, which depended on the whims of the opera-
tors as well as the upkeep of lines and relay stations (and the occasional financial consideration when rival newspapers were involved), was often unreliable. The first published reference to
Wild Bill's murder appeared in the Deadwood *Black Hills Pioneer* of August 5, which reported that McCall had shot him
through the back of the head while he was "unaware of the danger" and went on to describe McCall's capture. On August 12,
the Cheyenne *Daily Leader* announced, " 'Wild Bill' Tamed by a
Bullet" and briefly described his killing. Four days later, the editor of the *Daily Leader* remarked that "Hickok, like all of his victims 'died with his boots on,' and the world has not suffered
anything like any irreparable loss." Others, however, were genuinely saddened. On August 17, the *Ellis County Star,* published
at Hays City, noted that this

> is the long-looked for ending of the career of one who deserved a
> better fate. . . . While here he killed several men; but all their ac-
> quaintances agreed that he was justified in so doing. He never pro-
> voked a quarrel, and was a generous, gentlemanly fellow . . . had
> the fellow that shot him given him a fair fight, and not taken the
> cowardly advantage that he did, Wild Bill would not have been
> killed.

On August 18, the Abilene *Chronicle* devoted a short paragraph to the subject, but later, on September 1, it quoted a lengthy account published in the St. Louis *Globe-Democrat*. Indeed, a perusal of the obituaries reveals that while admitting that "a man of his stamp" had his faults and foibles, Wild Bill was considered to be a courageous individual respected both for his ability as a fighting man and for his strength of character. Many of these recollections and tributes were based upon the reactions of people who had known Hickok personally and not merely from hearsay.

When news of Wild Bill's death reached his family back in Troy Grove, they at first dismissed it as yet another rumor. But when someone appeared with a copy of the Chicago *Inter-Ocean* of August 17, 1876, which carried a graphic account of his death and burial, they were devastated. In later years it was rumored that Wild Bill's sister Lydia had had a premonition on the day that her brother died but did not at first link it with his murder. Later, however, when her husband brought home a newspaper reporting the death, she knew in her heart that James was indeed dead. An examination of her one surviving letter on the subject does not suggest a premonition, rather an awful dread and the fervent hope that the papers had got it wrong yet again. Writing from Kansas on August 17, Lydia addressed her letter to "Dear Brother" (which could have been Horace or Lorenzo, and in which she inexplicably used the name "Bill"), and in it, she wrote that her husband had come home to say he had read the *Inter-Ocean* account of her brother's death:

Is it true? It seems too awful hard as [to] be true but I want you to write and tell all you have heard or all that you do or hear about it. Oh Bill I do wish I was there with Mother. Now if this is true, it will nearly kill her[.] Oh dear I feel so bad down here alone[.] I would much rather he had been killed with Custer[.] Tell me what his wife writes about it, and give me her address[.] I have felt so hard toward her because I thought Jim loved her better than he did us and now it is all over with the poor boy[.] I cant feel any rest till I hear from you dear brother and how Mother is[.] I wish I was up there, I feel so awful Bill but it may not be so after all, tho[ugh] Barnes [her husband] said the paper gave names dates and all the particulars but he could not get the paper to bring home to me[.] I am so anxious and I have been most down sick

Celinda and Lydia Hickok, sisters of Wild Bill, from a photograph made in the 1860s. The original is a tintype and has been reproduced in reverse to correct the mirror image. Lydia, with finger to cheek, bears a strong resemblance to her brother James and was also like him in temperament. Both sisters died in 1916. (Courtesy the late Ethel Hickok; original plate is now owned by the Kansas State Historical Society)

ever since Barnes got better[,] he is not well yet. Baby is well. Brother if Ma gets sick you must let me know right off. My head is bursting, good night Dear Mother[.] There is few women love their brothers as I do even if I do not always show it. I feel most crazy about Jim.

Attached to her letter was a note from her husband confirming what had appeared in the Chicago paper and adding, "There is not the ghost of a chance for a mistake this time but I hope it is a mistake as they have made . . . many before."[25]

In 1896, in a feature in the Chicago *Daily Record* of December 26, Lydia described how the news reached Troy Grove:

Mother had been a sufferer from inflammatory rheumatism for two years before that, and had not taken a step for eighteen months. My sister [Celinda] was standing at the gate when a neighbor came by and brought the Chicago paper giving an account of Bill's death. He handed it to my sister. She took it up and hurried into the house, hiding the paper in the kitchen behind a mirror on a shelf. Then composing herself, she went in where mother was sitting.

"Mother," she said, "I am going over to the store a minute, and will be right back."

She put on her bonnet and ran to the little store . . . [and returned with her two brothers]. . . . When they entered the sitting room there sat mother, the newspaper lying at her side, slowing rocking back and forth, while the blood from a haemorrhage of the lungs dyed the front of her light dress. . . .

She never fully recovered from it and she died two years later still mourning over Bill's terrible death.

Agnes Lake Thatcher wrote on November 12 promising to visit them when she could, as she intended to see Wild Bill's grave. Declaring her love for the dead plainsman, she said: "I can see him Day and night before me. The longer he is Dead the worse I feel."[26]

Once the initial shock of Wild Bill's death had worn off, the family would face years of agonizing over his reputation and the constant stream of requests from the public for information or relics. Although Agnes was able to visit his grave in 1877, none of the close family could afford to do so, and they relied a great deal upon others to help with its upkeep. Charlie Utter kept his promise and paid for the lot. Later, Capt. Jack Crawford also contributed towards preserving Wild Bill's grave. In 1879, however, there was a crisis. The city authorities at Deadwood decided to move the bodies from the original cemetery at Ingleside, a picturesque spot on the south side of town, to a new location set aside on Mount Moriah.

Once word got out that the move was afoot, alarming stories appeared in the press. One claimed that Hickok's grave had been

robbed and that his two revolvers "made expressly for him and
. . . finished in a manner unequalled by any ever before manufactured in this or any other country" had been stolen.[27] This rumor
was refuted by Charlie Utter, who stated that Hickok had been
buried with his favorite rifle and no revolvers. But other stories
began to circulate once the actual exhumation and reburial took
place on August 3, 1879. Thanks to the percolation of dissolved
minerals into the coffin, Wild Bill was reported to have become
"petrified," and his body now weighed about 300 pounds. Despite some denials, the allegation inspired a humorously macabre
reaction among some editors. At Hays City, it was reported that a
request had been made to Deadwood to return Wild Bill in order
that he could be erected outside the newly built courthouse for
"it is not every man who is qualified to serve as a statue on his
own tomb." Doubtless Hickok himself appreciated the humor of
the situation, for it was also reported that when his features were
examined, there was a distinct smile upon his face.[28]

In 1892, Charlie Utter, who had paid for a marble headstone
when Wild Bill was reburied, was infuriated by a report that
claimed he had not paid for the plot and that, consequently, the
cemetery owners were planning to sell Hickok's remains to a
New York museum agent. Charlie rushed to Deadwood, where
the old cemetery records verified that he had indeed ensured
that Wild Bill's final resting place was secure.[29]

One of the people involved in the reburial of Wild Bill was
Louis B. Schoenfield. His claim to have masterminded the event
angered Charlie Utter, who described Schoenfield as a "deadbeat
and a bilk . . . a tender foot" seeking notoriety.[30] Schoenfield,
however, managed to convince Lorenzo Hickok that he had his
late brother's interests at heart. On September 6, 1879, he assured Lorenzo that "your Brother was a good friend of mine"
and went on to confirm that until 1877 the land where Wild Bill
lay was the public cemetery. When Mount Moriah Cemetery was
laid out, many people removed their dead before the county let
out a contract to remove them. He decided to buy a plot himself,
for he knew that "he [Wild Bill] would have done the same for
me." Schoenfield also wrote that he had "invited" Charlie Utter
to the removal and when Charlie next appeared in Deadwood he
would show him Lorenzo's letter. This letter was followed by a

note advising Lorenzo that he had been inundated by requests from the press for stories about Wild Bill. He also offered to retrieve a lock of Wild Bill's hair that he had given away. He further claimed to have a "deed to the lot where Wild Bill was buried" and he would have it recorded so that no one could disturb him. As for the "petrification," he said that he had got down into the grave and raised the coffin lid and that Wild Bill "looked natural & there was no odor at all[.] upon further examination the body was found to be very hard and the experts claimed that it was petrification[.] it was exposed to the air for four hours & no visible change had taken place."[31]

On April 19, 1880, Schoenfield again wrote Lorenzo to inform him that messengers (guards) on the Sidney coach had informed him that some Easterners had recently arrived in Sidney with the avowed intention of digging Wild Bill up and stealing him away. Schoenfield then begged Lorenzo to try and arrange for his brother's removal, for "I can assure you the remains are not offensive in any way." He himself would have undertaken the task but he was short of cash. He suggested a "metallic lined coffin for about seventy-five dollars and twenty dollars will send it to Fort Pierre or Sidney and the Post to take it home by railroad won['']t be much." He then alleged that "with the exception of the few dollars that Utter paid I did the whole work before and would willingly do it again if I was financially fixed." He then suggested that Lorenzo send money to Daugherty Wardnen & Co., Freighters, to pay for all expenses.[32]

A curious footnote to that correspondence came to light in 1966, when it was reported that an "elderly gentleman who had spent at least a part of his boyhood in Mendota" claimed that he and a companion had sneaked out one night on some boyish escapade and were at the railroad depot when the late train came in. Several members of the Hickok family then removed a large case, which he later believed contained Wild Bill's body. It took eight strong men to lift it. A stone was later placed at the grave. Understandably, present-day members of the family refute the yarn, especially the suggestion of a "stone" being placed over the grave.[33]

On April 12, 1885, Schoenfield again wrote to Lorenzo from Louisville, Kentucky, asking for a letter of introduction to Buffalo

Bill, who was due in the city with his Wild West Exhibition. Lorenzo accordingly sent him a letter, but on May 19, he was advised that owing to an indisposition Schoenfield had been unable to see Buffalo Bill.[34]

On June 29, 1893, Horace Hickok received a letter from Henry Robinson, a Deadwood undertaker who had formerly acted as sexton and had cared for his brother's grave. Horace had apparently written to Robinson's predecessor enclosing a press clipping containing some alarming news. He first assured Horace that Charlie Utter had indeed paid for the plot. But as for the alleged "petrification," that was "all bosh & untrue." He added that "the story of Louis Schoenfield about the bombs being placed around the body is also untrue." The suggestion of bombs may have prompted Horace's letter—or perhaps it was simply mentioned in passing. At any rate, it must have disturbed the family. Worse was to come. Robinson then revealed that Schoenfield had been forced to leave the country, charged with stealing corpses from the graveyard and "therefore there is no dependence to be placed upon anything he tells you. I have heard a great many people say that they believed that Schoenfield took the body of Wild Bill, but this is only Rumour. . . . The grave has never been disturbed in the past 14 years." He added that Capt. Jack Crawford had visited the grave and arranged to place a wall and an iron fence around it, which cost $40. Crawford left $20 on account and still owed the remainder. Robinson claimed to have a piece of the original headboard erected by Charlie Utter that Crawford wanted, but he would not send it to him until he received the balance due. Robinson also mentioned the damage relic hunters had done to Wild Bill's monument erected by J. H. Riordan in 1891.[35]

On November 8, 1893, Col. E. E. Clough, president of the South Dakota Soldiers' Home at Hot Springs, advised Horace that Capt. Jack Crawford had enlisted his aid in arranging an entertainment, the proceeds of which would go toward the erection of a fence around Wild Bill's grave. Jack had purchased the materials in Chicago. The entertainment netted $29, of which $7 was spent on freighting the fence. Horace, early in 1894, dispatched $15 to Henry Robinson, presumably to help pay off Crawford's outstanding debt.[36]

Calamity Jane died on August 1, 1903, and it was proposed that she be buried next to Wild Bill. That news caused the Hickok family further distress. However, on August 28, Sol Star, the county clerk, wrote to assure Lorenzo that their "records show that a lot was purchased alongside and outside of the lot (fenced) of your Brother's for the burial of Calamity Jane, and said lot does in no wise conflict or disturb the resting place of J. B." Henry Robinson wrote to Lorenzo on May 25, 1904, stating that Sol Star had shown him Lorenzo's letter concerning Calamity Jane and confirming that she had indeed been buried in an adjoining lot at her own request. The monuments over his brother's grave had been demolished by souvenir hunters, though the latest one by Alvin Smith, a full-size figure of Wild Bill, was protected by a heavy iron cage with screen wire from Montgomery Ward that cost $100. The cost had been partially recovered from most of Wild Bill's friends, but so far he had only raised $72. Lorenzo promptly dispatched $10, which was gratefully received.[37]

In recent years, several attempts have been made to have Wild Bill's remains removed from Deadwood to Kansas and Illinois, but without success. In 1953, the Topeka *Capital* ran several items on the subject. On June 26, it reported that the "Battle of the Bones" was a local affair. One G. I. Dobbin, secretary of the "Wild Bill Hickok Foundation," demanded the return of Hickok's bones because he had once stated that he "wishes to be buried" at Abilene. But on July 5, Frank Motz, editor of the Hays *Daily News* and son of the first mayor of Hays City, declared that Hays had prior claim. This article was followed on the ninth by a hint from Dobbin that his organization might end up stealing Hickok's bones! No one has so far thought to carry out an examination of the grave to establish whether or not Wild Bill still occupies it. Regardless, the gravesite continues to attract tourists and visitors anxious to stand close to the resting place of the man who inspired the myth.

If the real Wild Bill was allowed to rest in death, his myth and his family were not. His controversial reputation continued to affect them. Within weeks of his death they began to receive letters from so-called friends and close acquaintances of Wild Bill offering condolences and help in bringing McCall to justice. But examination of some of this correspondence has revealed that most of these "friends" were only after money, on the pretext of pursuing McCall or assisting Wild Bill's wife in her efforts to get McCall into court.

With the years, others approached the family, some with offers for relics and others anxious for information for publication. One such individual was J. W. Buel. In 1879 he had published a short history of Wild Bill, which led to a correspondence with Agnes Lake concerning errors. He visited her and obtained firsthand information, including, so he claimed, Wild Bill's personal diary. In his letter of March 9, 1881, Buel reminded Horace and Lorenzo of previous kindnesses and asked for details of Wild Bill's birthplace and a sketch of it. He remarked that they had omitted "any account of James between the time he was constable of Monticello township, Johnson County, Kansas, and 1860 when he vanquished the McCandlass gang at Rock Creek." He also asked for details of James's childhood, apologizing for not appearing in person because the distance was so great (he lived in St. Louis). He promised to send each brother a copy of the book on publication. As late as 1974, no copy of the book had been found, though one copy was located in Ethel Hickok's collection following her death.[38]

By the turn of the century, the Hickoks were becoming used to requests for information, and periodically, one of the brothers would write to newspapers correcting some of the nonsense still being written about James. Following the deaths of Horace and Lorenzo, Horace's sons, Horace and Howard, aided by their sisters, carried on the task. Horace was not as active as his brother Howard, but he did react when he thought his uncle's reputation was at stake. Howard, on the other hand, cooperated with William E. Connelley, who became something of a pest. On May 2, 1923, he wrote to Susan Andrews, a niece of Wild Bill's, concerning material about Wild Bill that her mother had furnished to the Colorado Historical Society. He claimed that she had obtained it from published books. He then declared: "I have all the books. There may be a few paragraphs on the first page of the material of your mother which have original information but I am sure most of it is from Buell's [sic] book. The statement made about the fight at Rock Creek is perfectly ridiculous and has been copied from some book."

Connelly went on to suggest that Edwin L. Sabin, another writer on the Hickok trail, had used her mother's fiction, and that he had informed the publishers of *Adventure Magazine* that there "was no truth in any of the statements made by Mr. Sabin." Worse, he felt sure her mother did not know that he (Wild Bill) "had been married to a half-breed Shawnee Indian." Andrews drafted a reply on the back of Connelley's original letter:

> Your letter dated May 2, should be ignored and would be only I feel some of your statements must not be published. Unless you send us the records and proof of Jas. B. Hickok's marriage to a Shawnee Indian you will be persecuted—[prosecuted]. I do not know what accounts . . . my mother furnished to Colorado Society, but do not feel that you are the one to criticise. You say you have all the books, so have we, a great many and many of them untrue and greatly exaggerated. Buell's book is the only one authorized by the Hickok family as a great deal of that account was furnished by the Hickok family. . . . You need not ask for pictures facts nor any other favors, we will furnish nothing. We didn't ask to have any history written and from your letter it seems that you would like to receive much and give little. If the Kansas State Historical Society want a history written they had better employ one who has about him at least common decency. Your statements are ridiculous and shows your immense ego. How did you secure true accounts of [the] fight at Rock Creek? Jas. Hickok has relatives living in Kansas a niece and nephew and until eight years ago a sister. I'm sorry he has no brothers nor sisters to answer your impudent letter.[39]

Andrews's reaction indicates that the family at that time still believed that Buel's account was accurate, but they did not appreciate Connelley's arrogance. By 1927, however, Howard indicated that he, at least, was sympathetic to Connelley. On August 13, the Topeka *Capital* mentioned that Howard had visited with Connelley to learn more about his uncle's exploits. "Nothing was done," Connelley was quoted as saying; "I just told him a few facts about the life of Hickok which I happen to know." Howard, it was reported, was "seeking facts to refute statements that his famous uncle was a coward and killed innocent people." Evidently, his meeting with Connelley bore fruit, and he began an exchange of letters and apparently loaned Connelley materials to copy, for on January 25, 1928, Connelley thanked Howard for the loan of letters. He then asked for more material, adding, "Please tell your folks that they will be ashamed of themselves one of these days for their attitude." It is doubtful that the letter was ever shown to the family, for on January 30, 1928, Howard wrote, mentioning that he was enclosing further letters written by his uncle that Connelley could copy and return. He also announced the discovery of a "fine daguerreotype of J.B. at age of 21." He suggested, "If you could tell me how this could be copied I could get it copied but no chance of me getting it now, that is permanent possession of it." In a postscript, Howard emphasized how much he wished he could help Connelley. But so far as is known, he did not part with any prized relics of Wild Bill.[40]

On June 12, 1929, Howard wrote to Connelley to find out how his book was coming along. In his reply of July 15 Connelley wrote requesting the "gun carried by your uncle and copies of all papers and letters that he wrote." Howard's reply has not been found, but on January 2, 1930, Connelley did have the grace to state that he agreed that the relatives had been imposed upon so often that they could hardly be blamed for thinking somebody wants to exploit them.[41]

The family still gets requests for information, and occasionally receives insults from the more rabid anti-Wild Bill brigade. Others, not meaning to offend, but nonetheless insensitive, ask for details about all the men he killed!

The public's view of Hickok has changed little since the 1920s, except that people now tend to explore his motivations rather than make firm, blinkered judgments—a healthy sign. Nevertheless, he remains an enigma, despite the emergence in recent years of previously unknown documentation concerning the real James Butler Hickok. That he did perform many of the feats attributed to him is no longer in doubt. But why does his mythical counterpart continue to enthrall the public? Few of his contemporaries thought him heroic. Rather, he was regarded as a character, which, in the parlance of the time, meant a colorful, sometimes desperate, but courageous individual whose dangerous "scrapes" were admired.

The legendary Wild Bill, however, was a different matter, a larger than life character that defies both his eulogizers and his critics. He was the role model that inspired later generations to admire gunfighting peace officers—as Buffalo Bill Cody had influenced the public's acceptance of a "heroic" cowboy (a tradition carried into the movie era). And it is the heroic Wild Bill that is uppermost in the public's mind. Historians and sociologists may well disagree over the Hickok phenomenon, but they cannot ignore the potency of his myth. In my years of research I have read many attempts to explain Wild Bill the myth and the man. Only one writer (one of his severest yet fairest critics) came close when he wrote: That Wild Bill's "legend lives—and will live, so long as men talk of courage. Whatever else we may say of him, this much is true: He shot straight, and asked few favors . . . and he walked like a man in the presence of his enemies."[42]

WILD BILL.

The first published illustration of Wild Bill as it appeared in Harper's New Monthly Magazine *for February 1867. This woodcut is based on a Charles W. Scholten carte de visite. (Author's collection)*

Appendix

Harper's New Monthly Magazine, "Wild Bill" (February 1867)

S
everal months after the ending of the civil war I visited the city of Springfield in Southwest Missouri. Springfield is not a burgh of extensive dimensions, yet it is the largest in that part of the State, and all roads lead to it—which is one reason why it was the *point d'apari* as well as the base of operations for all military movements during the war.

On a warm summer day I sat watching from the shadow of a broad awning the coming and going of the strange, half-civilized people who, from all the country round, make this a place for barter and trade. Men and women dressed in queer costumes; men with coats and trowsers made of skin, but so thickly covered with dirt and grease as to have defied the identify of the animal when walking in the flesh. Others wore homespun gear, which oftentimes appeared to have seen lengthy service. Many of those people were mounted on horse-back or mule-back, while others urged forward the unwilling cattle attached to creaking, heavily-laden wagons, their drivers snapping their long whips with a report like that of a pistol-shot.

In front of the shops which lined both sides of the main business street, and about the public square, were groups of men lolling against posts, lying upon the wooden sidewalks, or sitting in chairs. These men were temporary or permanent denizens of the city, and were lazily occupied in doing nothing. The most marked characteristic of the inhabitants seemed to be an indisposition to move, and their highest ambition to let their hair and beards grow.

Here and there upon the street the appearance of the army blue betokened the presence of a returned Union soldier, and the jaunty, confident air with which they carried themselves was all the more striking in its contrast with the indolence which appeared to belong to the place. The only indication of action was the inevitable revolver which every body, excepting, perhaps, the women, wore about their persons. When people moved in this lazy city they did so slowly and without method. No one seemed in haste. A huge hog wallowed in luxurious ease in a nice bed of mud on the other side of the way, giving vent to gentle grunts of satisfaction. On the platform at my feet lay a large wolf-dog literally asleep with one eye open. He, too, seemed contented to let the world wag idly on.

The loose, lazy spirit of the occasion finally took possession of me, and I sat and gazed and smoked, and it is possible that I might have fallen into a Rip Van Winkle sleep to have been aroused ten years hence by the cry, "Passengers for the flying machine to New York, all aboard!" when I and the drowsing city were roused into life by the clatter and crash of the hoofs of a horse which dashed furiously across the square and down the street. The rider sat perfectly erect, yet following with a grace of motion seen only in the horsemen of the plains, the rise and fall of the galloping steed. There was only a moment to observe this, for they halted suddenly, while the rider springing to the ground approached the party which the noise had gathered near me.

"This yere is Wild Bill, Colonel," said Captain Honesty, an army officer addressing me. He continued:

"How are yer, Bill? This yere is Colonel N——, who wants ter know yer."

Let me at once describe the personal appearance of the famous Scout of the Plains, William Hitchcock, called "Wild Bill," who now advanced toward me, fixing his clear gray eyes on mine in a quick, interrogative way, as if to take "my measure."

The result seemed favorable, for he held forth a small, muscular hand in a frank, open manner. As I looked at him I thought his the handsomest *physique* I had ever seen. In its exquisite manly proportions it recalled the antique. It was a figure Ward would delight to model as a companion to his "Indian."

Bill stood six feet and an inch in his bright yellow moccasins. A deer-skin shirt, or frock it might be called, hung jauntily over his shoulders and revealed a chest whose breadth and depth were remarkable. These lungs had had growth in some twenty years of the free air of the Rocky Mountains. His small, round waist was girthed by a belt which held two of Colt's navy revolvers. His legs sloped gradually from the compact thigh to the feet, which were small and turned inward as he walked. There was a singular grace and dignity of carriage about that figure which would have called your attention meet it where you would. The head which crowned it was now covered by a large sombrero, underneath which there shone out a quiet, manly face; so gentle is its expression as he greets you as utterly to belie the history of its owner; yet it is not a face to be trifled with. The lips thin and sensitive, the jaw not too square, the cheek bones slightly prominent, a mass of fine dark hair falls below the neck to the shoulders. The eyes, now that you are in friendly intercourse, are as gentle as a woman's. In truth, the woman nature seems prominent throughout, and you would not believe that you were looking into eyes that have pointed the way to death to hundreds of men. Yes, Wild Bill with his own hands has killed hundreds of men. Of that I have not a doubt. "He shoots to kill," as they say on the border.

In vain did I examine the scout's face for some evidence of murderous propensity. It was a gentle face, and singular only in the sharp angle of the eye, and without any physiognomical reason for the opinion, I have thought his wonderful accuracy of aim was indicated by this peculiarity. He told me, however, to use his own words:

"I allers shot well; but I come ter be perfect in the mountains by shootin at a dime for a mark, at best of half a dollar a shot. And then until the war I never drank liquor nor smoked," he continued, with a melancholy expression; "war is demoralizing it is."

Captain Honesty was right. I was very curious to see "Wild Bill, the Scout," who, a few days before my arrival in Springfield, in a duel at noonday in the public square, at fifty paces, had sent one of Colt's pistol-balls through the heart of a returned Confederate soldier.

Whenever I had met an officer or soldier who had served in the Southwest I heard of Wild Bill and his exploits, until these stories became so frequent and of such an extraordinary character as quite to outstrip personal knowledge of adventure by camp and field; and the hero of these strange tales took shape in my mind as did Jack the Giant Killer or Sinbad the Sailor in childhood's days. As then, I now had the most implicit faith in the existence of the individual; but how one man could accomplish such prodigies of strength and feats of daring was a continued wonder.

In order to give the reader a clearer understanding of the condition of this neighborhood, which could have permitted the duel mentioned above, and whose history will be given hereafter in detail, I will describe the situation at the time of which I am writing, which was late in the summer of 1865, premising that this section of country would not to-day be selected as a model example of modern civilization.

At that time peace and comparative quiet had succeeded the perils and tumult of war in all the more Southern States. The people of Georgia and the Carolinas were glad to enforce order in their midst; and it would have been safe for a Union officer to have ridden unattended through the land.

In Southwest Missouri there were old scores to be settled up. During the three days occupied by General Smith—who commanded the Department and was on a tour of inspection—in crossing the country between Rolla and Springfield, a distance of 120 miles, five men were killed or wounded on the public road. Two were murdered a short distance from Rolla—by whom we could not ascertain. Another was instantly killed and two were wounded at a meeting of a band of "Regulators," who were in the service of the State, but were paid by the United States Government. It should be said here that their method of "regulation" was slightly informal, their war-cry was, "A swift bullet and a short rope for returned rebels!"

I was informed by General Smith that during the six months preceding not less than 4000 returned Confederates had been summarily disposed of by shooting or hanging. This statement seems incredible; but there is the record, and I have no doubt of its truth. History shows few parallels to this relentless destruction of human life in time of peace. It can be explained only upon the ground that before the war, this region was inhabited by lawless people. In the outset of the rebellion the merest suspicion of loyalty to the Union cost the patriot his life; and thus large numbers fled the land, giving up home and every material interest. As soon as the Federal armies occupied the country these refugees returned. Once securely fixed in their old homes they resolved that their former persecutors should not live in their midst. Revenge for the past and security for the future knotted many a nerve and sped many a deadly bullet.

Wild Bill did not belong to the Regulators. Indeed, he was one of the law and order party. He said:

"When the war closed I buried the hatchet, and I won't fight now unless I'm put upon."

Bill was born of Northern parents in the State of Illinois. He ran away from home when a boy, and wandered out upon the plains and into the mountains. For fifteen years he lived with the trappers, hunting and fishing. When the war broke out he returned to the States and entered the Union service. No man probably was ever better fitted for scouting than he. Joined to his tremendous strength he was an unequalled horseman; he was a perfect marksman; he had a keen sight, and a constitution which had no limit of endurance. He was cool to audacity, brave to rashness, always possessed of himself under the most critical circumstances; and above all, was such a master in the knowledge of woodcraft that it might have been termed a science with him—a knowledge which, with the soldier, is priceless beyond description. Some of Bill's adventures during the war will be related hereafter.

The main feature of the story of the duel was told me by Captain Honesty, who was unprejudiced, if it is possible to find an unbiased mind in a town of 3000 people after a fight has taken place. I will give the story in his words:

"They say Bill's wild. Now he isn't any sich thing. I've known him gong on ter ten year, and he's as civil a disposed person as you'll find he-e-arabouts. But he won't be put upon."

"I'll tell yer how it happened. But come inter the office; thar's

"Putting upon him," from Harper's New Monthly Magazine *34:201 (February 1867).*

a good many round hy'ar as sides with Tutt—the man that's shot. But I tell yer 'twas a fair fight. Take some whisky? No! Well, I will, if yer'l excuse me.

"You see," continued the Captain, setting the empty glass on the table in an emphatic way, "Bill was up in his room a-playing seven-up, or four-hand, or some of them pesky games. Bill refused ter play with Tutt, who was a professional gambler. Yer see, Bill was a scout on our side durin the war, and Tutt was a reb scout. Bill had killed Dave Tutt's mate, and, atween one thing and other, there war an onusual hard feelin atwixt 'em.

"Ever sin [*sic*] Dave come back he had tried to pick a row with Bill; so Bill wouldn't play cards with him any more. But Dave stood over the man who was gambling with Bill and lent the feller money. Bill won bout two hundred dollars, which made Tutt spiteful mad. Bime-by he says to Bill:

" 'Bill, you've got plenty of money—pay me that forty dollars yer owe me in that horse trade.'

"And Bill paid him. Then he said:

" 'Yer owe me thirty-five dollars more; yer lost it playing with me t'other night.'

"Dave's style was right provoking; but Bill answered him perfectly gentlemanly:

"'I think yer wrong, Dave. It's only twenty-five dollars. I have a memorandum of it in my pocket down stairs. Ef it's thirty-five dollars I'll give it yer.'

"Now Bill's watch was lying on the table. Dave took up the watch, put it in his pocket, and said: 'I'll keep this yere watch till yer pay me that thirty-five dollars.

"This made Bill shooting mad; fur, don't yer see, Colonel, it was a-doubting his honor like, so he got up and looked Dave in the eyes, and said to him: 'I don't want ter make a row in this house. It's a decent house, and I don't want ter injure the keeper. You'd better put that watch back on the table.'

"But Dave grinned at Bill mighty ugly, and walked off with the watch, and kept it several days. All this time Dave's friends were spurring Bill on ter fight; there was no end ter the talk. They blackguarded him in an underhand sort of a way, and tried ter get up a scrimmage, and then they thought they could lay him out. Yer see Bill has enemies all about. He's settled the accounts of a heap of men who lived round here. This is about the only place in Missouri whar a reb can come back and live, and ter tell yer the truth, Colonel———" and the Captain, with an involuntary movement, hitched up his revolver-belt, as he said, with expressive significance, "they don't stay long round here!

"Well, as I was saying these rebs don't like ter see a man walking round town who they knew in the reb army as one of their men, who they now know was on our side, all the time he was sending us information, sometimes from Pap Price's own headquarters. But they couldn't provoke Bill inter a row, for he's afeared of hissel when he gits *awful* mad; and he allers left his shootin irons in his room when he went out. One day these cusses drew their pistols on him and dared him to fight, and they told him that Tutt was a-goin ter pack that watch across the squar [sic] next day at noon.

"I heard of this, for every body was talking about it on the street, and so I went after Bill and found him in his room cleaning and greasing and loading his revolvers.

"'Now, Bill,' says I, 'you're goin to get inter a fight.'

"'Don't you bother yerself, Captain,' says he. 'It's not the first time I have been in a fight; and these d——d hounds have put on me long enough. You don't want me ter give up my honor, do yer?'

" 'No, Bill,' says I, 'yer must keep yer honor.'

"Next day, about noon, Bill went down on the squar. He had said that Dave Tutt shouldn't pack that watch across the squar unless dead men could walk.

"When Bill got onter the squar he found a crowd stanin in the corner of the street by which he entered the squar, which is from the south, yer know. In this crowd he saw a lot of Tutt's friends; some were cousins of his'n, just back from the reb army; and they jeered him, and boasted that Dave was a-goin to pack that watch across the squar as he promised.

"Then Bill saw Tutt stanin near the court-house, which yer remember is on the west side, so that the crowd war behind Bill.

"Just then Tutt, who war alone, started from the court-house and walked out into the squar, and Bill moved away from the crowd toward the west side of the squar. Bout fifteen paces brought them opposite to each other, and about fifty yards apart. Tutt then showed his pistol. Bill had kept a sharp eye on him, and before Tutt could pint it Bill had hi'sn out.

"At that moment you could have heard a pin drop in that squar. Both Tutt and Bill fired, but one discharge followed the other so quick that it's hard to say which went off first. Tutt was a famous shot, but he missed this time; the ball from his pistol went over Bill's head. The instant Bill fired, without waitin ter see ef he had hit Tutt, he wheeled on his heels and pointed his pistol at Tutt's friends, who had already drawn their weapons.

" 'Aren't yer satisfied, gentlemen?' cried Bill, as cool as an alligator. 'Put up your shootin-irons or there'll be more dead men here.' And they put 'em up, and said it war a far fight."

"What became of Tutt?" I asked of the Captain, who had stopped at this point of his story and was very deliberately engaged in refilling his empty glass.

"Oh! Dave? He was as plucky a feller as ever drew trigger; but Lord bless yer! it was no use. Bill never shoots twice at the same man, and his ball went through Dave's heart. He stood stock-still for a second or two, then raised his arm as if ter fire again, then he swayed a little, staggered three or four steps, and then fell dead.

"Bill and his friends wanted ter have the thing done regular, so we went up ter the Justice, and Bill delivered him self up. A jury was drawn; Bill was tried and cleared the next day. It was proved that it was a case of self-defense. Don't yer see, Colonel?

I answered that I was afraid that I did not see that point very clearly.

"Well, well!" he replied, with an air of compassion, "you haven't drunk any whisky, that's what's the matter with yer." And then, putting his hand on my shoulder with a half-mysterious half-conscious look in his face, he muttered, in a whisper:

"The fact is, thar was an undercurrent of a woman in that fight!"

The story of the duel was yet fresh from the lips of the Captain when its hero appeared in the manner already described. After a few moments' conversation Bill excused himself, saying:

"I am going out on the prarer a piece to see the sick wife of my mate. I should be glad to meet yer at the hotel this afternoon, Kernel."

"I will go there to meet you," I replied.

"Good-day, gentlemen," said the scout as he saluted the party;

"Are you satisfied?" from Harper's.

"For life or death," from Harper's.

and mounting the black horse, who had been standing quiet, un-hitched, he waved his hand over the animal's head. Responsive to the signal, she shot forward as the arrow leaves the bow, and they both disappeared up the road in a cloud of dust.

"That man is the most remarkable character I have met in four years' active service," said a lieutenant of cavalry, as the party resumed their seats. "He and his mate—the man who scouted with him—attempted the most daring feat that I ever heard of."

As there appeared to be no business on hand at the moment the party urged the lieutenant to tell the story.

"I can't tell the thing as it was," said the young officer. "It was beyond description. One could only hold their breath and feel. It happened when our regiment was attached to Curtis's command, in the expedition down into Arkansas. One day we were in the advance, and began to feel the enemy, who appeared in greater strength than at any time before. We were all rather uneasy, for there were rumors that Kirby Smith had come up from Texas with all his force; and as we were only a strong reconnoitring party a fight just then might have been bad for us. We made a big noise with a light battery, and stretched our cavalry out in the open and opposite to the rebel cavalry, who were drawn up in line of battle on the slope of the prairie about a thousand yards away. There we sat for half an hour, now and then banging at each other, but both parties keeping pretty well their line of battle. They waited for us to pitch in. We were waiting until more of our infantry should come.

"It was getting to be stupid work, however, and we were all hoping something would turn up, when we noticed two men ride out from the centre of their line and move toward us. At the first instant we paid little heed to them, supposing it some act of rebel bravado, when we saw quite a commotion all along the enemy's front, and then they commenced firing at the two riders, and then their line was all enveloped with smoke, out of which horsemen dashed in pursuit. The two riders kept well together, coming straight for us. Then we knew they were trying to escape, and the Colonel deployed our company as skirmishers to assist them. There wasn't time to do much, although, as I watched the pursued and their pursuers and found the two men had halted at what I could now see was a deep wide ditch, the moments seemed to be hours; and when they turned I thought they were going to give themselves up. But no; in the face of that awful fire they deliberately turned back to get space for a good run at the ditch. This gave time for two of their pursuers to get within a few yards of them, when they stopped, evidently in doubt as to the meaning of this retrograde movement. But they did not remain long in doubt, for the two men turned again, and, with a shout, rushed for the ditch, and then we were near enough to see that they were Wild Bill and his mate. Bill's companion never reached the ditch. He and his horse must have been shot at the same time, for they went down together and did not rise again.

"Bill did not get a scratch. He spoke to Black Nell, the mare we saw just now, who knew as well as her master that there was life and death in that twenty feet of ditch, and that she must jump it; and at it she went with a big rush. I never saw a more magnificent sight. Bill gave the mare her head, and turning in his saddle fired twice, killing both of his pursuers, who were within a few lengths of him. They were out of their saddles like stones, just as Black Nell flew into the air and landed safely on our side of the ditch. In a moment both the daring scout and the brave mare were in our midst, while our men cheered and yelled like mad.

"We asked Bill why he ran such a risk, when he could have stolen into our lines during the night?

" 'Oh,' said he, 'mate and I wanted to show them cussed rebs what a Union soldier could do. We've been with them now for more than a month, and heard nothing but brag. We thought we'd take it out of them. But'—and Bill looked across the green-sward to where his companion still lay motionless—'if they have killed my mate they shall pay a big price for it.'

"Bill must have brought valuable information," continued the lieutenant, "for he was at once sent to the General, and in an hour we had changed position, and foiled a flank movement of the rebels."

I went to the hotel during the afternoon to keep the scout's appointment. The large room of the hotel in Springfield is perhaps the central point of attraction in the city. It fronted on the street, and served in several capacities. It was a sort of exchange for those who had nothing better to do than to go there. It was reception-room, parlor, and office; but its distinguished and most fascinating characteristic was the bar, which occupied one entire end of the apartment. Technically, the "bar" is the counter upon which the polite official places his viands. Practically, the bar is represented in the long rows of bottles, and cut-glass decanters, and the glasses and goblets of all shapes and sizes suited to the various liquors to be imbibed. What a charming and artistic display it was of elongated transparent vessels containing every known drinkable fluid, from native Bourbon to imported Lacryma Christi!

The room, in its way, was a temple of art. All sorts of pictures budded and blossomed and blushed from the walls. Six penny portraits of the Presidents encoffined in pine-wood frames; Mazeppa appeared in the four phases of his celebrated one-horse act; while a lithograph of "Mary Ann" smiled and simpered in spite of the stains of tobacco-juice which had been unsparingly bestowed upon her originally encarmined countenance. But the hanging committee of this undersigned academy seemed to have been prejudiced—as all hanging committees of good taste might well be—in favor of *Harper's Weekly;* for the walls of the room were covered with wood-cuts cut from that journal. Portraits of noted generals and statesmen, knaves and politicians, with boun-

teous illustrations of battles and skirmishes, from Bull Run number one to Dinwiddie Court House. And the simple-hearted com-
ers and goers of Springfield looked upon, wondered, and
admired these pictorial descriptions fully as much as if they had
been the master-pieces of a Yvon or Vernet.

A billiard-table, old and out of use, where caroms seemed to
have been made quite as often with lead as ivory balls, stood in
the centre of the room. A dozen chairs, filled up the complement
of the furniture. The appearance of the party of men assembled
there, who sat with their slovenly shod feet dangling over the
arms of the chairs or hung about the porch outside, was in perfect harmony with the time and place. All of them religiously
obeyed the two before-mentioned characteristics of the people
of the city—their hair was long and tangled, and each man ful-
filled the most exalted requirement of laziness.

I was taking a mental inventory of all this when a cry and mur-
mur drew my attention to the outside of the house, when I saw
Wild Bill riding up the street at a swift gallop. Arrived opposite
the hotel, he swung his right arm around with a circular motion.
Black Nell instantly stopped and dropped to the ground as if a
cannon-ball had knocked life out of her. Bill left her there,
stretched upon the ground, and joined the group of observers on
the porch.

"Black Nell hasn't forgot her old tricks," said one of them.

"No," answered the scout. "God bless her! she is wiser and
truer than most men I know on. That mare will do any thing for
me. Won't you, Nelly?"

The mare winked affirmatively the only eye we could see.

"Wise!" continued her master; "why, she knows more than a
judge. I'll bet the drinks for the party that she'll walk up these
steps and into the room and climb up on the billiard-table and lie
down."

The bet was taken at once, not because any one doubted the
capabilities of the mare, but there was excitement in the thing
without exercise.

Bill whistled in a low tone. Nell instantly scrambled to her
feet, walked toward him, put her nose affectionately under his
arm, followed him into the room, and to my extreme wonder-
ment climbed upon the billiard-table, to the extreme astonish-

"Black Nell," from Harper's.

ment of the table no doubt, for it groaned under the weight of the four legged animal and several of those who were simply bifurcated, and whom Nell permitted to sit upon her. When she got down from the table, which was as graceful a performance as might be expected under the circumstances, Bill sprang upon her back, dashed through the high wide doorway, and at a single bound cleared the flight of steps and landed in the middle of the street. The scout then dismounted, snapped his riding-whip, and the noble beast bounded off down the street, rearing and plunging to her own intense satisfaction. A kindly-disposed individual who must have been a stranger, supposing the mare was running away, tried to catch her, when she stopped, and as if she resented his impertinence, let fly her heels at him and then quietly trotted to her stable.

"Black Nell has carried me along through many a tight place," said the scout, as we walked toward my quarters. She trains easier than any animal I ever saw. That trick of dropping quick which you saw has saved my life time and again. When I have been out scouting on the prarer or in the woods I have come across parties of rebels, and have dropped out of sight in the tall grass before they saw us. One day a gang of rebs who had been hunting for me, and thought they had my track, halted for half an hour within fifty yards of us. Nell laid as close as a rabbit, and didn't even whisk her tail to keep the flies off, until the rebs moved off, supposing they were on the wrong scent. The mare will come at my whistle and foller me about just like a dog. She won't mind any one else, nor allow them to mount her, and will kick a harness and wagon all ter pieces ef you try to hitch her in one. And she's right, Kernel," added Bill, with the enthusiasm of a true lover of horse sparkling in his eyes. "A hoss is too noble a beast to be degraded by such toggery. Harness mules and oxen, but give a hoss a chance ter run."

I had a curiosity, which was not an idle one, to hear what this man had to say about his duel with Tutt, and I asked him:

"Do you not regret killing Tutt? You surely do not like to kill men?"

"As ter killing men," he replied, "I never thought much about it. The most of the men I have killed it was one or t'other of us, and at sich times you don't stop to think; and what's the use after it's all over? As for Tutt, I had rather not have killed him, for I want ter settle down quiet here now. But thar's been hard feeling between us a long while. I wanted ter keep out of that fight; but he tried to degrade me, and I couldn't stand that, you know, for I am a fighting man, you know."

A cloud passed over the speaker's face for a moment as he continued:

"And there was a cause of quarrel between us which people round her don't know about. One of us had to die; and the secret died with him."

"Why did you not wait to see if your ball had hit him? Why did you turn round so quickly?"

The scout fixed his gray eyes on mine, striking his leg with his riding-whip, as he answered,

"I *knew* he was a dead man. I never miss a shot. I turned on the crowd because I was sure they would shoot me if they saw him fall."

"The people about here tell me you are a quiet, civil man. How is it you get into these fights?"

"D——d if I can tell," he replied, with a puzzled look which at once gave place to a proud, defiant expression as he continued— "but you know a man must defend his honor."

"Yes," I admitted, with some hesitation, remembering that I was not in Boston but on the border, and that the code of honor and mode of redress differ slightly in the one place from those of the other.

One of the reasons for my desire to make the acquaintance of Wild Bill was to obtain from his own lips a true account of some of the adventures related of him. It was not an easy matter. It was hard to overcome the reticence which makes men who have lived the wild mountain life, and which was one of his valuable qualifications as a scout. Finally he said:

"I hardly know where to begin. Pretty near all these stories are true. I was at it all the war. That affair of my swimming the river took place on that long scout of mine when I was with the rebels five months, when I was sent by General Curtis to Price's army. Things had come pretty close at that time, and it wasn't safe to go straight inter their lines. Every body was suspected who came from these parts. So I started off and went way up to Kansas City. I bought a horse there and struck out onto the plains, and then went down through Southern Kansas into Arkansas. I knew a rebel named Barnes, who was killed at Pea Ridge. He was from near Austin in Texas. So I called myself his brother and enlisted in a regiment of mounted rangers.

"General Price was just then getting ready for a raid into Missouri. It was sometime before we got into the campaign, and it was mighty hard work for me. The men of our regiment were awful. They didn't mind killing a man no more than a hog. The officers had no command over them. They were afraid of their own men, and let them do what they liked; so they would rob and sometimes murder their own people. It was right hard for me to keep up with them, and not do as they did. I never let on that I was a good shot. I kept that back for big occasions; but ef you'd heard me swear and cuss the blue-bellies, you'd a-thought me one of the wickedest of the whole crew. So it went on until we came near Curtis's army. Bime-by they were on one side Sandy River and we were on t'other. All the time I had been getting information until I knew every regiment and its strength; how much cavalry there was, and how many guns the artillery had.

"You see 'twas time for me to go, but it wasn't easy to git out, for the river was close picketed on both sides. One day when I was on picket our men and the rebels got talking and cussin each other, as you know they used to do. After a while one of the Union men offered to exchange some coffee for tobacco. So we went out onto a little island which was neutral ground like. The minute I saw the other party, who belong to the Missouri cavalry, we recognized each other. I was awful afraid they'd let on. So I blurted out:

" 'Now, Yanks, let's see yer coffee—no burnt beans, mind yer—but the genuine stuff. We know the real article if we is Texans.'

" 'The boys kept mum, and we separated. Half an hour afterward General Curtis knew I was with the rebs. But how to git across the river was what stumped me. After that, when I was on picket I didn't trouble myself about being shot. I used to fire at our boys, and they'd bang away at me, each of us taking good care to shoot wide. But how to git over the river was the bother. At last, after thinking a heap about it, I came to the conclusion that I always did, that the boldest plan is the best and safest.

"We had a big sargent in our company who was allus a-braggin that he could stump any man in the regiment. He swore he had killed more Yanks than any man in the army, and that he could do more daring things than any others. So one day when he was talking loud I took him up, and offered to bet horse for horse that I would ride out into the open, and nearer to the Yankees than he. He tried to back out of this, but the men raised a row, calling him a funk, and a bragger, and all that; so he had to go. Well, we mounted our horses, but before we came within shootin distance of the Union soldiers I made my horse kick and rear so that they could see who I was. Then we rode slowly to the river bank, side by side.

"There must have been ten thousand men watching us; for, besides the rebs who wouldn't have cried about it if we had both been killed, our boys saw something was up, and without being seen thousands of them came down to the river. Their pickets kept firing at the sargent; but whether or not they were afraid of putting a ball through me I don't know, but nary a shot hit him. He was a plucky feller all the same, for the bullets zitted about in every direction.

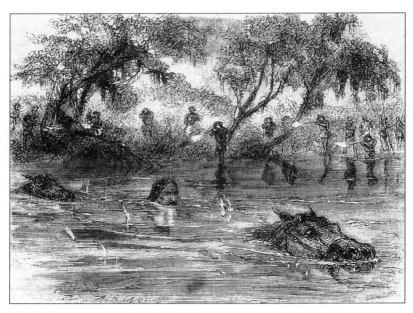

"Taking to the water," from Harper's.

"Bime-by we got right close ter the river, when one of the Yan-kee soldiers yelled out, 'Bully for Wild Bill!'

" 'Then the sargent suspicioned me, for he turned on me and growled out, 'By God, I believe yer a Yank!' And he at onst drew his revolver; but he was too late, for the minute he drew his pistol I put a ball through him. I mightn't have killed him if he hadn't suspicioned me. I had to do it then.

"As he rolled out of the saddle I took his horse by the bit, and dashed into the water as quick as I could. The minute I shot the sargent our boys set up a tremendous shout, and opened a smashing fire on the rebs who had commenced popping at me. But I had got into deep water, and had slipped off my horse over his back, and steered him for the opposite bank by holding onto his tail with one hand, while I held the bridle rein of the sargent's horse in the other hand. It was the hottest bath I ever took. Whew! For about two minutes how the bullets zitted and skipped on the water. I thought I was hit again and again, but the reb sharp-shooters were bothered by the splash we made, and in a little while our boys drove them to cover, and after some tumbling at the bank got into the brush with my two horses without a scratch.

"It is a fact," said the scout, while he caressed his long hair, "I felt sort of proud when the boys took me into camp, and General Curtis thanked me before a heap of generals.

"But I never tried that thing over again; nor I didn't go a scouting openly in Price's army after that. They all knew me too well and you see 'twouldn't a been healthy to have been caught."

The scout's story of swimming the river ought, perhaps, to have satisfied my curiosity; but I was especially desirous to hear him relate the story of a sanguinary fight which he had with a party of ruffians in the early part of the war, when, single handed, he fought and killed ten men. I had heard the story as it came from an officer of the regular army who, an hour after the affair, saw Bill and the ten dead men—some killed with bullets, others hacked and slashed to death with a knife.

As I write out the details of this terrible tale from notes which I took as the words fell from the scout's lips, I am conscious of its extreme improbability; but while I listened to him I remembered the story in the Bible, where we are told that Samson "with the jawbone of an ass slew a thousand men," and as I looked upon this magnificent example of human strength and daring, he appeared to me to realize the powers of a Samson and Hercules combined, and I should not have been inclined to place any limit upon his achievements. Besides this, one who has lived for four years in the presence of such grand heroism and deeds of prowess as was seen during the war is in what might be called a "receptive" mood. Be the story true or not, in part, or in whole, I belived then every word Wild Bill uttered, and I believe it to-day.

" 'I don't like to talk about that M'Kandlas affair," said Bill, in answer to my question. "It gives me a queer shiver whenever I think of it, and sometimes I dream about it, and wake up in a cold sweat.

"You see this M'Kandlas was the Captain of a gang of desperadoes, horse-thieves, murderers, regular cut-throats, who were the terror of every body on the border, and who kept us in the mountains in hot water whenever they were around. I knew them all in the mountains, where they pretended to be trapping, but they were hiding from the hangman. M'Kandlas was the biggest scoundrel and bully of them all, and was allers a-braggin of what he could do. One day I beat him shootin at a mark, and then threw him at the back-holt. And I didn't drop him as soft as you would a baby, you may be sure. Well, he got savage mad about it, and swore he would have his revenge on me some time.

"This was just before the war broke out, and we were already takin sides in the mountains either for the South or the Union. M'Kandlas and his gang were border-ruffians in the Kansas row, and of course they went with the rebs. Bime-by he clar'd out, and I shouldn't have thought of the feller agin ef he hadn't crossed my path. It 'pears he didn't forget me.

"It was in '61, when I guided a detachment of cavalry who were comin in from Camp Floyd. We had nearly reached the Kansas line, and were in South Nebraska, when one afternoon I went out of camp to go to the cabin of an old friend of mine, a Mrs. Waltman. I took only one of my revolvers with me, for although the war had broke out I didn't think it necessary to carry both my pistols, and, in all or'nary scrimmages, one is better than a dozen ef you shoot straight. I saw some wild turkeys on the road as I was goin down, and popped one of 'em over, thinkin he'd be just the thing for supper.

"Well, I rode up to Mrs. Waltman's, jumped off my horse, and went into the cabin, which is like most of the cabins on the prarer, with only one room, and that had two doors, one opening in front and t'other on a yard, like.

" 'How are you, Mrs. Waltman?' I said, feeling as jolly as you please.

"The minute she saw me she turned as white as a sheet and screamed: 'Is that you, Bill? Oh, my God! they will kill you! Run! run! They will kill you!'

" 'Who's a-goin to kill me?' said I. 'There's two can play at that game.'

" 'It's M'Kandlas and his gang. There's ten of them, and you've no chance. They've jes gone down the road to the corn rack. They came up here only five minutes ago. M'Kandlas was draggin poor Parson Shipley on the ground with a lariat round his neck. The preacher was most dead with choking and the horses stamping on him. M'Kandlas knows yer bringin in that party of Yankee cavalry, and he swears he'll cut yer heart out. Run, Bill, run—But it's too late; they're comin up the lane.'

"While she was a-talkin I remembered I had but one revolver,

"The warning," from Harper's.

and a load gone out of that. On the table there was a horn of powder and some little bars of lead. I poured some powder into the empty chamber and rammed the lead after it by hammering the barrel on the table, and had just capped the pistol when I heard M'Kandlas shout:

"'There's that d——d Yank Wild Bill's horse; he's here; and we'll skin him alive!'

"If I had thought of runnin before it war too late now, and the house was my best holt—a sort of fortress, like. I never thought I should leave that room alive."

The scout stopped his story, rose from his seat, and strode back and forward in a state of great excitement.

"I tell you what it is, Kernel," he resumed, after a while, "I don't mind a scrimmage with those fellers round here. Shoot one or two of them and the rest run away. But all of M'Kandlas's gang were reckless, blood-thirsty devils, who would fight as long as they had strength to pull a trigger. I have been in tight places, but that's one of the few times I said my prayers.

"'Surround the house and give him no quarter!' yelled M'Kandlas. When I heard that I felt as quiet and cool as if I was a-goin to church. I looked round the room and saw a Hawkins rifle hangin over the bed.

" 'Is that loaded?' said I to Mrs. Waltman.

" 'Yes,' the poor thing whispered. She was so frightened she couldn't speak out loud.

" 'Are you sure?' said I, as I jumped to the bed and caught it from its hooks. Although my eye did not leave the door, yet I could see she nodded 'Yes' again. I put the revolver on the bed, and just then M'Kandlas poked his head inside the doorway, but jumped back when he saw me with the rifle in my hand.

" 'Come in here, you cowardly dog!' I shouted. 'Come in here, and fight me!'

"M'Kandlas was no coward, if he was a bully. He jumped inside the room with his gun leveled to shoot; but he was not quick enough. My rifle-ball went through his heart. He fell back outside the house, where he was found afterward holding tight to his rifle, which had fallen over his head.

"His disappearance was followed by a yell from his gang and then there was a dead silence. I put down the rifle and took the revolver, and I said to myself: 'Only six shots and nine men to kill. Save your powder, Bill, for the death-hug's a-comin!' I don't know why it was, Kernel," continued Bill, looking at me inquiringly, "but at that moment things seemed clear and sharp. I could think strong.

"There was a few seconds of that awful stillness, then the ruffians came rushing at both doors. How wild they looked with their red, drunken faces and inflamed eyes, shouting and cussing! But I never aimed more deliberately in my life.

"One—two—three—four; and four men fell dead.

"That didn't stop the rest. Two of them fired their bird guns at me. And then I felt a sting run all over me. The room was full of smoke. Two got in close to me, their eyes glaring out of the clouds. One I knocked down with my fist. 'You are out of the way for a while,' I thought. The second I shot dead. The other three clutched me and crowded me onto the bed. I fought hard. I broke with my hand one man's arm. He had his fingers round my throat. Before I could get to my feet I was struck across the breast with the stock of a rifle, and I felt the blood rushing out of my nose and mouth. Then I got ugly, and I remember that I got hold

"The struggle for life," from Harper's.

of a knife, and then it was all cloudy like, and I was wild, and I struck savage blows, following the devils up from one side to the other of the room and into the corners, striking and slashing until I knew that every one was dead.

"All of a sudden it seemed as if my heart was on fire. I was bleeding everywhere. I rushed out to the well and drank from the bucket, and then tumbled down in a faint."

Breathless with the intense interest with which I had followed this strange story, all the more thrilling and weird when its hero, seeming to live over again the bloody events of that day, gave way to its terrible spirit with wild, savage gestures. I saw then—what my scrutiny of the morning had failed to discover—the tiger which lay concealed beneath that gentle exterior.

"You must have been hurt almost to death," I said.

"There were eleven buck-shot in me. I carry some of them now. I was cut in thirteen places. All of them had enough to have let out the life of a man. But that blessed old Dr. Mills pulled me safe through it, after a bed siege of many a long week."

"That prayer of yours, Bill, may have been more potent for your safety than you think. You should thank God for your deliverance."

"To tell you the truth, Kernel," responded the scout with a certain solemnity in his grave face, "I don't talk about sich things ter the people round here, but I allers feel sort of thankful when I get out of a bad scrape."

"In all your wild, perilous adventures," I asked him, "have you ever been afraid? Do you know what the sensation is? I am sure you will not misunderstand the question, for I take it we soldiers comprehend justly that there is no higher courage than that which shows itself when the consciousness of danger is keen but where moral strength overcomes the weakness of the body."

"I think I know what you mean, Sir, and I'm not ashamed to say that I have been so frightened that it 'peared is if all the strength and blood had gone out of my body, and my face was as white as chalk. It was at the Wilme Creek fight. I had fired more than fifty cartridges, and I think fetched my man every time. I was on the skirmish line, and was working up closer to the rebs, when all of a sudden a battery opened fire right in front of me, and it sounded as if forty thousand guns were firing, and every shot and shell screeched within six inches of my head. It was the first time I was ever under artillery fire, and I was so frightened that I couldn't move for a minute or so, and when I did go back the boys asked me if I had seen a ghost? They may shoot bullets at me by the dozen, and it's rather exciting if I can shoot back, but I am always sort of nervous when the big guns go off."

"I would like to see you shoot."

"Would yer?" replied the scout, drawing his revolver; and approaching the window, he pointed to a letter O in a sign-board which was fixed to the stone-wall of a building on the other side of the way.

"That sign is more than fifty yards away. I will put these six balls into the inside of the circle, which isn't bigger than a man's heart."

In an off-hand way, and without sighting the pistol with his eye, he discharged the six shots of his revolver. I afterwards saw that all the bullets had entered the circle.

As Bill proceeded to reload his pistol, he said to me with a naivete of manner which was meant to be assuring:

"Whenever you get into a row be sure and not shoot too

"The farewell," from Harper's.

quick. Take time. I've known many a feller slip up for shootin' in a hurry."

It would be easy to fill a volume with the adventures of that remarkable man. My object here has been to make a slight record of one who is one of the best—perhaps the very best—example of a class who more than any other encountered perils and privations in defense of our nationality.

One afternoon as General Smith and I mounted our horses to start upon our journey toward the East, Wild Bill came to shake hands good-by, and I said to him:

"If you have no objection I will write out for publication an account of a few of your adventures."

"Certainly you may," he replied. "I'm sort of public property. But, Kernel," he continued, leaning upon my saddle bow, while there was a tremulous softness in his voice and a strange moisture in his averted eyes, "I have a mother back there in Illinois who is old and feeble. I haven't seen her this many a year, and haven't been a good son to her, yet I love her better than any thing in this life. It don't matter much what they say about me here. But I'm not a cut-throat and vagabond, and I'd like the old woman to know what'll make her proud. I'd like her to hear

that her runaway boy has fought through the war for the Union
like a true man."

[William Hitchcock—called *Wild Bill, the Scout of the
Plains*—shall have his wish. I have told his story precisely as it
was told to me, confirmed in all important points by many witnesses; and I have no doubt of its truth.—G. W. N.]

Notes

Preface

1. Elmo Scott Watson as a witness in a Western "court" that sat in judgment in "The Case of James Butler Hickok, alias 'Wild Bill'," *The Westerners Brand Book* (Chicago; 1945–1946), vol. 3, (April–May 1946), nos. 2–3, 5; Richard O'Connor, *Wild Bill Hickok* (New York, 1959), 9, 108; Richard O'Connor to Joseph G. Rosa, September 18, 1968. O'Connor wrote that he had destroyed the materials he used when he wrote his Hickok book.

2. Frank McLynn, "Riding into Legend on the Back of a Bullet," *Times Higher Education Supplement* (London), June 15, 1990.

3. Mari Sandoz, *The Buffalo Hunters* (London, 1960), 87; Mari Sandoz to Joseph G. Rosa, November 24, 1956.

4. Mari Sandoz, *The Cattlemen: From the Rio Grande Across the Far Marias* (New York, 1958), 319.

Chapter One
In Search of "Wild Bill"

1. Lydia Hickok Barnes to Harry S. Young, September 7, 1915. Copy courtesy of David Dary.

2. Homer W. Wheeler, *The Frontier Trail* (Los Angeles, 1923), 98–102.

3. Manhattan (Kans.) *Independent,* October 26, 1867.

4. North Topeka (Kans.) *Times,* August 31, 1876 (see also the Tacoma (Wash.) *Daily Tribune,* February 15, 1911); Charles F. Gross to J. B. Edwards, April 26, 1926, Manuscripts Division, Kansas State Historical Society, Topeka, Kans. (hereafter cited as KSHS); Kansas City, Mo.,

city directories (1872–1876); Darrell Garwood, *Crossroads of America: The Story of Kansas City* (New York, 1948), 125.

5. Samuel D. Henry, "Wild Bill—Some Personal Recollections," Coon Rapids (Iowa) *Enterprise,* June 10, 1927.

6. W. E. Webb, "Air Towns and Their Inhabitants," *Harper's New Monthly Magazine,* November 1875, 828–835.

7. William E. Curtis, *A Summer Scamper Along the Old Santa Fe Trail and Through the Gorges of Colorado to Zion* (Chicago, 1883), 58–59.

8. Hays (Kans.) *Daily News,* June 20, 1931.

9. Joseph G. Rosa, *They Called Him Wild Bill: The Life and Adventures of James Butler Hickok* (Norman, Okla., 1964 and 1974), 227–234. I am indebted to James McLaird for details of the Newson play.

10. Ibid., 237; Charles Gross to J. B. Edwards, April 13, 1922, and June 15, 1925, KSHS.

11. Elizabeth Bacon Custer, *Following the Guidon,* (New York, 1890), 160–161.

12. Chicago *Tribune,* August 25, 1876.

13. Undated clipping in the newspaper scrapbooks, KSHS.

14. Rosa, *They Called Him Wild Bill,* 237–241; it was only following publication that I was shown a copy of Agnes's certificate of marriage to Carson in 1877. No evidence of a divorce has been found.

15. I am indebted to Fred Kline for bringing the photograph and poem to my attention and for presenting me with copies. Robin May found the Saxe poem, and Iris Wylie of the Green County Library discovered "Salina Stubbs."

16. Joseph G. Rosa, *They Called Him Wild Bill,* 10–14; for a complete history of the Hickok family, see Edith Harmon, *Pioneer Settlers of Troy Grove, Ill.* (Mendota, Illinois, 1973). I am also indebted to Edith Harmon, Hickok's grandniece, for additional information on the family.

17. Copy supplied by Edith Harmon.

18. Conversations with the late Ethel Hickok and Edith Harmon.

19. James Butler Hickok to Polly Butler Hickok, September 28, 1856. The original is now owned by KSHS.

20. Polly Butler Hickok to Horace Hickok, August 16, 1859, KSHS.

21. James Butler Hickok to Horace Hickok, November 24, 1856, KSHS.

22. Lorenzo Butler Hickok to Polly Butler Hickok, December 2, 1867, KSHS.

23. Webb, "Air Towns and Their Inhabitants," 833.

24. Richard Dunlop, "Wild Bill Donovan on the Mexican Border,"

The Westerners Brand Book, vol. 39 (Chicago, November–December, 1982), no. 5, 33–35.

25. Leavenworth *Daily Conservative,* August 4, 1863.

26. Martin Ismert to Joseph G. Rosa, September 11, 1957.

27. Leo E. Huff, "Guerrillas, Jayhawkers and Bushwhackers in Northern Arkansas During the Civil War," *Arkansas Historical Quarterly* 24:2 (Summer 1965): 137; Olathe (Kans.) *Mirror,* February 27, 1864.

28. Rosa, *They Called Him Wild Bill,* 120.

29. Wayne Spiller to Patricia Wagner, editor of *True West,* May 27, 1972. She kindly supplied the author with a copy.

30. For a detailed examination of this killing, see Rosa, *They Called Him Wild Bill,* 207–221; San Francisco *Daily Evening Bulletin,* September 18, 1871 (citing the Omaha *Herald* of September 6); copy supplied by William B. Secrest.

31. Mary Jo Cooper, Austin, Tex., Public Library, to Joseph G. Rosa, June 20, 1990, enclosing copies of census returns.

32. Case no. 84, the *U.S. v. J. Hickox,* indictment for contempt, U.S. District Court Records, Kansas Territory, 1855–1859, Archives Division, KSHS.

33. J. W. Buel, *Heroes of the Plains* (New York and St. Louis, 1882), 28–29; *U.S. v. William Hanschien, alias "Shanghai Bill,"* U.S. District Court Records, Kansas Territory, 1855–1859, Archives Divisions, KSHS.

34. "The Hickok Legend," typescript, together with other papers prepared by Howard L. Hickok, presented to the author by his son, the late James Butler Hickok, United States Marine Corps. George W. Hance, "The Truth About Wild Bill," Topeka *Mail and Breeze,* December 20, 1901; "George W. Hance Recounts Interesting Story of 'Wild Bill' Hickok," Rolla (Mo.) *Herald,* January 18, 1912.

35. William Pound, U.S. Attorney, to the Hon. Alphonso Taft, Attorney General, February 7, 1877. Records of the Office of the Pardon Attorney, No. F-307, Records Group No. 204, National Archives, Washington, D.C.

Chapter Two
A Hero of Harper's

1. George Ward Nichols, "Wild Bill," *Harper's New Monthly Magazine* 34 (February, 1867): 274. See Appendix for the complete text of this article.

2. Charles W. Scholten's studio was on the south side of the public

square, and he is believed to have made several plates of Hickok. Apart from the famous woodcut, which is based on a *carte de visite,* only one other of his photographs has come to light. It is reproduced in this volume.

3. His opinion was shared by J. B. Edwards, who had known Hickok at Abilene: "I want to go on record and say this, Wild Bill never used the words and language which said [Nichols's] write up claims he used their [sic] or any other time to anybody during his life time." (J. B. Edwards to William E. Connelley, September 13, 1927, Manuscripts Division, KSHS).

4. Original copies of these are now rare. Some issues are held by the Library of Congress.

5. This letter and letters from James, Lorenzo, Oliver, and other members of the family are now on file at the KSHS.

6. Springfield *Missouri Weekly Patriot,* July 27, 1865.

7. Nichols, "Wild Bill," 285; Horace D. Hickok to the editor of the Topeka *Mail and Breeze,* September 27, 1901.

8. Records of the Quartermaster General, 1861–1865, National Archives, Washington, D.C.

9. I am indebted to Jo Lohoefener, Oberlin, Kansas, a grandniece of Lydia Hickok Barnes, for a copy of this letter.

10. The original letter is now on file at the KSHS; Records of the Quartermaster General, 1861–1865, National Archives, Washington, D.C.

11. Records of the Quartermaster General, 1861–1865, National Archives, Washington, D.C.

12. John B. Sanborn, *The Campaign in Missouri in September and October, 1864* (n.p., n.d.), 32. Copy kindly supplied by the University of Missouri, Rolla.

13. F. A. Carpenter, *History of the 17th Illinois Cavalry Volunteers* (n.p., ca. 1886), not paginated. Copy supplied by Rodney Staab.

14. Records of the Seventeenth Illinois Volunteer Cavalry, copy of Alfred Brock's service record supplied by the Illinois State Historical Society; G. Beighey to Joseph G. Rosa, October–December, 1984; Michael E. Pilgrim, Military Service Branch, Military Archives Division, National Archives, Washington, D.C., to Joseph G. Rosa, June 3, 1985.

15. The original letter is now on file at the KSHS.

16. Records of the Quartermaster General, 1861–1865, National Archives, Washington, D.C.; *The War of the Rebellion: A Compilation of Official Records of the Union and Confederate Armies,* vol. 150, ser. 1, vol. 47, pt. 1, 810, 819.

17. Ibid.

18. Records of the Quartermaster General, 1861–1865, National Archives, Washington, D.C.

19. Nichols, "Wild Bill," 275.

20. Ibid., 279.

21. Ibid.; Springfield *Missouri Weekly Patriot,* January 31, 1867.

22. Nichols, "Wild Bill," 274, 279.

23. William E. Connelley, *Wild Bill and His Era* (New York, 1933), 70; Frank J. Wilstach, *Wild Bill Hickok: The Prince of Pistoleers* (New York, 1926), 106.

24. Records of the Quartermaster General, 1861–1865, National Archives, Washington, D.C.

25. Nichols, "Wild Bill," 281–282.

26. Leo E. Huff, "Guerrillas, Jayhawkers and Bushwhackers in Northern Arkansas During the Civil War," *Arkansas Historical Quarterly* 24:2 (Summer 1965): 128–129.

27. Ibid., 129–130; William W. Denison, "Early Days in Osage County," Kansas State Historical Society *Collections* 17 (1926–1928), 145–146.

28. Gary L. Cheatham, " 'Desperate Characters': The Development and Impact of the Confederate Guerrillas in Kansas," *Kansas History: A Journal of the Central Plains* 14:3 (Autumn 1991): 144–161

29. Huff, "Guerrillas," 128–129.

30. Sanborn, *The Campaign in Missouri,* 25; Donald R. Hale, *They Called Him Bloody Bill: The Life of William Anderson, Missouri Guerrilla* (Clinton, Mo., 1982), 77–78.

31. Michael Fellman, *Inside War: The Guerrilla Conflict in Missouri during the American Civil War* (New York, 1989), 247–248.

32. J. W. Buel, *Heroes of the Plains* (New York and St. Louis, 1882), 69–72.

33. In an effort to find Buel's papers, which might include the alleged "diary," I enlisted the aid of a computer expert/researcher. She checked every likely source within the United States and found nothing (Audrey Harmon to Joseph G. Rosa, February 20, 1995).

34. Frances B. Heitman, *Historical Register and Dictionary of the United States Army* (Washington, D.C., 1903), 747; Nichols devoted much of his later years to music, and upon his death from tuberculosis on September 15, 1885, he was the much-respected founder and president of the College of Music at Cincinnati.

35. Extracts were kindly provided by his great-grandson, Prof. Robert W. Hatton.

Chapter Three
Tall Tales and Tangled Truths

1. St. Louis *Weekly Missouri Democrat,* April 16, 1867.
2. J. W. Buel, *Heroes of the Plains* (New York and St. Louis, 1883), 36–38.
3. Ibid., 445.
4. Ibid., 471–473.
5. George Ward Nichols, "Wild Bill," *Harper's New Monthly Magazine* (February 1867): 282–284.
6. I am indebted to William B. Secrest for details of this affair.
7. Edwin P. Mitchell, *Memoirs of an Editor: Fifty Years of American Journalism* (New York and London, 1924), 104–105; Lewiston (Maine) *Evening Journal,* February 4, 1874, announced the appearance of the Combination at the Lyceum Hall on the evening of the sixth).
8. Topeka (Kans.) *Mail and Breeze,* June 21 and July 5, 1901.
9. Cheyenne *Wyoming State Tribune,* December 24, 1948; Cheyenne (Wyo.) *Leader,* August 18, 1903.
10. J. W. ("Doc") Howard, *"Doc" Howard's Memoirs* (Denver, Colo., 1931), 19–20.
11. William F. Cody, *The Life of Hon. William F. Cody, Known as Buffalo Bill* (Hartford, Conn., 1879), 332.
12. Hays (Kans.) *Ellis County News,* March 28, 1929.
13. Hays (Kans.) *Daily News,* March 12, 1931.
14. Sir Richard Burton, *The Look of the West 1860: Across the Plains to California* (Lincoln, Nebr., 1965), 11.
15. Major Albert Barnitz, diary, Barnitz Papers, Beinecke Library, Yale University, copy supplied by Robert M. Utley.
16. Luther North, *Man of the Plains* (Lincoln, Nebr., 1961), edited by Donald F. Danker, 250–251; see also Herbert Cody Blake, *Blake's Western Stories* (Brooklyn, N.Y., 1929), 11. The late Don Russell, who spent some time analyzing Luther's statements, wrote, "Luther North did a lot of shouting about things that aren't so. Don't take him too seriously" (Don Russell to Joseph G. Rosa, September 17, 1958); Cheyenne *Wyoming State Tribune,* July 13, 1910, and December 7, 1943.
17. Charles B. Roth to Joseph G. Rosa, July 18, 1956.
18. Charles F. Gross to J. B. Edwards, June 15, 1925, Manuscripts Division, KSHS.
19. D. R. Gorden to George Hance, June 25, 1929, Manuscripts Department, Nebraska State Historical Society.
20. Thomas J. Dimsdale, *The Vigilantes of Montana* (Norman, Okla., 1953), 25.

21. W. E. Webb, *Buffalo Land* (Cincinnati and Chicago, 1872), 146.

22. *New York Clipper,* September 13, 1873.

23. Buel, *Heroes,* 213–214.

24. For a complete review of Hickok's pistol skills and further information on the pistols he used, see Joseph G. Rosa, *They Called Him Wild Bill: The Life and Adventures of James Butler Hickok* (Norman, Okla., 1964 and 1974), 338–349.

25. W. W. Greener, *The Gun and Its Development* (London, 1910), 538–539.

26. William B. ("Bat") Masterson, "The Tenderfoot's Turn," *Guns Quarterly* 2 (Summer 1960): 10–13, 66–67.

27. Ed McGivern, *Fast and Fancy Revolver Shooting* (Chicago, 1975), 95–113, 302.

28. *Description and Rules for the Management of the Springfield Rifle, Carbine, and Army Revolvers* (Washington, D.C., 1898), 67–68.

Chapter Four
"The Scout of the Plains"

1. J. W. Buel, *Heroes of the Plains* (New York and St. Louis, 1882), 98–100; *Buffalo Bill's Wild West and Congress of Rough Riders of the World* (souvenir program, 1893), 14–15.

2. Howard R. Lamar, ed., *The Reader's Encyclopedia of the American West* (New York, 1977), 102–103.

3. The original letter is now located in the Manuscripts Division, KSHS.

4. Ibid.; in October 1990, Gregory Hermon walked me over the site of the Battle of Bull Creek and explained how the action took place.

5. Robert H. Williams, *With the Border Ruffians* (London, 1907), 101.

6. Leavenworth *Kansas Weekly Herald,* January 30, 1858.

7. Gregory Hermon to Joseph G. Rosa, March 7, 1990. Mr. Hermon has studied the original land grants.

8. I am indebted to Hickok's grandniece Edith Harmon for the text of the letter from Guy Butler. The letter from Jones & Cartwright is now in the author's collection; "Julia Cody Goodman's Memoirs of Buffalo Bill," edited by Don Russell, *Kansas Historical Quarterly* 27:4 (Winter 1962): 484.

9. Records of the Quartermaster General, 1861–1865, National Archives, Washington, D.C; Charles Dawson, *Pioneer Tales of the Oregon*

Trail (Topeka, Kans., 1912), 106–107; *Buffalo Bill's Wild West* (souvenir program), 1893, 15.

10. St. Louis *Weekly Missouri Democrat,* May 21, 1867; Marysville (Kans.) *Enterprise,* May 18,1867.

11. George A. Custer, *My Life on the Plains* (New York, 1876), 130.

12. Ibid., 178.

13. Leavenworth (Kans.) *Daily Conservative,* March 17, 1868; Leavenworth (Kans.) *Daily Times,* November 16, 1870; William E. Connelley, *Wild Bill and His Era* (New York, 1933), 103–105.

14. Custer, *My Life,* 131.

15. *Trail* 1:11 (April 1909): 14–18; Denver *Rocky Mountain News,* September 14, 1868; Central City *Register,* September 8, 1868.

16. *Compendious History of Ellsworth County, Kansas: From Its Early Settlement to the Present Time,* printed at the office of the Ellsworth *Reporter,* 1879, 19–20.

17. Elizabeth Bacon Custer, *Following the Guidon* (New York, 1890), 160–161; Elizabeth Bacon Custer, *Tenting on the Plains* (New York, 1887), 622.

18. Custer, *My Life,* 33–34.

19. Ibid.

20. Letters Dispatched (1867), Fort Harker, National Archives, Washington, D.C.; Robert M. Utley, ed., *Life in Custer's Cavalry: Diaries and Letters of Albert and Jennie Barnitz, 1867–1868* (New Haven and London, 1977), 37–38.

21. Francis Cragin, "Early West Notebook," Francis Cragin Collection, Colorado Springs Pioneer Museum.

22. George A. Armes, *Ups and Downs of an Army Officer* (Washington, D.C., 1900), 271–272.

23. Gen. E. A. Carr, "Carr's Campaign of 1868–69" (manuscript in the possession of James T. King); Letters Dispatched (1869), Records of Fort Dodge, National Archives, Washington, D.C.

24. Ibid.;William F. Cody, *The Life of the Hon. William F. Cody, Known as Buffalo Bill* (Hartford, Conn., 1879), 227.

25. Hiram Robbins, "Wild Bill's Humors," *Arkansaw Traveler,* n.d.

26. William E. Connelley, *Wild Bill and His Era* (New York, 1933), 113.

27. David Dixon, "A Scout with Custer: Edmund Guerrier on the Hancock Expedition of 1867," *Kansas History* 4:3 (Autumn 1981): 155–156.

28. Ibid., 160–161.

29. Custer, *My Life,* 47.

30. Theodore R. Davis, "Henry M. Stanley's Indian Campaign in

1867," *The Westerners Brand Book* (1945–1946), vol. 2 (Chicago, 1947), 106–107; *Harper's Weekly,* June 29, 1867, 406.

31. John S. Gray, "Will Comstock—The Natty Bumppo of Kansas," *The Westerners Brand Book,* vol. 18 (Chicago, February 1962), no. 12, 89–91, 93–96.

32. Ibid.

33. William F. Cody to John W. Crawford, August 23, 1885, William F. Cody Papers, Box 1, Western History Collection, Denver Public Library; see also Darlis A. Miller, *Captain Jack Crawford: Buckskin Poet, Scout, and Showman* (Albuquerque, N.M.), 1993.

34. George Ward Nichols, "Wild Bill," *Harper's New Monthly Magazine* 34 (February 1867): 274; Meadville (Pa.) *Evening Republican,* November 4, 1873; Troy (N.Y.) *Times,* February 25, 1874; Wilbert Eisele, *The Real Wild Bill Hickok* (Denver, Colo., 1931), 5.

35. *Compendious History of Ellsworth County,* 21–22.

Chapter Five
"A Bad Man to Fool With"

1. St. Louis *Weekly Missouri Democrat,* April 16, 1867.

2. Ibid.; George Ward Nichols, "Wild Bill" *Harper's New Monthly Magazine* 34 (February 1867), 274.

3. Francis Cragin, "Early West Notebook," Francis Cragin Collection, Colorado Springs Pioneer Museum; Luther North, *Man of the Plains: Recollections of Luther North, 1856–1882,* edited by Donald F. Danker (Lincoln, Nebr., 1961), 310; Pueblo (C.T.) *Chieftain,* January 28, 1869; John Malone, who later became active in politics, cited in the Wichita (Kans.) *Eagle,* September 14, 1876.

4. Manhattan (Kans.) *Independent,* October 26, 1867.

5. William Francis Hooker to Addison E. Sheldon, February 10, 1936, Manuscripts Department, Nebraska State Historical Society.

6. Hamilton Cochran, *Noted American Duels and Hostile Encounters* (Philadelphia, 1963), 14–25. Revolving breeched arms have been known since the sixteenth century, but not until the introduction of the percussion cap and Samuel Colt's Revolving Pistol were they taken seriously.

7. Philip D. Jordan, *Frontier Law and Order* (Lincoln, Nebr., 1970), 2.

8. Edgar Beecher Bronson, *The Red-blooded Heroes of the Frontier* (New York, 1910), 70.

9. Kansas City (Mo.) *Journal,* November 15, 1881.

10. W. B. ("Bat") Masterson, *Famous Gun Fighters of the Western Frontier,* annotated and illustrated by Jack DeMattos (Monroe, Wash., 1982), 11–12.

11. Nichols, "Wild Bill," 283.

12. Topeka (Kans.) *Daily Commonwealth,* December 6, 1871.

13. Leavenworth (Kans.) *Daily Times,* March 13, 1873.

14. Springfield (Mo.) *Weekly Patriot,* January 31, 1867; Atchison (Kans.) *Daily Champion,* February 5, 1867.

15. George A. Custer, *My Life on the Plains* (New York, 1876), 34.

16. Leavenworth (Kans.) *Appeal,* August 25, 1876.

17. Lawrence (Kans.) *Republican Journal,* October 7, 1871.

18. Austin (Tex.) *Democratic Statesman,* October 26, 1871.

19. Joseph G. McCoy, *Historic Sketches of the Cattle Trade of the West and Southwest,* edited and annotated by Ralph P. Bieber (Lincoln, Nebr., 1985), 204; cited by William E. Connelley in *Wild Bill and His Era* (New York, 1933), 153.

20. Chicago *Tribune,* August 25, 1876.

21. Wichita (Kans.) *Weekly Beacon,* October 28, 1874.

22. Topeka (Kans.) *Daily Commonwealth,* December 16, 1869.

23. Leavenworth (Kans.) *Daily Times,* March 13, 1873.

24. Mendota (Ill.) *Bulletin,* April 11, 1873; Annie Tallent, *The Black Hills: Or the Last Hunting Ground of the Dakotas* (St. Louis, 1899), 100–101.

25. Kansas City (Mo.) *Times,* August 30, 1876; Hays City (Kans.) *Sentinel,* February 2, 1877.

26. Joe B. Frantz, "The Frontier Tradition: An Invitation to Violence," in Hugh Davis Graham and Ted Robert Gurr, *The History of Violence in America* (New York, 1969), 132–133.

27. Richard Marohn, *The Last Gunfighter: John Wesley Hardin* (College Station, Tex., 1995), 312. Richard Marohn, "John Wesley Hardin, Adolescent Killer: The Emergence of a Narcissistic Behavior Disorder," *Annals of the American Society for Adolescent Psychiatry* 14 (1987): 271–296.

28. Charles F. Gross to J. B. Edwards, June 15, 1925, Manuscripts Division, KSHS.

29. Nichols, "Wild Bill," 282–284.

30. Atchison (Kans.) *Daily Champion,* February 5, 1867.

31. Mark Dugan, "The Mystery of Sarah Shull," in his *Tales Never Told Around the Campfire* (Athens, Ohio, 1990), 29–78.

32. For general coverage of the so-called McCanles Massacre, see George W. Hansen, "The True Story of Wild Bill–McCanles Affray in Jefferson County, Nebraska, July 12, 1861" (with supporting articles by Addison E. Sheldon and William Monroe McCanles), *Nebraska History*

Magazine 10:2 (April–June, 1927); William E. Connelley, "Wild Bill—James Butler Hickok: David C. McCanles at Rock Creek," Kansas State Historical Society *Collections* 17 (1926–1928); Joseph G. Rosa, *They Called Him Wild Bill* (Norman, Okla., 1964 and 1974), 34–52.

33. Major Albert Barnitz, diary, Second Ohio Cavalry, Barnitz Papers, Beinecke Library, Yale University.

34. Springfield (Mo.) *Weekly Patriot,* August 10, 1865; *State of Missouri v. James Hickok* on a charge of manslaughter, Boxes 486 and 498; *State of Missouri v. Davis K. Tutt* on a charge of gambling, Box 584, Records of the Circuit Court, Greene County, Mo., Regular Term, 1865 (Greene County Archive, Springfield, Mo.).

35. Kansas City (Mo.) *Daily Journal of Commerce,* August 25, 1869.

36. J. W. Buel, *Heroes of the Plains* (New York and St. Louis, 1882), 116–117.

37. Blaine Burkey, *Wild Bill Hickok the Law in Hays City* (Hays, Kans., 1975), 10–12.

38. A. D. Bellport to G. W. Hansen, March 15, 1929, Manuscripts Department, Nebraska State Historical Society.

39. John Ryan, "Ten Years with General Custer Among the American Indians," *Newton Circuit,* July 9, 1909.

40. James D. Drees, "The Hays City Vigilante Period, 1868–1869," M.A. thesis, Fort Hays State University. Copy supplied by the author.

41. Buel, *Heroes of the Plains,* 116–117.

42. Service records of privates John Kile and Jeremiah Lonergan, U.S. Seventh Cavalry Regiment, National Archives, Washington, D.C.; some companies of the Seventh Cavalry were issued the Remington "New Model" Army pistol. During the Civil War, the Ordnance Department advised the War Department that a number of these .44 caliber revolvers had failed to meet their tests. In 1867 Gen. C. C. Auger, commanding the Department of the Platte, complained that many of the Remington pistols issued to his command had exploded or misfired. He reported that they had not experienced similar problems with Colt pistols (Records Group 156, Records of the Office of the Chief of Ordnance, National Archives, Washington, D.C.); Junction City (Kans.) *Union,* July 23, 1870; Records of Fort Hays, Kans., National Archives, Washington, D.C.

43. Buel, *Heroes of the Plains,* 118–122.

44. Olathe (Kans.) *Mirror and Newsletter,* February 23, 1882.

45. Charles F. Gross to J. B. Edwards, June 15, 1925, Manuscripts Division, KSHS.

46. The late Martin Ismert advised me in the late 1950s that Robert W. Snyder, Jr., an early-day Kansas City historian was told by the Wil-

liams family that Wild Bill explained to Michael's widow Mary what happened. Further proof that Williams had connections with the Abilene police force was found in the Warrensburg (Mo.) *Standard* of October 12, 1871, which carried a report of the Coe-Williams shooting copied from the Kansas City *News* of October 6: "One of the victims was Mike Williams, who until recently was a resident of this city, for a long time keeping the saloon at the corner of 12th and Walnut streets, and afterwards bartender at Dennis Halpine's saloon, on 4th street. About four months ago he went to Abilene and took a position on the police force, leaving his wife in this city, now living with a brother in McGee's addition." The 1870 census of Jackson County, Mo., disclosed that Michael Williams was 28 and his wife Mary was 18. They lived in the same dwelling (no. 841) as John Williams (age 29), his wife, Mary C. Williams, age 19, and their son, George M. Williams, age five months. Another couple, Theodore and Eliza Steinbach also lived at the same address, which suggests that it was a boarding house.

47. Abilene (Kans.) *Chronicle,* October 12, 1871; Topeka (Kans.) *Daily Commonwealth,* November 25, 1871; this item, headed "Attempt to kill Marshal Hickok," was later published in the *Chronicle* of November 30 without any comment; Records of the City Council of Abilene (1871), microfilm copy, Manuscripts Division, KSHS.

48. Mendota (Ill.) *Bulletin,* April 11, 1873.

Chapter Six
"A Terror to Evil-Doers"

1. James Butler Hickok to his family, August 20, 1858. The original is on file at the KSHS; Case No. 84, the *U.S. v. J. Hickox,* indictment for contempt, Records of the U. S. District Court, Kansas Territory, KSHS.

2. Case No. 482, the *U.S. v. John Tobin and William Wilson,* larceny, District Court, District of Kansas, Records Group No. 21, Federal Archive Center, Kansas City, Mo.

3. Available records in the National Archives indicate that Hickok served sporadically as a deputy U.S. marshal from August 1867 until early in 1870; Nyle H. Miller and Joseph W. Snell, *Why the West Was Wild* (Topeka, Kans., 1963), 630.

4. Lawrence *Kansas Daily Tribune,* March 5, 1868; Iola (Kans.), *Allen County Courant,* March 7, 1868. I am indebted to James Drees for bringing these items to my attention.

5. Dodge City (Kans.) *Ford County Globe,* November 22, 1881.

6. Joe B. Frantz, "The Frontier Tradition: An Invitation to Violence," in

in Hugh Davis Graham and Ted Robert Gurr, *The History of Violence in America* (New York, 1969), 129–132.

7. John B. Edwards, *Early Days in Abilene* (Abilene, Kans., 1940), 7; Topeka (Kans.) *Daily Commonwealth,* September 27, 1872.

8. Robert C. Dykstra to Joseph G. Rosa, July 4, 1959; see also his *The Cattle Towns* (New York, 1968).

9. Wayne Gard, *Frontier Justice* (Norman, Okla., 1949), 149–67.

10. Wayne Gard, *The Chisholm Trail* (Norman, Okla., 1954), 73–84.

11. Wichita city records, journal A, 69 and 187.

12. Undated sheet found among letters from James Hickok to his family (1858?). Original on file at KSHS.

13. Original on file at KSHS.

14. Records of the Quartermaster General, National Archives, Washington, D.C.; Junction City (Kans.) *Union,* July 27, 1867; Hays City (Kans.) *Railway Advance,* November 9, 1867.

15. Joseph G. Rosa, "J. B. Hickok, Deputy U.S. Marshal," *Kansas History: A Journal of the Central Plains* 2:4 (Winter 1979): 231–251.

16. Records of Fort Hays (letters sent), 1869, National Archives, Washington, D.C.

17. Buel, *Heroes of the Plains,* 133–134.

18. The Abilene (Kans.) *Chronicle,* August 17, 1871, published the ordinance in full; Records of the City Council of Abilene, microfilm copy, Manuscripts Division, KSHS.

19. Arthur Chapman, "The Men Who Tamed the Cow-Towns," *Outing* 45 (November 1904): 131–139.

20. Emerson Hough, *The Story of the Outlaw: A Study of the Western Desperado* (New York, 1907). Chapter 7 is devoted to Hickok.

21. Typed copy supplied to the writer in the late 1950s. Later, when attempts were made to trace the original document, it had disappeared. It was presumed misfiled or perhaps stolen by an autograph collector anxious to acquire a specimen of Hickok's signature.

22. Stuart Henry, *Conquering Our Great American Plains* (New York, 1930), 274–275.

23. Joseph G. McCoy, *Historic Sketches of the Cattle Trade of the West and Southwest* (Kansas City, Mo., 1874), 204.

24. A. T. Andreas, *History of the State of Kansas* (Chicago, 1883), 688.

25. Dwight D. Eisenhower, "Remarks upon Receiving the America's Democratic Legacy Award at B'nai B'rith Dinner in Honor of the 40th Anniversary of the Anti-Defamation League," November 23, 1953, *Public Papers of the Presidents of the United States: Dwight D. Eisenhower,*

vol. 1 (January 20 to December 31, 1953), Eisenhower Library, Abilene, Kans.

Chapter Seven
A Blood and Thunder Hero

1. David Daly and Joseph Persky, "The West and the Western," pt. 1, "Myth," *Journal of the West* 29:2 (April 1990): 6.

2. Ibid., pt. 2, "Heroes," 40–41.

3. I am indebted to Edward T. LeBlanc for copies of some of the dime novels that featured Wild Bill, together with copies of *Dime Novel Roundup;* my thanks also to Victor A. Beach for information concerning Paul Preston and Thomas Picton. And a special thanks to Kevin Carpenter for a copy of the complete text of "Buffalo Bill, The King of the Border Men" as published in *Boys of England.* For a claim that Cody actually wrote the story, see William F. Cody, as told to Ned Buntline, *Buffalo Bill, King of the Border Men,* edited and with an afterword by William Roba (Davenport, Iowa, 1987).

4. J. Edward Leithead, "Buckskin Men of Forest and Plain," pt. 5, *Dime Novel Roundup,* vol. 21:10 (October 1953), 74–75.

5. Hiram Robbins, "Wild Bill's Humors," an undated clipping supplied by the late Don Russell, credited to the *Arkansaw Traveler;* I am also indebted to Dr. Robert Pepper for information on Texas Jack's saloon.

6. Don Russell, *The Lives and Legends of Buffalo Bill* (Norman, Okla., 1960), 153–155.

7. A copy of the letter from Horace Hickok was supplied by his grandniece Edith Harmon. The letter from Buffalo Bill is now in the author's collection.

8. For further details of Cody's early exposure to the stage, see Russell, *Lives;* Herschel C. Logan, *Buckskin and Satin* (Harrisburg, Pa., 1954); and William F. Cody, *The Life of Hon. William F. Cody, Known as Buffalo Bill* (Hartford, Conn., 1879).

9. Nothing has so far come to light to suggest when Cody approached Wild Bill with an offer to tour Europe, which suggests that it was speculation on Cody's part.

10. Cody, *Life,* 329; Joseph G. Rosa, *They Called Him Wild Bill: The Life and Adventures of James Butler Hickok* (Norman Okla., 1964 and 1974), 163–169.

11. One of the "thrills" associated with Wild West plays was the large amount of black powder and the many percussion caps exploded

during each performance. At times audiences must have viewed the action through a fog of powder smoke.

12. Little Rock *Arkansaw Democrat,* January 23, 1899. Hiram Robbins was born at New Lisbon, near Cincinnati, Ohio, on April 8, 1844. His family was deeply religious, but his aspirations lay elsewhere. He worked on railroads before becoming a playwright. Later he was a sewing machine salesman and finally a judge. In 1897 he spent some time in the Klondyke, but failed to strike it rich. For details of his plays, see *Dramatic Compositions Copyrighted in the United States (1870–1916),* Library of Congress, Washington, D.C.

13. Dr. Robert Pepper informed me of Cody's sojourn at West Chester. I am indebted to Sandra K. Sagala for details of this and other performances of the Combination; see also her article "An Unlikely Trio: Buffalo Bill, Wild Bill, and Texas Jack—Actors," *True West* 40:6 (June 1993): 23–27.

14. The identity of "Dashing Charley" was divulged by George O'Dell in his *Annals of the New York Stage,* 15 vols. (n.p., 1927–1949). He also discovered that in 1872 a play entitled *Wild Bill* was produced with D. F. Ralton in the title role. Similarly, he reports that even as Maeder's play with Cody playing himself was being performed, a burlesque called "Buffalo Bill, with his Great Buffalo Bull" was going the rounds. O'Dell described these events as "an epidemic of border drama." (Paul Fees, curator of the Buffalo Bill Museum, to Joseph G. Rosa, March 4, 1986).

15. Paul Fees, curator of the Buffalo Bill Museum, to Joseph G. Rosa, March 4, 1986. Dr. Fees added that Julian Kent had a "trained bear" as a part of his act.

16. W. F. Cody to Sam Hall, July 5, 1879, cited by Sarah J. Blackstone in *The Business of Being Buffalo Bill: Selected Letters of William F. Cody, 1879–1917* (New York, Westport, and London, 1988), 2.

17. Paul Eisloeffel and Andrea I. Paul, "Hollywood on the Plains: Nebraska's Contribution to Early American Cinema," *Journal of the West* 33:2 (April 1994): 13–19.

18. David Cruickshanks to Joseph G. Rosa, December 6, 1978. Cruickshanks was quoting from interviews given by Adelia to Henry G. Conrad in 1934.

19. Undated clipping supplied by Edith Harmon.

20. Howard L. Hickok, notes accompanying his "The Hickok Legend," copy on file in author's collection; Mendota (Ill.) *Reporter,* November 5, 1936.

21. Interview with the late Colonel King, a history professor who studied Hickok, at Denver airport, October 1983.

22. John Tuska, *The American West in Film: Critical Approaches to the Western* (Lincoln, Nebr., 1988), 180.

23. Kirk Honeycutt, "Bridges has looks, six-gun for 'Wild Bill,' " *Hollywood Reporter,* March 28, 1994; "Walter Hill Rides Again," interview by Irene Lacher, Los Angeles *Times,* January 3, 1995.

Chapter Eight
"The Deadman's Hand"

1. William Francis Hooker to the editor of *Adventure Magazine,* August 3, 1920; William Francis Hooker to A. E. Sheldon, February 1936, Manuscripts Department, Nebraska State Historical Society; Hope A. Hilton, *Wild Bill Hickman and the Mormon Frontier* (Salt Lake City, 1988). In correspondence with me, May 4, 1992, Hilton admitted that her great-grandfather had never been known as "Wild Bill" during his lifetime but that the publishers decided the name would increase sales.

2. Karl F. Stephens, M.D., "How Blind Was Hickok?" *The English Westerners' Brand Book, 1975–1976* (1977), 7–10; for a full discussion of this subject, see Joseph G. Rosa, *They Called Him Wild Bill* (Norman, Okla., 1964 and 1974), 265–271); Laramie County Clerk of Court Criminal Appearance Docket Book 2, 23, June 17, 1875–August 1876; Cheyenne *Daily Leader,* August 16, 1876; Kansas City *Star,* August 29, 1918 (review of Hooker's *The Prairie Schooner*); William Francis Hooker to Addison E. Sheldon, February 19, 1936; Kansas City *Times,* January 19, 1875; J. W. Buel, *Heroes of the Plains* (New York and St. Louis, 1882), 170, 181.

3. The Cheyenne press also gave space to Hickok's plans (see Cheyenne *Daily Sun,* April 30, 1876, and *Daily Leader,* May 3, 1876).

4. Buel, *Heroes of the Plains,* 188; Rosa, *They Called Him Wild Bill,* 299. The original letter, together with the marriage certificate and other Hickok items, was presented in the 1920s by Gilbert Robinson, Jr., husband of Agnes's daughter Emma, to the United States Playing Card Company's museum, Cincinnati, Ohio.

5. St. Paul (Minn.) *Press and Tribune,* September 8, 1876.

6. In evidence at the McCall trial at Yankton, Carl Mann, a part owner of Saloon No. 10, stated that McCall owed money to Hickok from a previous game (Yankton *Press & Dakotaian,* December 5, 1876); for a full account of the McCall trial, see Joseph G. Rosa, *Alias Jack McCall: A Pardon or Death?* (Kansas City, Mo., 1967).

7. In 1993, a Colt .45 caliber Single Action Army revolver (a "Peacemaker") was auctioned in England. Serial numbered 2079, the 7–1/2"

barreled pistol was manufactured in 1874. Accompanying the pistol was a batch of correspondence which purported to "authenticate" the weapon as the one used by McCall to murder Hickok. But a personal examination of this material (in particular a letter allegedly written by the late Raymond W. Thorp) convinced me that the weapon was a fake. It failed to reach its reserve price ($50,000) in the first sale; in its second appearance it went for about $20,000. Had it been *the* pistol that killed Wild Bill, it is most unlikely that it would have been removed from the United States for sale. According to the trial documents, McCall's pistol was described as "Navy size."

8. Chicago *Inter-Ocean,* August 17, 1876; Frank J. Wilstach, *Wild Bill Hickok: The Prince of Pistoleers* (New York, 1926), 284–285.

9. William Rodney Massie was quite a character. Born in 1829 near Berger, Franklin County, Missouri, he spent his life on the Mississippi and Missouri rivers. He died at St. Louis in 1910.

10. Frank L. Forster to Joseph G. Rosa, May 15, 1971.

11. Wilstach, *Wild Bill,* 284.

12. *Tombstone Epitaph* (national edition), September and December 1978.

13. Wilstach quoted this text, which was also cited by Capt. Jack Crawford in the *Virginia Evening Chronicle* of August 4, 1877. Buel's text was based upon Crawford's version. He gave no hint that he had ever seen the original letter. I have quoted the original text, but have added the place, date, and signature to conform with Hickok's July 17 letter.

14. St. Paul (Minn.) *Press & Tribune* (citing the Denver *News*), September 8, 1876.

15. Henry Onsgard, "The Romance of the Black Hills," *South Dakota Historical Collections* 13 (1926): 32.

16. Shortly before McCall was hanged, the U.S. marshal received a letter from Mary A. McCall of Louisville, Kentucky, confirming that Jack was her brother and that he had left his parents and three sisters several years before. When shown the letter Jack admitted the relationship and wrote to her. He also prepared a statement to be published after his death, but destroyed it (see Rosa, *Alias Jack McCall,* 26).

17. Telephone conversation with Robert Rybolt in 1986; Robert Rybolt, "Wild Bill's Murder Plot," *True West,* July 1985, 42–45.

18. A search of the Kansas City press for the weeks following Hickok's murder failed to find any firsthand reports by Whitehead.

19. Deadwood (D.T.) *Black Hills Pioneer,* September 9, 1876; Rosa, *Alias Jack McCall,* 5.

20. Cheyenne (Wyo.) *Daily Leader,* August 26, 1876.

21. Yankton (D.T.) *Press & Dakotaian,* November 23, 1876.

22. Cheyenne *Daily Leader,* November 23, 1876.

23. The late Ethel Hickok told me on several occasions that "Uncle Lorenzo" had often spoken of his meeting with Jack McCall, and although he was not a violent man, he declared himself "outraged" by McCall's apparent indifference to his crime.

24. Records of the Pardon Attorney, No. F-307, Records Group No. 204, National Archives, Washington, D.C.

25. The original letter is now on file in the Manuscripts Division, KSHS.

26. Ibid.

27. Cheyenne (Wyo.) *Daily Leader,* July 1, 1879.

28. Hays City *Sentinel,* August 15 and 29, 1879.

29. Agnes Wright Spring, *Colorado Charley, Wild Bill's Pard* (Boulder, Colo., 1968), 124.

30. Charlie Utter to Dick and Brant Street, Denver, January 20, 1880. Original in the Manuscripts Division, KSHS.

31. Manuscripts Division, KSHS.

32. Ibid.

33. J. Arthur Thompson to Mrs. Jessica Nashold, Mendota, Ill., November 3 and 14, 1966. Author's collection.

34. Manuscripts Division, KSHS.

35. Ibid.

36. Ibid.

37. Ibid.

38. Original in the possession of Hickok's grandniece, Edith Harmon, who is Mrs. Andrews's daughter.

39. Ibid.

40. Original in the author's collection.

41. Original in the William E. Connelley Collection, Western History Department, Denver Public Library.

42. E. B. Mann, "Wild Bill Hickok," *American Rifleman* 95:4 (April 1947): 15–17, 30.

Bibliography

Books and Pamphlets

Andreas, A. T. *History of the State of Kansas.* Chicago, 1883.

Armes, George A. *Ups and Downs of an Army Officer.* Washington, D.C., 1900.

Blackstone, Sarah J. *The Business of Being Buffalo Bill: Selected Letters of William F. Cody, 1879–1917.* New York, Westport, and London, 1988.

Blake, Herbert Cody. *Blake's Western Stories.* Brooklyn, N.Y., 1929.

Bronson, Edgar Beecher. *The Red-blooded Heroes of the Frontier.* New York, 1910.

Buel, J. W. *Heroes of the Plains.* New York and St. Louis, 1882.

Burkey, Blaine. *Wild Bill Hickok the Law in Hays City.* Hays, Kans., 1975.

Burton, Sir Richard. *The Look of the West 1860: Across the Plains to California.* Lincoln, Nebr., 1965.

Carpenter, F. A. *History of the 17th Illinois Cavalry Volunteers.* N.p., ca. 1886.

Cochran, Hamilton. *Noted American Duels and Hostile Encounters.* Philadelphia, 1963.

Cody, William F. *The Life of the Hon. William F. Cody, Known as Buffalo Bill.* Hartford, Conn., 1879.

Cody, William F., as told to Ned Buntline. *Buffalo Bill, King of the Border Men.* Edited, with an Afterword by William Roba. Davenport, Iowa, 1987.

Compendious History of Ellsworth County, Kansas: From Its Early Settlement to the Present Time. Ellsworth, Kans., 1879.

Connelley, William E. *Wild Bill and His Era.* New York, 1933.

Curtis, William E. *A Summer Scamper Along the Old Santa Fe Trail and Through the Gorges of Colorado to Zion.* Chicago, 1883.

Custer, Elizabeth Bacon. *Following the Guidon*. New York, 1890.

Custer, George A. *My Life on the Plains*. New York, 1876.

Dawson, Charles. *Pioneer Tales of the Oregon Trail*. Topeka, Kans., 1912.

Description and Rules for the Management of the Springfield Rifle, Carbine, and Army Revolvers. Washington, D.C., 1898.

Dimsdale, Thomas J. *The Vigilantes of Montana*. Norman, Okla., 1953.

Dugan, Mark. *Tales Never Told Around the Campfire*. Athens, Ohio, 1990.

Dykstra, Robert C. *The Cattle Towns*. New York, 1968.

Edwards, John B. *Early Days in Abilene*. Abilene, Kans., 1940.

Eisele, Wilbert. *The Real Wild Bill Hickok*. Denver, Colo., 1931.

Fellman, Michael. *Inside War: The Guerrilla Conflict in Missouri During the American Civil War*. New York, 1989.

Gard, Wayne. *The Chisholm Trail*. Norman, Okla., 1954.

————. *Frontier Justice*. Norman, Okla., 1949.

Garwood, Darrell. *Crossroads of America: The Story of Kansas City*. New York, 1948.

Graham, Hugh Davis, and Ted Robert Gurr. *Violence in America: Historical and Comparative Perspectives*. New York, 1969.

Greener, W. W. *The Gun and Its Development*. London, 1910.

Hale, Donald R. *They Called Him Bloody Bill: The Life of William Anderson, Missouri Guerrilla*. Clinton, Mo., 1982.

Harmon, Edith. *Pioneer Settlers of Troy Grove, Illinois*. Mendota, Ill., 1973.

Heitman, Francis B. *Historical Register and Dictionary of the United States Army*. Washington, D.C., 1903.

Henry, Stuart. *Conquering Our Great American Plains*. New York, 1930.

Hilton, Hope A. *Wild Bill Hickman and the Mormon Frontier*. Salt Lake City, 1988.

Hooker, William Francis. *The Prairie Schooner*. Chicago, 1918.

Hough, Emerson. *The Story of the Outlaw: A Study of the Western Desperado*. New York, 1907.

Howard, J. W. ("Doc"). *"Doc" Howard's Memoirs*. Denver, Colo., 1931.

Jordan, Philip D. *Frontier Law and Order*. Lincoln, Nebr., 1970.

Lamar, Howard R., ed. *The Reader's Encyclopedia of the American West*. New York, 1977.

Logan, Herschel C. *Buckskin and Satin*. Harrisburg, Pa., 1954.

McCoy, Joseph G. . *Historic Sketches of the Cattle Trade of the West and Southwest*. Edited and annotated by Ralph P. Bieber. Lincoln, Nebr., 1985.

McGivern, Ed. *Fast and Fancy Revolver Shooting*. Chicago, 1975.

Marohn, Richard. *The Last Gunfighter: John Wesley Hardin*. College Station, Tex., 1995.

Masterson, W. B. ("Bat"). *Famous Gun Fighters of the Western Frontier*. Annotated and illustrated by Jack DeMattos. Monroe, Wash., 1982.

Miller, Darlis A. *Captain Jack Crawford: Buckskin Poet, Scout, and Showman*. Albuquerque, N.M., 1993.

Miller, Nyle H., and Joseph W. Snell. *Why the West Was Wild*. Topeka, Kans., 1963.

Mitchell, Edwin P. *Memoirs of an Editor: Fifty Years of American Journalism*. New York and London, 1924.

North, Luther. *Man of the Plains: Recollections of Luther North, 1856–1882*. Edited by Donald F. Danker. Lincoln, Nebr., 1961.

O'Connor, Richard. *Wild Bill Hickok*. New York, 1959.

O'Dell, George. *Annals of the New York Stage*. 15 vols. N.p., 1927–1949.

Rosa, Joseph G. *Alias Jack McCall: A Pardon or Death?* Kansas City, Mo., 1967.

———. *The Gunfighter: Man or Myth?* Norman, Okla., 1969.

———. *They Called Him Wild Bill—The Life and Adventures of James Butler Hickok*. Norman, Okla., 1964 and 1974.

———. *The West of Wild Bill Hickok*. Norman, Okla., 1982 and 1994.

Russell, Don. *The Lives and Legends of Buffalo Bill*. Norman, Okla., 1960.

Sanborn, John B. *The Campaign in Missouri in September and October, 1864*. N.p., n.d. Copy supplied by University of Missouri, Rolla.

Sandoz, Mari. *The Buffalo Hunters*. London, 1960.

———. *The Cattlemen: From the Rio Grande Across the Far Marias*. New York, 1958.

Spring, Agnes Wright. *Colorado Charley, Wild Bill's Pard*. Boulder, Colo., 1968.

Tallent, Annie. *The Black Hills; Or the Last Hunting Ground of the Dakotas*. St. Louis, 1899.

The Westerners Brand Book (1945–1946). Chicago, 1946.

Tuska, John. *The American West in Film: Critical Approaches to the Western*. Lincoln, Nebr., 1988.

Utley, Robert M., ed. *Life in Custer's Cavalry: Diaries and Letters of Albert and Jennie Barnitz, 1867–1868*. New Haven and London, 1977.

Webb, W. E. *Buffalo Land*. Cincinnati and Chicago, 1872.

Wheeler, Homer W. *The Frontier Trail*. Los Angeles, 1923.

Williams, Robert H. *With the Border Ruffians*. London, 1907.

Wilstach, Frank J. *Wild Bill Hickok: The Prince of Pistoleers.* New York, 1926.

Dime Novels

Buffalo Bill, The King of the Border Men. Boys of England. London, 1870.

Buffalo Bill's Wild West and Congress of Rough Riders of the World. Souvenir program, 1893.

Buntline, Ned (E. Z. C. Judsen). *Buffalo Bill, the King of the Border Men.* Serialized in the *New York Weekly,* beginning December 1869.

————. *Wild Bill's Last Trail.* Diamond Dick Library, no. 192. New York, July 4, 1896.

Hickok, William. *Wild Bill's First War Trail: A Stirring Tale of Real Life on the Border.* The Campfire Library. N.d.

Ingraham, Prentiss. *Wild Bill, The Pistol Dead Shot; Or, Dagger Don's Double.* Beadle's Dime Library, vol. 13, no. 168. New York, January 11, 1882.

————. *Wild Bill, the Pistol Prince.* Beadle's Pocket Library, no. 383. May 13, 1891.

Leithead, J. Edward. *Buckskin Men of Forest and Plain,* pt. 5. *Dime Novel Roundup,* vol. 21, no. 10. October 1953.

Preston, Paul. *Wild Bill the Indian Slayer.* DeWitt's Ten Cent Romances, no. 3. March (?) 1867.

"Wild Bill." Budget Story Books, vol. 220. London, 1895.

Wild Bill's First Trail, as told by himself. DeWitt's Ten Cent Romances, no. 10. October (?) 1867.

Wilder, Wm. West ("Wyoming Will"). *Wild Bill's Sable Pard.* Beadle's Popular Library, no. 48. February 24, 1892.

Articles

Chapman, Arthur. "The Men Who Tamed the Cow-Towns." *Outing* 45 (November 1904).

Cheatham, Gary L. " 'Desperate Characters!': The Development and Impact of the Confederate Guerrillas in Kansas." *Kansas History: A Journal of the Central Plains* 14:3 (Autumn 1991).

Connelley, William E. "Wild Bill—James Butler Hickok: David C. McCanles at Rock Creek." Kansas State Historical Society *Collections,* 17 (1926–1928).

Crawford, Jack. "The Death of Wild Bill." *City Life,* New York, May 18, 1895.

——. "The Truth About Calamity Jane." *Journalist,* New York, ca. 1900.

Daly, David, and Joseph Persky. "The West and the Western," *Journal of the West* 29:2 (April 1990).

Davis, Theodore R. "Henry M. Stanley's Indian Campaign in 1867." *The Westerners Brand Book (1945–46).* Chicago, 1947.

Denison, William W. "Early Days in Osage County," Kansas State Historical Society *Collections* 18 (1926–1928).

Dixon, David. "A Scout with Custer: Edmund Guerrier on the Hancock Expedition of 1867." *Kansas History* 4:3 (Autumn 1981).

Dunlop, Richard. "Wild Bill Donovan on the Mexican Border." *The Westerners Brand Book,* 39. Chicago, November–December 1982.

Eisenhower, Dwight D. "Remarks upon Receiving the America's Democratic Legacy Award at B'nai B'rith Dinner in Honor of the 40th Anniversary of the Anti-Defamation League," November 23, 1953. Public Papers of the Presidents of the United States: Dwight D. Eisenhower, vol. 1 (January 20 to December 31, 1953). Eisenhower Library, Abilene, Kans.

Eisloeffel, Paul J., and Andrea I. Paul, "Hollywood on the Plains: Nebraska's Contribution to Early American Cinema." *Journal of the West* 33:2 (April 1994).

Frantz, Joe B. "The Frontier Tradition: An Invitation to Violence." In Hugh Davis Graham and Ted Robert Gurr, *The History of Violence in America.* New York, 1969.

Gomer, Alva. "Against Fearful Odds: A True Story." *Trail* 1 (April 1909).

Gray, John S. "Will Comstock—The Natty Bumppo of Kansas." *The Westerners Brand Book,* vol. 18. Chicago, February 1962.

Hance, George W. "George W. Hance Recounts Interesting Story of 'Wild Bill' Hickok." Rolla (Mo.) *Herald,* January 18, 1912.

——. "The Truth About Wild Bill." Topeka *Mail and Breeze,* December 20, 1901.

Hansen, George W. "The True Story of Wild Bill–McCanles Affray in Jefferson County, Nebraska, July 12, 1861. *Nebraska History Magazine,* 10:2 (April–June 1927).

Hatton, Robert W. "Just a Little Bit of the Civil War, As Seen by W. J. Smith, Company M, 2nd O.V. Cavalry." Cincinnati Historical Society *Bulletin* (Fall 1980).

Henry, Samuel D. "Wild Bill—Some Personal Recollections," Coon Rapids (Iowa) *Enterprise,* June 10, 1927.

Huff, Leo E. "Guerrillas, Jayhawkers and Bushwhackers in Northern

Arkansas During the Civil War." *Arkansas Historical Quarterly* 24 (Summer 1965).

Lacher, Irene. "Walter Hill Rides Again." Los Angeles *Times,* January 3, 1995.

Lewis, Alfred Henry. "How Mr. Hickok Came to Cheyenne, or, the Epic of an Unsung Ulysses." *Saturday Evening Post,* March 12, 1904.

Little, E. C. "A Son of the Border." Topeka *Mail and Breeze,* September 13, 1901.

McLynn, Frank. "Riding into Legend on the Back of a Bullet." *Times Higher Education Supplement* (London), June 15, 1990.

Mann, E. B. "Wild Bill Hickok." *American Rifleman,* 95:4 (April 1947).

Marohn, Richard. "John Wesley Hardin, Adolescent Killer: The Emergence of a Narcissistic Behavior Disorder." *Annals of the American Society for Adolescent Psychiatry* 14 (1987).

Masterson, W. B. ("Bat"). "The Tenderfoot's Turn." *Guns Quarterly* 2 (Summer 1960).

Nichols, George Ward. "Wild Bill." *Harper's New Monthly Magazine* 34 (February 1867).

Onsgard, Henry, "The Romance of the Black Hills." *South Dakota Historical Collections.* 13 (1926).

Robbins, Hiram. "Wild Bill's Humors." *Arkansaw Traveler* (n.d.).

Rosa, Joseph G. "J. B. Hickok, Deputy U.S. Marshal." *Kansas History: A Journal of the Central Plains* 2:4 (Winter 1979).

————. "George Ward Nichols and the Legend of Wild Bill Hickok." *Arizona and the West* 19:2 (Summer 1977).

Russell, Don, ed. "Julia Cody Goodman's Memoirs of Buffalo Bill." *Kansas Historical Quarterly* 27 (Winter 1962).

Ryan, John. "Ten Years with General Custer Among the American Indians." *Newton Circuit,* July 9, 1909.

Rybolt, Robert. "Wild Bill's Murder Plot." *True West,* July 1985.

Stephens, Karl F. "How Blind Was Hickok?" *The English Westerners' Brand Book, 1975–76* (1977).

Webb, W. E. "Air Towns and Their Inhabitants." *Harper's New Monthly Magazine* (November 1875).

Manuscripts and Other Materials

Barnes, Lydia Hickok, to Harry S. Young, September 7, 1915. Copy courtesy of David Dary.

Barnitz, Major Albert. Diary and Journals covering the period 1861–1870. Barnitz Papers, Beinecke Library, Yale University.

Bellport, A. D., to G. W. Hansen, March 15, 1929. Manuscripts Department, Nebraska State Historical Society, Lincoln, Nebr.

Carr, Gen. E. A. "Carr's Campaign of 1868–69." Manuscript in the possession of James T. King.

Cody, W. F., to John Wallace Crawford, August 23, 1885. William F. Cody Papers, Box 1, Western History Collection, Denver Public Library.

Cody, W. F., to Horace Hickok, March 23, 1880. Author's collection.

Court Records: Those relative to the Rock Creek affair are housed at the Nebraska State Historical Society. Records concerning the Tutt killing at Springfield., Mo., are retained by the Greene County Archive, Springfield. Documents, including warrants and subpoenas concerning Hickok's service as a deputy U. S. marshal are held at the Kansas City, Mo., branch of the National Archives (which also has the McCall trial papers). The records of the McCall Pardon File (Office of the Pardon Attorney, No. F-307, Records Group No. 204) are filed at the National Archives, Washington, D.C.

Cragin, Francis. "Early West Notebook" Francis Cragin Collection. Colorado Springs Pioneer Museum.

Drees, James D. "The Hays City Vigilante Period, 1868–1869." M.A. thesis, Fort Hays State University, Hays, Kans.

Edwards, J. B., to William E. Connelley, September 13, 1927, Manuscripts Division, KSHS.

Gross, Charles F., to J. B. Edwards (1922–1926 correspondence). Manuscripts Division, KSHS.

Hickok, Howard L. "The Hickok Legend." Typescript, author's collection.

Hickok, Howard L., to William E. Connelley, January 30, 1928. Author's collection.

Hickok, James Butler, to various members of his family at Troy Grove (see also letters from Lorenzo, Oliver, and Polly Butler Hickok). Manuscripts Division, KSHS.

Hickok, James Butler, to Lydia Hickok Barnes, July 8, 1862. Original owned by his grandniece Jo Lohoefener.

Hooker, William Francis, to Addison E. Sheldon, various years. Manuscripts Department, Nebraska State Historical Society, Lincoln, Nebr.

Jones & Cartwright, Leavenworth, Kans., to Horace Hickok, June 6, 1861. Author's collection.

Marriage Certificate, George Carson and Agnes Lake Hickok. Wyoming State Archive, Cheyenne.

Newspaper Scrapbooks. The Library, KSHS.

Ordnance Department Records. National Archives, Washington, D.C.

Records of the City Council of Abilene, 1870–1872. Microfilm copy, Manuscripts Division, KSHS.

Records of Fort Hays, Kans., 1867–1870. National Archives, Washington, D.C.

Records of the Quartermaster General, Civilians Hired as Scouts, Couriers and Teamsters for the period 1861–1870. National Archives, Washington, D.C.

Service records of privates Jeremiah Lonergan and John Kile. U.S. Seventh Cavalry Regiment, National Archives, Washington, D.C.

Thompson, J. Arthur, to Mrs. Jessica Nashold, Mendota, Ill., November 3 and 14, 1966. Author's collection.

Newspapers

The following newspapers were checked at random for the years 1856 until the early 1900s except the Kansas papers, which were searched for the period 1856–1879.

Abilene (Kans.) *Chronicle*
Atchison (Kans.) *Daily Champion*
Cheyenne (W.T.) *Daily Leader*
Cheyenne (W.T.) *Democratic Leader*
Cheyenne (Wyo.) *Wyoming State Tribune*
Cheyenne (W.T.) *Sun*
Chicago *Daily News*
Chicago *Daily Record*
Chicago *Inter-Ocean*
Chicago *Tribune*
Deadwood (D.T.) *Black Hills Pioneer*
Denver *Rocky Mountain News*
Dodge City (Kans.) *Ford County Globe*
Ellsworth (Kans.) *Reporter*
Fort Scott (Kans.) *Weekly Monitor*
Hays (Kans.) *Daily News*
Hays (Kans.) *Ellis County News*
Hays City (Kans.) *Ellis County Free Press*
Hays City (Kans.) *Ellis County Star*
Hays City (Kans.) *Hays City Railway Advance*
Hays City (Kans.) *Sentinel*
Iola (Kans.) *Allen County Courant*
Johnson County (Kans.) *Democrat*

Junction City (Kans.) *Daily*
Junction City (Kans.) *Weekly Union*
Kansas City (Mo.) *Daily Journal of Commerce*
Kansas City (Mo.) *Journal*
Kansas City (Mo.) *Times*
Lawrence (Kans.) *Republican*
Leavenworth (Kans.) *Appeal*
Leavenworth (Kans.) *Daily Conservative*
Leavenworth (Kans.) *Daily Times*
Leavenworth (K.T.) *Kansas Weekly Herald*
Lewiston (Maine) *Evening Journal*
Little Rock (Ark.) *Arkansaw Democrat*
London (England) *The Times*
Longview (Tex.) *Democrat*
Manhattan (Kans.) *Independent*
Meadville (Pa.) *Evening Republican*
Mendota (Ill.) *Bulletin*
New York *New York Clipper*
North Topeka (Kans.) *Times*
Olathe (Kans.) *Mirror*
Olathe (Kans.) *Mirror and Newsletter*
Omaha (Nebr.) *Daily Bee*
Omaha (Nebr.) *Herald*
Rolla (Mo.) *Herald*
St. Louis *Globe-Democrat*
St. Louis *Republican*
St. Louis *Times*
St. Louis *Weekly Missouri Democrat*
St. Paul (Minn.) *Press & Tribune*
Saline (Kans.) *County Journal*
San Francisco *Daily Alta California*
San Francisco *Daily Evening Bulletin*
Springfield (Mass.) *Republican*
Springfield (Mo.) *Missouri Weekly Patriot*
Tacoma (Wash.) *Daily Tribune*
Tombstone (Ariz.) *Epitaph* (1978)
Topeka (Kans.) *Daily Commonwealth*
Topeka (Kans.) *Mail and Breeze*
Troy (N.Y.) *Times*
Wichita (Kans.) *Weekly Beacon*
Yankton (D.T.) *Press and Dakotaian*

Index